Subdued by the Sword

A Line Officer in the 121st New York Volunteers

JAMES M. GREINER

State University of New York Press

Published by
State University of New York Press, Albany

For information, address State University of New York Press,
90 State Street, Suite 700, Albany, NY 12207

Production by Judith Block
Marketing by Anne Valentine

Library of Congress Control Number
Greiner, James M., 1954–
    Subdued by the sword : a line officer in the 121st New York Volunteers /
James M. Greiner.
        p. cm.
    Includes bibliographical references (p.) and index.
    ISBN 0-7914-5867-9 (alk. paper) — ISBN 0-7914-5868-7 (pbk. : alk. paper)
    1. Kidder, John S., d. 1905.   2. Kidder, John S., d. 1905—Correspondence.
3. United States. Army. New York Infantry Regiment, 121st (1861–1865)
4. New York (State)—History—Civil War, 1861–1865—Regimental histories.
5. New York (State)—History—Civil War, 1861–1865—Personal narratives.
6. United States—History—Civil War, 1861–1865—Regimental histories.
7. United States—History—Civil War, 1861–1865—Personal narratives.
8. Kidder, Harriet, d. 1922—Correspondence.   9. Soldiers—New York
(State)—Laurens—Biography.   10. Laurens (N.Y.)—Biography.   I. Title.

E523.512st .G74 2003
973.7'81—dc21
                                                                    2002045251

10 9 8 7 6 5 4 3 2 1

For
Jerry Reed
and the entire Kidder family

Contents

"... it will be too bad to have those suffer with them [the Confederates] who are good Union People but I look for such a state of things. It will come as sure as the sun rises and sets unless this rebellion is subdued by the sword. People may laugh at my opinion but they will live to see my words proven true."

Captain John S. Kidder
121st New York Volunteers

Acknowledgments

My initial intention was to rewrite the regimental history of the 121st New York Volunteers, a Civil War unit that drew men from my own Herkimer and neighboring Otsego County. While looking for new source material, I was struck by the fact that a Captain Kidder had served with the unit from its formation to the close of the war eventually rising to the rank of lieutenant colonel. A quick check of his service and pension records indicated that John S. Kidder was from nearby Laurens, New York and had died there in 1905. His wife, Harriet, also died in Laurens in 1922. Using Harriet's date of death as relatively recent, I then contacted Grace Crandall at the Ambrose V. Powell Library in Laurens. She told me that Mrs. Kidder's great-grandson would contact me. A few days later, the Laurens Village Historian, Dick Rose, called me and gave me a brief history of his family. He didn't hesitate to tell me who else to contact for more information on John and Harriet Kidder. I wasn't off the phone a second when another call came through. The caller was eighty-four-year-old Frances Warren of Mohawk, New York. She was the granddaughter of John and Harriet. Frances had many fond memories of her grandmother and invited me to her residence at the Mohawk Homestead.

A third call was received from Jerry Reed of Whitesboro, New York, a great-great-grandson of the Kidders. Someone once told me that in every family there is one member who takes it upon him or herself to preserve and record the family history. For the Kidder clan this person is Jerry Reed. Frances Warren said it best when I interviewed her in 1995: "We Kidders are a bunch of packrats, we never throw anything out. If it's out there, Jerry will find it. He's good, you know."

He certainly is! Tirelessly Jerry has pieced together and researched the family history. Newspaper clippings, scrapbook articles, letters, diaries, and a treasure trove of unpublished photographs are only a few of the items he was able to assemble and make available to me. Jerry, more than anyone, encouraged me to complete a book on John S. Kidder. His enthusiasm was contagious. It was so easy to set aside a regimental history project and concentrate on a biography of the remarkable husband and wife team of John and Harriet Kidder.

Most of the information about their lives is gleaned from the almost ninety existing letters that John wrote to Harriet during the Civil War. Like other soldiers of this era, both northern and southern, John S. Kidder was confronted for the first time in his life with the task of writing home on a regular basis. These letters were painstakingly transcribed for my use by another Kidder grandson, Harrie Washburn of Sharon Springs, New York. Writing in a semi-legible to an almost indecipherable scrawl, it can be said that John S. Kidder was a hurried letter writer in both thought as well as pen. From whole sheets of paper to tiny scraps, he recorded his thoughts, actions, and observations. He never wasted *any* writing space, filling in margins and writing upside down across the tops of the letters. He was a champion in the use of abbreviations. Never once did he spell completely Regiment (Regt.), Headquarters (Hdq.), or Company (Co.), just to name a few. Spelling was also not one of Kidder's fortes, so, for the sake of easier reading, I undertook the job of correcting the spelling and putting in punctuation within quotes.

An insatiable gossip, John S. Kidder constantly asked his wife for news of Laurens and its inhabitants. It was not uncommon for him to mention as many as ten names in a single letter. What makes his letters different from many letters of this era is their almost total lack of sentiment, beginning with a simple "Dear Wife" and ending with, "As Always." Perhaps the reason for this lack of affection is that John S. Kidder was continually writing for a small audience. He encouraged Harriet to share his letters with others. His father and stepmother were alive at this time and so was Harriet's father. A frequent visitor to the Kidder household at this time was Dr. Addison P. Strong. A widower, Dr. Strong had been married to Adeline T. Matteson, Harriet's oldest sister. Letters of any personal nature were always identified with a bold "Confidential" written across the envelope by Kidder. These letters were for Harriet's eyes only and unfortunately do not exist today.

This book would have been very difficult to research had it not been for the very dedicated staffs of many libraries. The staff at the Carlisle Military Barracks couldn't do enough for me. From books and manuscripts to rare photographs, it is certainly "one stop shopping" for the Civil War researcher. Local libraries right here in the Mohawk Valley were extremely helpful. Heidi Moody of the Frank J. Basloe Library in Herkimer and Patricia DiTata and Debbie Tracy of the West Canada Valley Central Schools Library went to great lengths tracking down old books and obtaining them for me through the library loan system. At the Little Falls Public Library, Marc Klimek was kind enough to let me use the original copies of the *Little Falls Journal and Courier*. The New York State Historical Association Library at Cooperstown not only has a good collection of Civil War and Otsego County related documents, but they also have a microfilm copy of the all important Regimental Day Books of the 121st New York. Although tedious in their nature, these books offer a wonderful view of the "paperwork" and "hurry up and wait" existence that the men of the 121st New York Volunteers endured during their tenure in the army. The Edward G. Minor Medical Library at the University of Rochester deserves a special thanks for assisting me with the research regarding the medical conditions that existed in war time Annapolis.

Scott Hartwig of the Gettysburg National Military Park was very helpful in deciphering the observations Kidder made at Gettysburg. Staff Historian, Donald Pfanz of the Fredericksburg-Spotsylvania National Military Park, helped clear up a lot of confusion regarding Colonel Upton's assault of May 10 at Spotsylvania. I am indebted to both of these gentlemen.

Tim Reese of Burkittsville, Maryland poured through census records and old maps researching Virginia families that Kidder mentioned. Carl Morrel and Richard Buchanan were my Elmira Prison experts. Both of these gentlemen provided research and information on this sometimes forgotten prison camp. Carl Sahre of Herkimer pulled together much of the information on Sayler's Creek and was continually offering advice and support for this project. I am extremely grateful to William D. Matter for his last minute assistance, and also, Joe Scalise for all of his "technical help."

Dr. Donald H. Stewart of Cortland—teacher, mentor, and, above all, friend—"Thank you for everything."

And last, but certainly not least, I would like to thank the person who had to hear about the Kidder family day after day, the same person who accompanied me on all those exciting trips to libraries, cemeteries, and historic sites. My wife Teresa, never a big history buff, probably knows as much as me about the Kidder family after having typed this manuscript a few times. Her advice and support were essential in the completion of this book.

ONE

The New Americans

1830–1862

Frustrated and disappointed at the condition and lack of military success on the part of the Army of the Potomac, newly appointed Capt. John S. Kidder declared: "I really think if it was not for the adopted soldiers we should not have an army."[1] He was exaggerating the condition and quality of soldiers when he wrote this in one of his first letters home in October 1862. Early in the Civil War, the Army of the Potomac had suffered several setbacks but, in time would prove itself in battle. The "adopted soldier" thirty-two-year-old Kidder so modestly referred to was, in reality, himself. John S. Kidder was always proud of the fact that he was an American by choice, not by birth.

Very little is known about his early life in England except that his father and mother, John and Mary Ann Payne Kidder, moved from village to village before finally settling in Charing, England, about fifty miles southeast of London. It was here that the elder Kidder established a small shop; it was also here that eight of the Kidder children, including John Swain, were born. For a dozen years, the elder Kidder supported his growing family by selling a variety of goods supplied by the British East India Company. His shop was well stocked with all kinds of spices, coffees, groceries, and, of course, teas.

Several factors influenced the elder Kidder's decision to immigrate to America. First, the economic climate of England had changed as the 1840s ushered in a depression. To help boost the sagging economy, Prime Minister Sir Robert Peel proposed a tax on all incomes in excess of £150 per year.[2] The burden of an extra tax may have strained the Kidder family budget. This was also the time of the Industrial Revolution. The unbearable pollution brought about by this revolution turned meandering streams into cesspools, for layers of soot blanketed the towns from factory smokestacks. If these were two good reasons to leave England, there was perhaps also a third. Two uncles, George and Thomas Kidder, had recently emigrated to America and settled in upstate New York. It is possible that the Kidder family had received glowing reports about the wide open spaces and the availability of affordable land in America.

Convinced that a better life lay ahead for himself and his family, the elder Kidder sold his shop and its contents. Although America was only an ocean away, the Atlantic crossing was still a dangerous undertaking in the 1840s. A wide variety of pamphlets were in circulation at the time warning the prospective immigrant about the obvious dangers in traveling to America. Dreadful stories of the Atlantic crossing were pub conversation throughout England. Tales of shipwrecks, unscrupulous sea captains preying upon the ignorance of passengers, and disease-ridden ships were common. For many, and this included the Kidders, the desire to emigrate far outweighed the dangers.

The fact that the Kidder family had a little money set them apart from other immigrants of the day. Instead of splitting the family up and coming to America piecemeal, which was common, they were able to travel as a family—a very large one at that. With John and Mary Ann were Salina, 14 years old; John, 12; George, 11; Frances, 10; William, 8; Mary, 6; Edward, 2; and Charlotte, 1 year old.[3]

Unlike the Irish, the Kidders were able to escape the slums of New York City and move into the interior of upstate New York. On May 19, 1842, the former merchant from Charing, Kent County, England, purchased a 129 acre farm from Richard Harrington in Pittsfield, Otsego County, New York. The $1,600 transaction was recorded in the County Clerks Conveyance Book as "hand paid."[4] Two summers later, the elder Kidder was able to obtain an excellent return on his investment when he sold seventy-eight acres of land to William Smith for $1,727.[5]

It is difficult to determine how successful John and Mary Ann Kidder were at farming. As the years went by, their children grew and left the farm in various stages. First to leave was Salina, the eldest daughter. She married Alexander Aires, and by 1848 was expecting her first child. Living with Salina and Alexander at this time was seven-year-old Charlotte. The reason Charlotte moved from the farm is a mystery. One can only surmise that it was an arrangement made to accommodate Salina after the birth of the baby. We shall never know.

We do know that at age eighteen, John Swain Kidder entered into an apprenticeship with James Kenyon, a carriage maker in the nearby village of Morris. After working one winter as a school teacher, John arranged to extend his apprenticeship for two more winters while continuing to work the family farm during the summers. As his apprenticeship became more involved, it was clear to him that this was the work he truly desired. Within a year, he left home and took up residence with the Kenyons. He never, at any time in his life, expressed any regret at leaving the family farm and seemed to develop a certain sympathy towards those who worked the soil for a living. Years later his own account books would reflect this by listing several farm accounts "on hold," as unable to pay.[6]

In a short while sixteen-year-old Frances Kidder joined her brother and was employed by the Kenyons as a live-in domestic. Now the only girl left on the family farm was twelve-year-old Mary. As John's absence meant one less farmhand, seventeen-year-old George and fourteen-year-old William took on more and more responsibilities, for Edward, age seven, was still too young to work. In 1844, Major Henry Payne Kidder, "H.P." as he was called, was born, the only Kidder, until that time, born in America.[7]

For the next several years John S. Kidder learned all aspects of the carriage business. Construction, repairs, custom work, and accounting were part of his training. It was not uncommon for him to put in ten to fifteen hours a day to earn his $50 annual salary as an apprentice. He even managed to include a few odd jobs such as painting, setting glass for windows, and cutting wood to make extra money. This was all hard work; however, he never worked on Sunday. On the Sabbath he could be found at the Baptist Church in Morris lending his voice to the choir. It was probably here that he met, and was totally captivated by, seventeen-year-old Harriet Matteson. On October 6, 1853, John and Harriet were married in Morris. It was a union that would last fifty-two years.[8]

Since John was still an apprentice at the time of his marriage, the newlyweds boarded at the Kenyons for $1.75 a week. The following year, apprenticeship finished, John and Harriet moved to Laurens, New York. In 1854, they rented a house owned by Harriet's father. With a capitol investment of $275, John entered into a business partnership with blacksmith, Elisha Fisher. This was the beginning of the Kidder and Fisher Carriage Shop.[9]

In their first year of business the two men built and sold six wagons. The next year they managed to sell eleven, and the year after that, sixteen. John and Elisha prided themselves on their ability to construct wagons and carriages to suit any purpose. An open buggy sold for $90, and two-horse buggies sold for $165. A sulky, a two-wheeled carriage, could be purchased for as little as $65; while the custom carriage of cotton milliner William C. Fields sold for $127.[10]

Remembering the days at Kenyons, work didn't stop with the sale of carriages. John S. Kidder and his partner sold paint and varnish, made repairs to wagons, and in time constructed their own blacksmith shop to do iron work. With the addition of the blacksmith shop came an increase in odd job repair work. No job was too big or too menial. They forged spindles for the cotton mill, made loom forks, and even mended the handle on the sausage machine at Drews Store. Business was steady even though there were times when the flow of money wasn't coming in. In many instances, people unable to pay their bills bartered for services. Kidder and Fisher traded for a variety of items, for example, cloth, leather, lumber, and even meat. On one occasion they accepted seventy-three pounds of lard for services rendered.[11]

When work slowed at his own shop, Kidder, characteristically, not one to sit idle when a dollar could be earned, found work elsewhere. An example of this happened in November 1861. Leaving Fisher at the shop, he traveled to Norwich to accept a temporary job with a wheelwright. Filing spindles and mortising (carving out) wheel hubs by day, he spent his evenings boarded above a local tavern. Joining him in this arrangement were two other married men presumably in the same work situation. "I cannot call it home," John confessed to Harriet in a short note. "I do not feel homesick because it is of no use, it would not better it any therefore we keep contented as possible."[12] He hoped to earn $10 a week for this work.

While John concerned himself with the carriage shop, Harriet's world centered around home and church. Still active in the church choir, she found time to teach Sunday school, and she continued to do so for the remainder of her life. A major concern for Harriet was maintaining a large household that now included her mother and father, Ruth and Joshua Matteson. As money conscious as her husband, Harriet looked for ways to save money within the family budget. A spare room in the house was always rented.

There was reason for John and Harriet's preoccupation with money. The village of Laurens, nestled safely beneath the rolling hills of Otsego County, had not escaped the economic depression brought on by the bank Panic of 1857. These were, as one Laurens resident recorded in her diary, "hard times."[13] The ripple effect caused by the Panic was still being felt by many as late as 1860. While farmers worried about the price of hops, Kidder, too, was concerned about the lack of wagon orders.

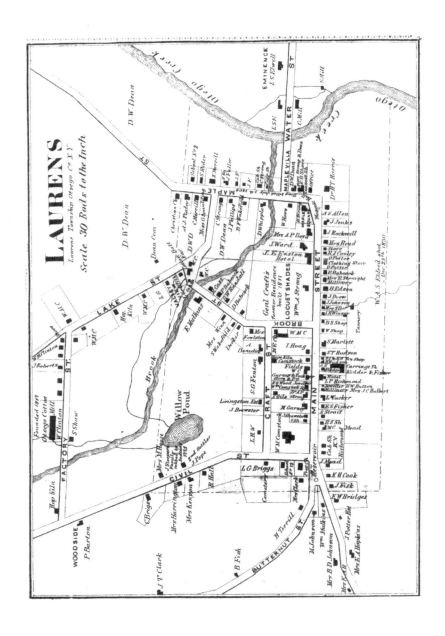

Despite these difficult times, the Kidders did have cause to celebrate. After suffering three consecutive miscarriages, Harriet gave birth to a healthy baby girl, Clara Amelia, on March 13, 1861. To her adoring father, Clara would always be referred to as "my little diamond" or "my queen diamond." The happiness they shared was interrupted a month later by events that took place a world away. A federal fort in Charleston Harbor, Fort Sumter, had surrendered to the southern Confederacy. The Civil War had begun.

John S. Kidder did not immediately volunteer his services after the fall of Fort Sumter, or even after the Union defeat at First Bull Run three months later. As the summer of 1862 arrived, however, it was clear that those who had predicted a short war were terribly wrong. The fearful casualties out west at Shiloh and the failure of Army of the Potomac Commander, George B. McClellan, to capture Richmond, the Confederate capitol, convinced many that the war would be long and costly. The sooner fresh troops could be brought into the field, the quicker the rebellion could be stamped out. On July 2, 1862, President Abraham Lincoln called on the governors of the loyal states for an additional three hundred thousand troops, chiefly infantry, to serve three years.[14]

This proclamation by President Lincoln caused a great deal of excitement all over the country. In small communities such as Little Falls in Herkimer County, the local newspapers published patriotic editorials comparing this national crisis to a similar call for troops during the Revolutionary War. "Let not the emergency show that Old Herkimer of 1862, is less patriotic than Old Herkimer of 1776—nor less patriotic then she proved to be but twelve months ago. . . . We can be the first to answer the Governors Proclamation and now let us take hold and do it!" *The Little Falls Journal and Courier* which published this editorial also kept its readers up to date on the latest rumors of new regiments being organized in and around the county. "We are about to enlist another regiment to which the pronoun 'our' may be properly prefixed, and we ask those enlisting from this county if it is well to remember this."[15] The *Courier* even went as far as to publish the population figures, for Herkimer County (40,561) and neighboring Otsego County (50,157), to illustrate how feasible it would be for either county to raise a contingent of troops.[16]

The person with the real authority to raise troops and to specify what part of the state they would be drawn from was Governor Edwin D. Morgan in Albany. Morgan was in a position like that of a medieval king. As monarchs of old took it upon themselves to reward their faithful with titles of nobility for special services to the crown, so, too, could the governor of a state. He could reward those who helped raise troops with a high rank in the volunteer army. On July 19, 1862, Governor Morgan appointed Richard Franchot as colonel of a volunteer regiment to be raised in the 20th State Senatorial District, which included all of Herkimer and Otsego counties.[17]

A self-made man by the standards of this era, Franchot had done quite well for himself without a stint in the military. The son of a French immigrant, he had attended local schools in Otsego County (including Hartwick Academy) and later made his way to the Polytechnic Institute in Troy, New York. Returning to the town of Morris, he helped establish a wool and cotton factory while dividing his time between local politics, as the Town Supervisor, and other assorted business interests, becoming the first President of the Albany and Susquehanna Railroad. On March 4, 1861, Franchot took his seat in the Thirty-seventh Congress.[18]

When Franchot made his tour of Herkimer and Otsego counties that summer, he discovered he would have little trouble raising a standard ten company regiment consisting of one thousand men. In fact, there was a great deal of competition between the various towns and villages to see who would be the first to meet their quota. Hardly a newspaper in either county left the presses without an article entitled "War Meeting at . . ."

In less than twenty-five days, Colonel Franchot had enough men signed on to fill the ranks of a volunteer regiment. One reason for the speed in which the regiment was organized was the effort put forth by recruiting officers. Your position on the staff of the regiment was dependant upon the number of men you enlisted in your company. Anyone who harbored the desire to wear the shoulder straps of an officer was a busy man in both counties. It would help a great deal if you had good business contacts or were a well-respected member of your community. Clinton A. Moon and Thomas S. Arnold, soon to be captain and first lieutenant of Company C, were actively raising troops and were considered "most capable members of the legal profession," according to the *Journal and Courier*.[19] Most of the officers were lawyers or had good political connections.

In Laurens, John S. Kidder and Elisha Fisher had some serious discussions regarding the future of the carriage business in the summer of 1862. "We were in debt," Kidder later admitted. They had a large stock of wagons and people were not paying their bills. "Times were hard," he said.[20]

When it was announced that a new volunteer regiment was being raised in both counties with each county being held accountable for five companies, Kidder made his intentions known to his partner. Fisher objected to the idea immediately. "I don't care what Fisher says about my coming into the army," Kidder later recalled. "He felt that our creditors might give us trouble and want their money. I talked with most of them and they said they could wait on us and would not require us to pay until a reasonable time."[21]

With his creditors temporarily satisfied and Fisher in control of the carriage business, John S. Kidder began to actively recruit men in and around the village of Laurens. His goal was to enlist an entire company and thus attain the rank of captain. "That I expected a commission I do not deny," he later said, carefully adding, "but I am confident had I not obtained one when I started, I should have held the same position that I do at present."[22]

Of the hundred men needed to form a standard infantry regiment, Kidder was able to sign on seventy men, forty of which hailed from Laurens. Assisting him in this endeavor was a twenty-two-year-old country store clerk from nearby Worcester. Delavan Bates had once dreamed of a military career, however, in 1857 he failed in an attempt to secure an appointment to West Point. Years later he noted that the cadet who took his place, Henry B. Noble, never got beyond the rank of captain. "I think it may have been all for the best," said the future brigadier general and Medal of Honor recipient.[23] Bates scoured the Worcester district and was able to add twenty-five men to Kidder's Company.

On August 18, 1862, John S. Kidder was appointed captain of Company I of the 121st New York Volunteers. "I was commissioned second lieutenant," grumbled Delavan Bates, "while Colonel Franchot sandwiched in a relative as first lieutenant."[24] John D. P. Douw, a nephew of Col. Richard Franchot had, indeed, been appointed to the rank of first lieutenant.

For John S. Kidder and Delavan Bates this incident seemed to be a combination of army politics, favoritism, and nepotism. They didn't like it but there wasn't much they could do about it.

There was another reason for the sudden rush to the colors in that summer of 1862, and that was, simple economics. There was a fairly lucrative bounty being offered at the federal, state, and even the local level. This inducement of over $200 to sign on for three years could, in time, prove to be a veritable nest egg for a young man. In addition to this, it was not uncommon for communities or private individuals to come forth with additional funds. The village of Fairfield offered $500 to be divided equally among those who volunteered from the community, and claimed it was the largest single bounty offered by any village in the state.[25] Private individuals challenged others to make donations. When forwarding his check for $100, S. C. Franklin, a local resident declared: "I trust you will divide equally among the volunteers of this town who have so nobly responded to the call of the [U.S.] Government, to protect the Old Flag, the Constitution, and the property of some of our wealthy townsmen who will neither go forth as soldiers in the army of our country, nor contribute for its support."[26]

The lure of the bounty helped Kidder recruit in Laurens. In 1860, the average yearly wage for a farm laborer in the surrounding area of Laurens was $200. A young man could make this same amount by simply signing on for three years.[27] This large bounty seemed to offset the comparatively low pay the average soldier received—a scant $13 per month. Col. Silas Burt, who had served as the Assistant Inspector General of the New York State National Guard, defended the rate of pay. "At first glance," Burt said of the pay, it "seems paltry, but when it is considered that, in addition, he receives food, clothing, quarters and medical attendance, there seems no reason why he should spend more than $3 to $5 a month, and not allot the residue for the support of his dependents, or if free from that contingency, should not direct its deposit in a savings bank to accumulate as capital when he returns to the working world."[28] It was still a popular assumption that the war would soon come to an end, the Rebellion "crushed out," as claimed by the *Oneonta Herald*, "and the war concluded within a year. There are very few men, comparatively, that can secure a better income in any other way."[29]

In addition to troops, each senatorial district was expected to furnish a training facility. In the last week of July, Mohawk farmer Henry Schuyler agreed to rent a portion of his farm to the state for this purpose at the rate of $10 per acre. The location was perfect. Situated atop a small plateau in the Town of German Flatts, the field overlooked the Mohawk River and the Village of Herkimer. It was on the same side of the river as Mohawk, Ilion, and Frankfort and only a short distance from Richfield Springs in neighboring Otsego County. More importantly, Camp Schuyler was within walking distance of the railroad line that led to Albany.

By mid-August 1862, Kidder and Bates had moved their Company I boys north towards Camp Schuyler on the Mohawk River. Here, they would receive the remainder of their bounty and be officially sworn in as volunteer soldiers.

Throughout the month of August an endless parade of soldiers, politicians, family members, and well-wishers descended upon Camp Schuyler. By the time Kidder and Bates arrived, there were already several full companies present. The camp took on the appearance of a tent city complete with a dining hall that served three meals a day. As soon as Kidder reported for duty, he presented his men to the adjutant and saw to it that each man was properly outfitted with a uniform. It was a relaxed atmosphere and there was a certain degree of bending the rules on that first day. When eighteen-year-old Cassius Delavan completed his medical examination and signed his enlistment papers, he collected his uniform and left camp. "I and some other fellows went over to Mohawk and got some photographs taken," he recorded in his tiny diary. From there he went directly home. He didn't report back to camp for four days; there were still chores that had to be completed on the family farm in Norway.[30]

On the same day, August 21, 1862, the *Little Falls Journal and Courier* published the entire roster of the 121st New York Volunteers, and Silas Burt arrived at Camp Schuyler with the remainder of the state bounty.[31] Many soldiers like young Cassius Delavan were anxious to get the money and send it home. There were a few last minute enlistees who showed up at Camp Schuyler at the exact moment Burt arrived with cash in hand. When Homer Wilson of German Flatts arrived, Kidder quickly signed him up to fill a vacant spot in his own Company I. Wilson took the money and vanished. There wasn't much Kidder could do except record the embarrassing incident in the Regimental Day Books.[32] It was his first but certainly not his last encounter with deserters. When Burt finished, only one man in the entire regiment had refused a bounty. Reverend John R. Sage, twenty-nine-year-old former minister of the Universalist Church in Little Falls, enlisted as regimental chaplain and would only accept the pay of a private soldier. "*We* call this patriotic," declared the *Journal and Courier*.[33]

With Burt's departure, the regiment now made every effort to act like real soldiers. The men drilled the best they could since no weapons had been issued to them. They stood guard and performed some of the less glamorous tasks associated with a soldier's life. Cassius Delavan assured his sister that washing dishes for his entire company was, "not a small job."[34] Some of the men became immediately homesick and wrote letters in their spare time; others idled away the time playing cards. There were no more visits to the local saloons in Herkimer and Mohawk; the men were now required to be in uniform and forbidden to leave the camp. Officers were introduced to form after form of military paperwork and prided themselves in their daily company, inspections. Occasionally they marched their company, or the entire regiment out of camp toward the Old Fort Herkimer Church. Only a mile from camp, the stone church stood as a reminder of the part the region played in the American Revolution. Soon the 121st New York Volunteers would take part in another revolution of sorts, hundreds of miles away.

Amid all this excitement and activity, Col. Richard Franchot appeared as confident as ever. He was, as one person observed, "constantly at his post, most active and energetic and already the pride of his men."[35] Before leaving Camp Schuyler, a group of grateful citizens presented the politician turned soldier with "a fine sword, belt pistols, sash, shoulder straps, spurs and gauntlets, the whole costing $130."[36]

On August 30, 1862, the 121st New York was ordered to break camp and report to the seat of war. That same day, another Union defeat was recorded at Second Bull Run. Captain Kidder marched his Company I men out of Camp Schuyler. They camped on the village green in Mohawk and then proceeded to the train station in the village of Herkimer where the boxcars would take them out of the valley. The fact that the entire regiment had trained for less than a month at Camp Schuyler escaped many as equipment and men were loaded onto the train. Woefully unprepared for what lay ahead, they still had not been issued tents or rifles.

As the eastbound train made its way toward Albany, their first stop, Captain Kidder of Company I had time to think about the journey he was undertaking. So far, the greatest adventure in his life had been the Atlantic Ocean crossing. It had been quite an experience for a boy of twelve years. Now, twenty years later, he was embarking on another great adventure. The Civil War was an event that would change John S. Kidder and those closest to him, for it became a Kidder family affair. All of his brothers would eventually volunteer their services, as would several brothers-in-law. Joining him in the 121st New York Volunteers was brother Edward, and his sometimes troublesome brother-in-law Delos Lewis. Next came George Kidder who enlisted in the 152nd New York Volunteers, a unit that drew men from the same state senatorial district as the 121st New York. When youngest brother Major Henry Payne Kidder was of age, he enlisted, and from far away California, William Kidder enlisted. When William Kidder left the family farm in 1858, he traveled to Panama, crossed the Isthmus and made it to the Shasta gold fields in California. In March 1864, he enlisted in the 7th California Volunteers. Finally, there was Charley Matteson. Harriet Kidder's brother had enlisted in the 76th New York Volunteers. John S. Kidder always made a special effort to look after Charley whenever he could.

With Albany, New York City, Philadelphia, and Baltimore behind them, the 121st New York became yet another in a long line of volunteer regiments that streamed through the nation's capitol. Arriving in Washington on September 3, the regiment had time for a brief rest and then reported directly to Fort Lincoln. One of the many defensive forts that surrounded the capitol, the twelve-gunned Fort Lincoln wasn't much to look at, even from the untrained military eye of Second Lieutenant Delavan Bates. "The fort is merely a breastwork, thrown up with a ditch around it and some brush," he observed.[37]

It was here, at Fort Lincoln, that the regiment was finally issued their Enfield rifles, cartridge boxes, and one hundred rounds of ammunition. Now properly equipped with weapons, there seemed to be little urgency regarding their situation, even with a Rebel flag clearly visible in the distance. Some, like Cassius Delavan, managed to sneak down to the Potomac River to wash their clothes and go swimming.[38]

This inactivity would be short-lived. Col. Franchot was stirred into action when it was reported that the Confederate Army had invaded Maryland. Leaving Fort Lincoln on September 7, 1862, Franchot force marched the regiment in an effort to join the Army of the Potomac. It was a grueling experience that few ever forgot. Marching under the hot Maryland sun burdened by heavy knapsacks, rations, and weapons, men dropped by the roadside and slept beneath the stars since tents had not been issued. Roused by Franchot at 2:00 A.M., they continued their arduous trek. These forced marches were too much for soldiers who had never marched before, save for a few miles with light packs and no weapons a few weeks earlier at Camp Schuyler. Their inexperience and suffering did not go unnoticed. "There is a new regiment attached to our brigade, the One Hundred Twenty First New York," wrote Chaplain John Adams of the 5th Maine in his diary, ". . . and marching comes hard for them."[39]

Franchot seemed to drive his men all the harder now that cannon fire could be heard in the vicinity of Crampton Gap, just below South Mountain. The march was made even more intolerable by the taunts the men received from the older regiments they passed along the way. Insults regarding their bounty status ranged from the mild "Paid Hirelings," and "$200 Dollar Men," to the vicious "$200 Sons of Bitches."[40]

Newly assigned to the VI Corps, Franchot was anxious to prove the fighting ability of his men; he pleaded with First Division Commander and fellow New Yorker, Maj. Gen. Henry Warner Slocum to have the 121st New York placed in the first line of battle. Slocum wisely brushed aside the request of the inexperienced Franchot and placed the regiment in the second brigade commanded by Col. Joseph J. Bartlett.

Nestled in a ravine for safekeeping, Bartlett followed Slocum's lead and rested the exhausted troops, giving them a "reserve" role to play. The regiment had a perfect view of the Battle of Crampton's Gap. With very few exceptions, it was the first battle anyone in the 121st had ever witnessed. An excited Captain Kidder showed remarkable clarity when recording the scene and even went so far as to include, in his letter to Harriet, a crude map of the day's events.

> *About 9,000 of our men, comprised of Bartlett's, (Brig. Gen. John) Newton and part of (Brig. Gen. William) Smith's Brigades went up to fight the enemy and take the pass. Gen. Slocum said he would do it in half an hour after he got within reach of them. I think he carried it in less than that time after he commenced firing. They made a splendid charge up a hill as Cooley's and utterly routed them. It was an exciting scene to witness. The enemy were posted at the foot of the hill in the woods which is composed of trees, [there was] no under brush to obstruct the passage of our men. I was fearful it would be night before the attack could be made but the fight was finished before dark. We came over the field early this morning. I counted 156 dead Rebels and 39 of our men besides any quantity of wounded while coming up the hill. I think I counted about all the dead of our men, as most of them were killed before they reached the woods. The Rebels lay strewn all along up the hill; they had a very strong position and ought to have held the pass with 500 men with their batteries, but they ran like sheep.*[41]

The attack made at Crampton's Gap was a little late as Kidder stated, with Gen. Slocum launching his attack at 3:00 P.M. The Confederates resisted but with less than one thousand men, could hardly hold back the twelve thousand man VI Corps for very long. Three hours later, at dusk, the battle was over and the VI Corps held the mountain pass. The next day there was very little for green troops like the 121st New York to do except assist in rounding up stragglers, picking up abandoned arms, and any other useful material left on the field.

It was here in the serenity of Pleasant Valley, past the Gap they had secured, that the entire VI Corps camped while Confederate and Federal Forces slugged it out along the banks of Antietam Creek in what would be forever called "America's Bloodiest Day." It would be three days after the battle, on September 19, before the 121st New York would get to Antietam. Once more, they were relegated to the unglamorous task of collecting abandoned equipment from the field. While some soldiers gathered up these items, others wandered the field looking for the graves of neighbors and friends who had been killed in action near Dunker Church. Here, the 34th New York Volunteers, a regiment drawn from Herkimer County, suffered a staggering 154 casualties. The sight of the dead, both Union and

Confederate, lying in rows of thirty to fifty men, had a sobering effect on the boys of the 121st New York. "I was very glad when we left the vicinity," recorded eighteen-year-old Clinton Beckwith of Company B, in his diary. "Its horrors sickened me."[42] If the swift dash at Crampton's Gap gave the illusion of glory in war, then the sight of the Antietam Battlefield quickly put an end to any thoughts they may have had regarding a romanticized war.

From Antietam, the 121st moved to Bakersville where they were finally issued tents. Up until this time the regiment had improvised. According to Cassius Delavan, cornstalks and "all other such things" were used to provide shelter.[43]

During this time of respite, Captain Kidder found himself occasionally in the position of Officer of the Day. All of the officers took turns at this duty. Although it relieved them from some of the monotonous routines like drilling and marching, they still had other duties to perform. It was a chance to assume more responsibility, or as Kidder explained, "take charge of the camp, see that the streets are cleaned, the sinks kept in order and see also that the guard is properly mounted and posted, see there is an officer present in all companies at roll call."[44]

Kidder took *all* of this very seriously as his ultimate goal was to rise in rank. In order to achieve this, Kidder believed that he had to make Company I the best in the regiment. One of the first appointments John S. Kidder made was to place Private Charles Dean in the position of Company Clerk. The twenty-one-year-old former mechanic from Laurens had been an old friend, and Kidder felt fortunate to have someone who could and would perform this tedious duty. Captain Kidder may have been a businessman back home, but he abhorred paperwork. Dean was just the man, as Kidder noted. He was always "in the best of spirits and gently stroking his *huge moustache*."[45] Dean felt that his shoulder length moustache made him look every bit the soldier, "a la militaire" as he was fond of saying.[46]

With Lt. D. P. John Douw temporarily absent from the company (he was serving as an ordinance officer on the staff of General Slocum), Kidder began to rely more and more on the abilities of Delavan Bates. "He is a good Officer," he said of Bates. "I am pleased with him. I think I could not have a better man. My Orderly Sergeant, James Cronkite is the best Orderly in the Regiment."[47]

Utilizing the collection of military books belonging to Second Lieutenant Bates, Captain Kidder got to work drilling his men. With the assistance of Bates and Cronkite, the company gradually improved in both drill and discipline. After only a few weeks, he couldn't have been more pleased with the results. In a letter to Harriet he boasted of his accomplishments:

> *James Gardiner and some of my boys from Worcester are as tough as knots and make good soldiers. [James] McIntyre's health is better than it has been; he improves in drill. Also Henry Heniker and Mason Jenks, Samuel Fenton, George Teel, Robin Fox make first rate soldiers. . . . In fact, I am well-satisfied with my men. I was afraid I should have to reduce some of the Corporals and Sergeants to the ranks for incompetency, but they are improving rapidly. . . . Indeed I have heard that some of the Old Captains of other Regiments had said that Company I was the best drilled Company in the whole Regiment. Whenever we come on to drill or on dress parade, we are always the first company out. That is what military men like is promptness.*[48]

Toward the end of September, Captain Kidder's optimism regarding his company soon became overshadowed by a sick list that grew with each passing day. "There are a number of sick but none dangerously," he confided to Harriet.[49] He showed genuine concern and sympathy for those who were sick and contempt for those who feigned illness. When eighteen-year-old Charles Thurston vanished, Kidder was furious. Thurston, in supposed poor health, had made it all the way to Washington for the purpose of obtaining a medical discharge. "I think he will have a good time of it," fumed Kidder.

> *He has been more trouble to me than all the rest of the Company. He would leave rank when we were on the march and steal apples, peaches, or anything else, and, when we lay in the field overnight at the Battle of Crampton Gap, he was out all night and was taken sick the next day. He will be made to toe the mark when he gets back.*[50]

As if the growing problem of sickness wasn't bad enough, the regiment was now faced with a change in command. On September 14, 1862, Col. Richard Franchot submitted his resignation after exactly one month of service. This announcement brought few tears, and to some a sigh of relief. "Never had a regiment a worse commandant," said Assistant Surgeon Daniel M. Holt.[51] Eager to return to his seat in Congress, the politician was, indeed, out of his element. "Franchot told me the reason why he resigned," recalled Kidder. "It was for the best interest of the regiment. *I thought so myself* as he had no taste for it."[52]

Franchot's resignation was accepted immediately—the day after it was submitted. Years later there would be a bizarre postscript to the career of Franchot. On March 13, 1865, he was promoted for "gallant and meritorious service during the war." Franchot, who never fought in a battle, was promoted to the rank of brevet brigadier general.[53]

In typical army fashion, rumors now began to circulate around the campfires as to who would be the new colonel. It didn't take Kidder long to find out. "Our new Colonel is Captain Upton," he wrote to Harriet, "a West Point graduate that has been in the service a year."[54]

As exciting as this sounded, and it was true, Colonel Upton would not be able to report to the 121st New York until the last week of October. During this interim, the health of the regiment continued to decline and now there was a death. "A young Pearson of Roseboom belonging to Company G," Kidder solemnly recorded.[55] At the age of twenty-three, Helon Pearson became the first soldier of the regiment to die, succumbing to typhoid fever on the second day of October. He was buried with full military honors complete with a volley being fired over his grave.

By the time Col. Emory Upton arrived at the camp of the 121st New York Volunteers, there were only 722 enlisted men and twenty-eight officers present for duty. Some of these men were sick, only able, as Kidder put it, to perform "half duty." Upton's first act as colonel of the 121st New York was to move the sick men from their makeshift shelters into a brick barn that he commandeered as a hospital. He then ordered more medical supplies and relocated the rest of the men to a better campsite. This was a relief to Captain Kidder who now had sixteen of his Company I boys on the sick list. Some appeared to be on the road to recovery while others were too sick to be moved. Despite this, he continued to be optimistic. Hamilton Westcot had been sick but appeared to be improving. "The large men do not endure as well as the smaller boys," he noted. Both the Snediker boys were getting better, but he worried about the three Camp boys from the village of Morris. Charles, Hiram, and Nelson Camp "are sick most of the time . . . but they can get about."[56]

Eventually, David Bushnell, a Worcester boy signed on by Delavan Bates, became the first casualty of Company I. When Bushnell's brother received word that he was sick with the fever, he rushed to Maryland but was too late. It was Kidder's sad duty to escort him to his brother's grave. Already depressed, Capt. John S. Kidder returned to camp only to discover that more of his men were sick.[57]

It took a while for things to improve, but Colonel Upton's efforts did not go unnoticed by the regiment. Most agreed that their new regimental commander was a lot different than the last one. Half Franchot's age, the twenty-three-year-old Upton was a veteran of First Bull Run (where he was wounded in action), McClellan's Peninsular Campaign, and Antietam. His appointment to the 121st was a combination of timing and luck. In October 1862, Upton received orders to report to his alma mater to assist in the training of cadets. He loathed this sort of boring assignment, having already drilled recruits in Washington prior to First Bull Run.[58] While in Washington, in late September, he heard of Franchot's sudden departure. A native of Batavia, New York, the West Point graduate seized the opportunity to command a New York State infantry regiment. Serving in the artillery had earned him recognition, but it had not given him what he sincerely desired—rank! By attaching himself to a volunteer regiment, the former captain of the 5th Artillery moved up several grades to colonel of the 121st New York Volunteers. Upton brought with him the much needed leadership skills and combat experience that Franchot never possessed. He was, as Kidder said, "West Point," a professional,[59] and "worth four like Franchot," added Bates.[60]

Apart from the health of the regiment, a second great concern facing the freckle-faced Upton was the growing discontent within the ranks. As Kidder assumed the duties of Officer of the Day, Upton, in the company of Capt. John D. Fish, a former lawyer from Frankfort, New York of Company D, scouted the countryside on horseback in search of thirteen deserters. "I think it is disgraceful to the Herkimer Companies," said Kidder of the affair.

> I think there will have to be some shooting before desertions will cease. I think also that there must be more efficient measures used to catch these scoundrels. I think also that there is but very little patriotism among the troops. There are many that are waiting to get their pay who will desert as soon as they get it. We have lost by desertion about 70 men from this Regiment and not a man will help catch a deserter if he returned home. Shame on such Americans. I fear that there will be more deserters tonight. Men say they hope that those that have gone will not be caught and it is really discouraging to hear men talk. One would think they had lost all sense of honor and respect for the government. It seems as though they care not which side succeeds if they can only go home; the demoralization is general in all regiments. In fact I begin to lose all confidence in the troops, especially the Old Regiments. I think unless something is done soon our army will be useless. I am sorry to say but such are the facts. The men get nothing to read but that infamous sheet the N.Y. Herald which

*poisons their minds. Traitors of the north are writing to the men to desert.
That is they tell them that if they get home the government cannot hold
them, and I think such scoundrels ought to be arrested and hung.*[61]

Thankful for the moment that the Otsego companies, especially
Company I, were not deserting at the pace of the Herkimer companies,
Kidder, nonetheless, despised those who shirked their duty. Deserters
were traitors to John S. Kidder.

Sickness was still a big problem in the regiment, and as the last days
of October approached, another name was added to the sick list. While
visiting his own men at Burketsville, Captain Kidder fell ill and was declared unfit for duty. The extent of his illness will probably never be
known. Private Charlie Dean, in a letter to the *Oneonta Herald*, simply
called it "the fever."[62] The absence of Kidder left Company I with no officers. Second Lieutenant Bates had been stricken a few days earlier and was
in the hospital, and Lieutenant Douw was still on detached service on the
staff of Major General Slocum. All the company duties fell into the hands
of Orderly Sergeant James W. Cronkite. Tapping Cronkite for the position of orderly was a wise move on the part of Kidder. Soon Cronkite's
abilities came to the attention of Colonel Upton. Within a few weeks he
became a lieutenant in Company I, the first soldier to be promoted from
within the ranks.[63]

Kidder remained on the sick list and was absent from the regiment
for almost a month, not reporting back until November 28. Like most soldiers, he probably fell ill due to a combination of disease, poor nutrition,
and exposure to the elements. In his first letters home, he often complained about the unpredictable southern weather. This was a lot different
from the upstate New York weather he was accustomed to.

Avoiding the crowded hospitals that dotted the Maryland countryside after the Battle of Antietam, Captain Kidder was nursed back to
health at a private residence. Instead of an open air tent or straw strewn
barn floor for a bed, Kidder had his own room, a fireplace, and nurses
to wait upon him. He stayed with a Horine family for most of the month
of November and believed that the care given him by this family has-
tened his recovery. The Horine girls ("one 17 years and the other 19
years of age. Smart girls.") waited on him while their parents worked the
farm. "The old gentleman had but one hand . . . Mrs. Horine had but
one leg. So you see," he informed Harriet, "they were in a bad fix. But
they were . . . good Union folks. Only charged me $10 for the whole of
the time I was there."[64]

Second Lieutenant Bates had a similar experience. Nursed back to health by a Mrs. Maxwell, an appreciative Bates paid her $20 claiming, "I have no doubt she saved my life."[65]

Kidder never forgot his first experience on the sick list and became more and more concerned about his health. Fit and rested after his month long convalescence, he declared, "I am enjoying good health. I eat like a horse and my bowels are all right. I think I can help whip the Rebels as well as I ever could."[66]

Before reporting back to his regiment, Captain Kidder was ordered to Washington with instructions from Colonel Upton to check on the status of any men from the 121st New York Volunteers who were patients in hospitals. When he arrived at one hospital, he was immediately given a small supervisory assignment. He was to take charge of about two hundred fifty men that had recently been discharged from the hospital and were waiting to return to their respective regiments. Some of these men had been sick and others were recovering from wounds they had sustained at Antietam. The sight of these men stirred Kidder. There was no lack of patriotism here. "There was not over 3 or 4 that belonged to any one Regiment and a *Noble set* of men they were; some quite lame that had been shot in the legs but willing and anxious to join their regiments. Such Patriots are *worth their weight in gold.*"[67]

It was at one of these hospitals that Kidder came face-to-face with the errant Charles Thurston. After seeing men that had been wounded in battle, it was difficult for him to accept Thurston's worn out excuse that he was still too ill to return to the ranks. After interviewing several hospital attendants, who claimed that Thurston was fit for duty, Kidder decided to present his case to Upton when he returned to camp.[68]

As was his habit throughout the war, John S. Kidder always found time to make little side trips. While in Washington he sought out old friends from Laurens and made a special effort to visit the camp of the 152nd New York where his brother George was now a sergeant. When the 152nd left Camp Schuyler, it had been assigned to garrison duty in the defense of the nation's capitol. What most impressed the elder Kidder was the relative comfort the garrison troops enjoyed. The 121st New York had just been issued shelters—two pieces of canvas that buttoned together to form a wedgelike or "half-lap tent." Brother George was living in a walled tent complete with wood floor and stove. Some of the officers were billeted in houses. "Haven't waded in blood ankle deep, haven't been hungry, thirsty or tired as yet," quipped a 152nd New York officer of a soldier's life thus far.[69]

After leaving his brother in the comparative luxury of garrison life, John S. Kidder boarded a boat and proceeded to Aqua Creek Landing in Virginia. The 121st had moved several times during his absence and were presently encamped at Stafford Court House. He arrived at Aqua Creek only to discover there were no horses available for him to purchase or even borrow. So, with overcoat over one arm and carrying his valise, he set off on a four mile walk to camp. He fatigued quickly after being bedridden so long and was excited when a rider approached him with a spare horse. Arriving at camp, Kidder reported immediately to the tent of Colonel Upton. There were twenty-three men billeted in hospitals in and around the vicinity of Washington according to Kidder's estimate. This was great news to Upton. There was a chance that these men might recover and return to the regiment the way Kidder had done. Upton needed every man at this moment as the regiment numbered only 657 men present for duty.[70] Sickness and disease had ravaged the unit that had not yet seen a single battle.

Captain Kidder made it a point to tell Colonel Upton of his encounter with Charles Thurston. "If he was well enough to run about and walk over to Frederick [Maryland] or go to Baltimore he could have reported to the Regiment," said Kidder. Upton agreed and told him to list Thurston as a deserter. In the paper chase that ensued, the medical discharge papers got to Thurston before the charge of desertion. He was discharged in December 1862. The only part of this entire episode that bothered Kidder was that back home in Laurens his wife was involved in the Thurston problem. Harriet had met young Thurston's mother, and the woman was upset that the Captain [Kidder] had been "very hard" on her boy. One wonders how upset she really could have been. Her son collected a $200 bounty, had been in the army only four months and was home by Christmas, not having fired a single shot at the enemy.[71]

When Kidder reunited with his Company I boys, things were quite different with Upton at the helm. Still green compared to the standards of other regiments, the 121st New York was being drilled at a furious pace. Assisting Colonel Upton in this endeavor were the officers and men of the 5th Maine.

When the 121st was assigned to the VI Corps, they were placed in the Second Brigade of the First Division along with the 96th Pennsylvania, 5th Maine, 16th and 27th New York regiments. It didn't take long for these veteran regiments to bestow the sobriquet "Onesters" on the 121st, because of the number one-twenty-one they wore on their caps, and also because Onesters rhymed with "youngsters," an obvious reference to their lack of experience in soldiering. Years later at veteran reunions, the "One-sters" would look back on these days with fond memories.

The 121st respected the Pennsylvania "Coal Heavers" as fighters, but never developed a close friendship with them the way they did with the 5th Maine. The 5th Maine did much more than simply welcome the 121st New York into the brigade. The officers of the 5th Maine spent many hours assisting the officers of the 121st New York in the art of drill and march. The enlisted men of the 5th Maine also availed themselves. Freely circulating about the camps of the Onesters, they offered valuable advice on how to set up a proper camp, lighten backpacks in preparation for long marches, and, most importantly, how to cook over an open fire. Delavan Bates estimated that perhaps nine-tenths of the men on both sides, before the Civil War, had never cooked a meal in their lives, "not even fried a slice of pork or made a cup of coffee."[72]

John S. Kidder was no exception. From all accounts, he hated to cook and his diet reflected this with the assortment of foods he would consume at any given time. For dinner he might have corned beef, cheese, onions, bread, and rice after eating only fried potatoes for breakfast.[73] He finally gave up cooking altogether and assigned Leroy Hall, who had once worked for him in the carriage shop, as cook for the officers of Company I. This arrangement turned out to be a cost saving measure as officers were expected to purchase their own rations. "I think it costs us as little for board as any officers in the Regiment, the Captain being very economical," said Delavan Bates of this arrangement.[74] It was cheaper to cook for three or four than to cook individually.

Another reform that was easy to recognize was Colonel Upton's penchant for not wasting a single moment in the day. Rising at 5:30 A.M., the day began with breakfast, followed in quick succession with surgeon's call, camp and company inspection, battalion or regimental drill. There were frequent parades, complete with dress white gloves. "I feel proud of the 121st," John wrote to Harriet. "It would do you good to see them maneuver on battalion drill, then march to camp at right shoulder, shift arms, every man steps at the same instant."[75]

This sort of disciplined marching did not go unnoticed by the veteran regiments. In time, they would grant the 121st another nickname, "Upton's Regulars," because they acted like regular army troops, not as volunteers.

Upton not only wanted his men to behave like soldiers, but also to look like soldiers. "The Colonel ordered every man to have his whiskers shaved off. I tell you there are some queer looking chaps," said John J.

Ingraham of Company D. "I think if we stay here three years I can raise a moustache by that time."[76] With that, the beards came off and a variety of moustaches appeared. The only ones who seemed exempt from this strange order were members of the medical staff. Dr. William Bassett and Dr. Daniel M. Holt kept their beards, but all the other officers shaved. It looked as if Upton was indeed trying to mold the regiment into his own moustached image.

Another change that met with Kidder's approval was Upton's insistence that the authority of the officers be always respected. He was pleased to hear that, in his absence from Company I, James W. Cronkite had handled an incident in a proper fashion and received the support of Upton. The last instructions Kidder gave to Cronkite before he went on sick leave was, "not to take any insolence or disrespectful language from any member of the Company." Naturally, Kidder was pleased when he learned of the circumstances surrounding the court-martial of Charles Hogaboom. Cronkite, who had preferred the charges, wasn't even an officer at the time, but Upton looked upon him as doing an officer's duties. "Good for the Orderly," said Kidder of the incident. In addition to the court-martial, Hogaboom was ordered to pay a $13 fine and stand guard duty every other night for a week.[77]

Not all of Colonel Upton's reforms met with the approval of the officers of the 121st New York Volunteers. Shortly after taking command, Upton saw the need to weed out political, or opportunity seekers, who were wearing the shoulder straps of officers. He received permission from the State of New York not to have any more volunteer officers assigned to his command without first meeting his approval.[78] As to those officers who were already a part of the regiment prior to his arrival, Upton instituted a series of tests based on West Point standards. "Some of the Officers," John confided in a letter to Harriet, "have had to resign by request of the Colonel, who is a very strict man."[79] Those officers that stayed, like Kidder, now took their jobs all the more seriously. To John S. Kidder, to have to resign would be tantamount to failure and disgrace. Above all else, he wanted to succeed.

TWO

"You must not fret about me"

NOVEMBER 1862–APRIL 1863

Maj. Gen. George B. McClellan just wouldn't do. After weeks of inactivity following the Battle of Antietam, President Lincoln removed the popular general from command of the Army of the Potomac. On November 7, 1862, Lincoln gave the job to thirty-eight-year-old Maj. Gen. Ambrose E. Burnside. Entering the war as a colonel of Rhode Island Volunteers, Burnside performed well at First Bull Run and later led the attack on the coastal installations in North Carolina. At Antietam, he commanded the left wing of the army in a controversial attack over the bridge that will be forever associated with him.

Before John S. Kidder fell ill, he tried to reassure his wife that all was well. He didn't believe that there were any Rebels in the vicinity of Bakersville, Maryland, and, even if there were, the army was constantly being reinforced. "There are new Regiments continually coming in. We have a large army," he wrote Harriet on October 4. "You must not fret about me as our Regiment will be kept back and not brought into action before others as Slocum's Division is a *reserved* one."[1]

Their days as reservists were coming to an end, however. The entire Army of the Potomac was on the move. This was the start of a new campaign, not a move toward winter quarters like many of the 121st New York suspected. It didn't take Kidder long to find out their destination. For the first time, he had to close a letter to Harriet in much the same way other soldiers had to.

I expect to have a hand in the fight at Fredericksburg. If you should hear that I am killed or wounded you must not believe it until you hear from some reliable source. And if it should be my lot to fall, mourn not for me but take care of my girl and bring her up as she should be brought up. Educate her well by all means and she will be a comfort to you. . . . Yours as ever, J. S. Kidder.[2]

Captain Kidder of Company I was correct. Fredericksburg was the destination of the army. Holding high the "On to Richmond" banner of McClellan, the muttonchopped Burnside moved the army toward Fredericksburg, a key railroad junction due north of Richmond, the Confederate capitol. Hoping to make his job as commander of the army a little easier and less cumbersome, Burnside reorganized the army into three Grand Divisions. This was all very confusing to Harriet Kidder who couldn't understand the old way the army was organized.

"You ask about Brigades and Divisions," wrote John.

A Brigade is formed of 4 or 5 Regiments. We have 5
the 16th, 27th, 121st [New York], 96th Pennsylvania and 5th Maine,
A Division is formed of 3 Brigades
A Corps of several Divisions then
2 Corps form one Grand Division.[3]

The 121st was part of Maj. Gen. William B. Franklin's Grand Division.

For the men of the 121st, the Fredericksburg Campaign started on December 4, when they broke camp and marched toward the Rappahannock River. The beautiful day ("splendid day, as warm and smokey as your indian summer days in October," said Kidder) made the seventeen mile march over lots, creeks, fences, and ditches bearable.[4] The day that was unusually warm brought in a cool evening. As the officers' tents had not yet arrived, Captain Kidder, along with the other officers, slept under the stars with just a blanket.

The next day the weather turned. It started to rain and it didn't stop. The 121st was ordered to Belle Plain Landing and hadn't been on the road long when the rain turned to hail and snow. "Virginia," observed Kidder, "is nothing but a bed of quicksand."[5] At dusk, they arrived in Belle Plain Landing and almost all were in agreement that it was the very worst place they had ever been in. It was a miserable place for a camp. Some areas were partially flooded and others boasted about two inches of snow on the ground.

Colonel Upton sent many of the men to the nearby woods to look for firewood while the others tried the best they could to erect tents. "The boys went to work putting their tents up with their guns for they could not get any sticks and there was no wood to be seen and the boys stood around like a lot of cows in a cold storm, heads all down and humped up and shivering cold," recalled Private John J. Ingraham.[6]

Cold, wet, and miserable, the prospects of spending yet another night in the open without a tent did not appeal to Kidder. His tent and baggage still hadn't arrived. Fearful of falling ill once more, he was determined to seek some form of shelter for the night. He and Cronkite got lucky when they befriended the surgeons of the 130th Pennsylvania. "We took off our boots and wrung out our stockings," said Kidder. "We were wet up to our knees but dry otherwise . . . they lent us four blankets to sleep in, gave us some supper . . . they had nothing but crackers, coffee, sugar and syrup and raw pork, but we made a good meal."[7] He was grateful for this hospitality and felt sorry for those who, unlike himself, did not have a rubber coat. These men truly suffered and spent almost the entire night huddled by the fire trying to stay warm.

The bitter cold continued through the next day. "You ought to see the boys the next morning," said John J. Ingraham. "They looked like the last rose of summer. Their coats and blankets were frozed stiff as a rail."[8]

Captain Kidder was surprised to see that the bay at Belle Plain Landing was now partially frozen, hard enough, he said, for a man to stand on. He knew that this sudden blast of harsh weather would be extremely hard on those that were sick in the regiment. Although he still had seven of his men in hospitals in and around Stafford Court House, what concerned him was the handful of men that were ill and forced to make the journey to Belle Plain Landing. "All the men have coughs and bark like fury," recorded Kidder.[9]

Before the war, John S. Kidder made lists of everything that had to do with the operation of the carriage shop, for example, work orders, supplies, money owed, and money due. At this difficult time, they seemed like such trivial items. However, it now was necessary to make lists of the sick and dying in his company. They included: Amos Winton, Steven Bolt, and Sherman Peet. When James Hall mustered enough strength to sit before the fire, Kidder took it as a sign he was improving. He hoped that James, Leroy Hall's brother, might be able to join the rest of the company in drill. The soldier who worried him the most, however, was Chester Alger. The twenty-two-year-old former teacher at Hartwick was suffering from the effects of chronic diarrhea.

Kidder entrusted to Harriet the delicate task of informing loved ones back home concerning the condition of the men. "I suppose some folks think that I can be with all the sick and attend to their wants personally but that is an impossibility. I do the very best I can for them while they are here with the Regiment, but I do not know where they go when they are sent off to the hospital."[10] He went on to explain to Harriet that he had just been informed of the death of Freeman Rose who died three weeks earlier at a hospital in Washington.

In the next few weeks there would be more bad news to relay to Harriet. Chester Alger wasted away and died on December 16, and two days before Christmas, James Hall died. A distraught Kidder made preparations to send the body of the twenty-two year old home to his widowed mother in Laurens.

For a brief moment, Kidder's letter writing was interrupted by the distant sound of horse and wagon. "The boats are going up on wagons for the bridges past our camp. I expect we shall have a fight before long but it will depend on the weather."[11] The problem wasn't the weather, it was the bridges. Maj. Gen. Burnside waited seventeen critical days for the supply wagons to deliver his pontoon bridges.

On the morning of December 11, the men of the 121st New York woke with the sounds of the drummer boys with their steady rap-tap-tap beat. The coffee hadn't yet begun to boil when word passed from campfire to campfire that the regiment was to pack up and move toward the Rappahannock River. It took almost an hour to prepare for the move. Colonel Upton instructed his captains to place all unnecessary baggage, including tents, in supply wagons. The six mile journey took most of the morning, for the regiment had to step aside to let artillery pieces and wagons pass. As the brigade reached the heights that overlooked the river, the sound of cannons were heard in the distance.

When the brigade came to a halt, Captain Kidder, in the company of several other line officers, made his way to the front of the column to get a view of the river and the pontoon bridges they were to use in order to cross the river. Calling to mind his tactics lessons as one of Upton's pupils, he carefully surveyed his surroundings. There was the river itself, as he said, "about 25 to 30 rods wide and to look at it from the top of the hill it appears quite small." On a slip of paper from an unfinished letter to Harriet, Kidder sketched the Rappahannock River with a strong bold line. He added other points of interest to the crude map. "On the west side is a vast plain, about 3 miles across it ridges and [it] slopes gradually back a distance of 6 miles from the river." Above the plain he drew a small square. "We could see the Rebel camp on the distant hills out of reach of our guns."[12] The camp, he noted on his map, was part of Confederate General

James Longstreet's Corps. They had been making preparations to meet this new Yankee threat for most of the day.

Descending the heights and making their way to the river's edge, the Second Brigade of the First Division, of which the 121st New York was a part, crossed over on the pontoon bridges unscathed. This was not the case, however, for those soldiers who crossed the river two miles above this point. The real action was opposite the city of Fredericksburg and Kidder knew it. "We have 180 guns to protect our landing while crossing," he recalled. However, this did not stop the Rebel defenders within Fredericksburg.

> Our men made 5 pontoon bridges; all finished in good order in less than 2 hours excepting one opposite the city which was nearly done when the Rebs fired on our men from the houses with their rifles; and we had to abandon it [the bridges] and shell the scoundrels.[13]

Safely across the river, Kidder continued to look over the terrain before him, confident that, at last, the 121st New York would receive its baptism of fire. The brigade hadn't moved far inland when Colonel Upton arrived and informed them that there was a change in plans. The brigade was to recross the river. John Kidder was stunned. "Why such movements I do not understand, unless it was to deceive the Rebs."[14]

Enlisted men were just as baffled by this order. "The reason for our coming back I do not know," recorded Cassius Delavan in his diary.[15]

Doing an about face, the men, who had moments before cheered wildly at being on one side of the river, now marched back in the other direction. Grand Division Commander, Maj. Gen. William B. Franklin, left only a small force to guard the pontoon bridges on the west side of the river. "When we got down on the flat near the bank of the river, I never saw such a sight in my lifetime," said Kidder. By this time, Union artillery was shelling the city of Fredericksburg incessantly in an attempt to dislodge the Confederate sharpshooters. Well below the action, Kidder could see the results of this artillery display. "A grand sight it was," he later wrote. "Together with the shells flying and bursting, and the roar of cannon [it] put fight into the whole of us."[16]

That night, the Second Brigade camped on the east side of the river. An exhausted Captain Kidder, having been on his feet since 4:30 A.M., penned a few more lines before getting some much needed rest. "I can hear some horsemen crossing the bridges. You could hear them at a distance of 6 miles. I have information from Lieut. [Frank] Bolles that he had been in the city. . . . He says that we took 60 prisoners. While he was there many fine buildings were on fire."[17]

The next morning, December 12, the 121st New York Volunteers broke camp and crossed the Rappahannock River for the third time. Convinced that his Company I men would be in their first real fight, Kidder trimmed the unit, leaving behind those who might slow his progress. Sixty-one of his men tramped across the pontoon bridge. "To the honor of Company I, not withstanding all the cannonading during the morning," he proudly reported to Harriet. "Every man that I had marched over the bridge did not flinch or sneak back on by the wayside."[18]

Retracing their steps of the previous day, the brigade formed a line and proceeded to move further inland. Their destination was the Old Richmond Road near Deep Bottom Creek. As they neared the road, the brigade came within range of Confederate artillery. At first there were only a few shots fired; they did not appear to be dangerous. "I was standing on the bank [of the road] ordering my men to lay down, [when] a shell came directly over my head," recalled Kidder.

> I heard and saw it coming. I squatted down and let it pass over me. It struck in the road and passed over the Colonel's horse, which was lying down or it would have killed him immediately. Afterwards one came over just above and struck in the road and bounced, turned and went up the road.[19]

He was relieved that this shell narrowly missed Leroy Hall.

Shells struck or exploded nearby scaring some and amusing others. After two of his men finished bathing in the creek, a shell suddenly exploded covering them with dirt. Both men laughed and said that the Rebels would have to try again. "The men were perfectly cool and never offered to stir," said Kidder of this, his first real combat experience. "We did not have to order one back to his place as they all kept their places in perfect order as they do at any other time."[20]

Most of the shells passed harmlessly overhead, with one horrible exception. Private Edward Spicer of Company B was struck in the head by a shell fragment. It was the first real battle related death suffered by the 121st New York. "I didn't think he realized what struck him," said Clinton Beckwith, also of Company B. "Spicer's death threw a gloom over us. He was a fine fellow and liked by all of us." Amid the cannonade, Spicer's body was laid to rest where he fell, by the Old Richmond Road. A few prayers were read. Then Beckwith and the others got their supper and slept by their arms in preparation for the next day.[21]

By December 13, 1862, Maj. Gen. Burnside was ready for battle, having stretched his one hundred twenty-two thousand man force along a six mile front. It had taken the new federal commander almost a month to gather the necessary men and material for this campaign. His opposite number, Robert E. Lee, used this time wisely, carefully distributing his seventy-eight thousand man force so as to be ready to meet any new threat.

It began about 11:00 A.M. when Franklin's Grand Division launched an attack against the Confederate right flank, a position held by Stonewall Jackson's Corps. "They had a very hard battle on our left," said Kidder. "Capt. [Nelson] Wendell said that it was the worst firing he had ever heard from the time they were engaged, which was until dark."[22]

The attack Nelson Wendell referred to was moderately successful. The divisions of Generals John Gibbon and George G. Meade were able to break through Jackson's line. Jackson recovered and drove both intruders back across the field.

The second phase of the battle commenced about 1:00 P.M. when the Grand Divisions of Maj. Gen. Edwin Sumner and Maj. Gen. Joseph Hooker launched a series of brigade style assaults against the Confederate positions west of the city. The stone wall at Mayre's Heights afforded Lee's men excellent protection from their attackers. They poured volley after volley into the advancing blue wave inflicting terrible casualties. These suicidal attacks continued until late afternoon.

The 121st New York didn't take part in either of these actions, but was by no means idle. Having established a skirmish line along Old Richmond Road, the regiment spent most of the day dodging artillery shells and Rebel snipers. These activities required as much skill as luck. Using their Enfield rifles for the first time, the regiment stayed fairly active trading shots with the enemy. Confederate marksmanship was good and John S. Kidder begrudgingly granted the southerners a certain degree of respect. "The devils will lay down and crawl up to get a shot at our men and as soon as they [our men] discover them, they fire away at them," he noted. A private in Company G had his arm amputated as a result of this sniper activity. Only one of the Company I men was hit and Kidder considered this lucky. Private Moses Caryl received only a slight bruise to the arm when a Rebel ball passed through his overcoat and cape. No longer reservists, the 121st New York lost four men to snipers and artillery while reporting only seven as wounded.[23]

By the end of the day, Captain Kidder was aware of the fact that a tremendous battle had taken place above and below the position occupied by his brigade. Still a novice when it came to strategy and tactics, the untrained eye of the Laurens carriage maker could clearly see that the position held by the brigade was of no use to the army. The Confederates felled trees by a swamp making any advance toward their position extremely hazardous. "It would be impossible," Kidder said, "for us to charge on them without success." As to the outcome of the day's struggle, he was cautious, deciding not to put much faith in camp gossip. "What the result was we have not heard and probably shall not until we hear from the New York papers."[24] The wait wasn't long, as word soon reached them that a terrible battle had been fought with a fearful loss of life. Burnside's casualties amounted to some 12,700 men.

Two days later, on December 15, the VI Corps received new orders. For the 121st New York Volunteers, the day began at 1:00 A.M. and ended three hours later. Kidder felt sure that this would be the move where the army would regroup and shift southward to meet the enemy. "We were surprised that every man was [on] this side of the river, the bridges all up and out of the way of the Rebels. Why such a movement is a mystery to everyone, various rumors but none that are reliable."[25]

By midday the entire regiment was back in the same camp they were in before the campaign started.[26] It was as if the removal of the bridges made it official: the Fredericksburg Campaign was over.

Kidder pondered the next move. "I think we shall go down the river and flank them on the left or cut off their supplies or advance on Richmond. Then they will be compelled to come out of their forts and abandon them and fight us on equal grounds."[27] This was wishful thinking on his part, but it was 1862. After a major engagement like Fredericksburg, and a defeat no less, the Army of the Potomac fell back and licked its wounds. There would be time for flank movements and advances toward Richmond. This was not to happen however, until the spring of 1864.

This first big campaign tired the carriage maker who, by mid-December, was nursing a mild cold, although he dared not complain. "Our Colonel," he confided to Harriet, "sleeps on the ground without any tent the same as the rest of us do and is always on duty."[28] Just the same, John S. Kidder was relieved to see the baggage train show up with the tents, and looked forward to getting a decent night's rest.

I hope I shall sleep warm for I have not [slept] any night since I have been back to the Regiment. . . . Had to get up 2 or 3 times and [get] warm by the fire. I feel well but have a very hard cough. Send some good refined licorice or cough candy in a newspaper. You can send some occasionally, for it will be good for me.[29]

The licorice arrived about three weeks later and not only was his cough cured, but he also assured Harriet, "I eat like a horse." His appetite had returned. Licorice for a cough was just one of Kidder's "cure all" home remedies. Once, when he received a dozen onions from Lewis Cronkite [James Cronkite's father], Kidder was thoroughly delighted. He was convinced that onions would cure his diarrhea.[30]

Both armies remained in place through Christmas and New Year's Day. On January 2, 1863, an officer rode into the camp of the 121st and announced that the Rebels were crossing the Rappahannock River just south of their position. Colonel Upton sprang into action and quickly ordered out three companies to investigate. Companies A, D, and I were to, as Kidder recalled, "march down to the river and dispute its passage by the Rebs."[31] When they arrived, Captain Kidder deployed his Company I men in a skirmish line for the first time. He placed groups of three men about fifty yards apart in a long line. The only Rebels they saw were the ones on the opposite side of the river, huddled around their campfires. This didn't set too well with the men of the 121st, for they were not permitted to build fires that night; they were forced to stand guard from midnight till dawn. "It was a false alarm," said Kidder of the entire affair. "Some fool thought the Rebels were crossing because he heard a noise in the water."[32]

Back in camp, Kidder became convinced that the army was in no hurry to go anywhere. When he wasn't on duty and had all his paperwork completed, he took advantage of the apparent calm by venturing out to other regiments to visit old friends from Laurens. It was on one of these occasions that he made a visit to the 10th New York Cavalry. Here he was reacquainted with Captain Delos Carpenter. The forty-six-year-old Carpenter had been in the Cavalry since September 1861 and, by all accounts, was doing well. "He is fat and healthy," said Kidder. "Looks just like his sister Lydia."[33]

Accepting an invitation to dinner, Kidder was not only impressed by the menu ("We had beefsteak, onions, potatoes, pancakes and applesauce"), but also with the fact that Carpenter did his own cooking. Relying on the culinary skills of his friend, John S. Kidder was still out of his element when it came to cooking. "We thought you and Lydia would laugh to see us baking cakes," he wrote. After the meal, the two captains took a

Virginia 1862–1865

leisurely horseback ride; they were careful not to stay out too late on the unfamiliar Virginia roads.[34]

After leaving his friend, Kidder turned his horse toward the camp of the 121st and was halted by the sound of a brass band. This brought back memories. He thought of the Laurens Band and how well they played at the Otsego County Fair. "Such music I never heard," he said of the experience.[35] Kidder felt that this band was as good as the Laurens Band. A few months earlier, Kidder had asked Harriet to send him some sheet music. "Cut them out of the books and send them by mail. . . . We have good singers."[36] Harriet went to work removing music from old church hymnals, even managing to find a few pieces for male quartets.

> Lieut. Mather, Capt. Fish, Lieut. Gorton and a few others have a glee club; [they] want I should sing with them. They have the music that you sent. The Colonel, Major and Lieutenant Colonel want us to get up some good singing for the Sabbath and also glees for other occasions.[37]

Convinced that the army would be moving into winter quarters, Captain Kidder was determined to have his camp just as comfortable as his friend, Delos Carpenter's. Taking careful note of what others possessed and what he himself lacked, he put together a laundry list of supplies that stirred Harriet, as well as the entire carriage shop, into action. Kidder observed that many officers used a chest as a makeshift desk. Turning it on end, the drop leaf, or lid, served as a writing surface; the interior was used to store valuables and an assortment of required military papers and forms. To his business partner, Elisha Fisher, went the job of building one of these chests. Not surprised at his partner's specificity, Fisher received precise instructions as to its construction.

> Make it 2 foot 2 inches long, 18 inches wide and 14 inches deep on the inside. Tell him to send the keys in different letters so that if one should be lost we would stand a chance to get the others. . . . You can have the chest sent either by the American or Adams Express; I am not particular which—Cronkite thinks that Adams is the best.[38]

While Fisher busied himself with this project, apprentice James Cockett went to work making a variety of tin containers. His first creation was a two quart container with a large hole in the top that could be used to store maple molasses. Evidently, Kidder had already tried to pour molasses into a small army canteen with little success. When this tin was completed, Harriet filled it with syrup and fitted it with a tight cork. She even sent an extra cork just in case her husband lost the first one. A six pound tin container was filled with "white clover honey on the comb." The spaces between these tin pails were to be filled with dried apples. "Fill every nook and corner," he said, adding that if space permitted, to send along a half of cheese. All jells and jams were to be sent in old oyster cans that were simply soldered shut. From the experience of others, notably Captain Henry Galpin, Kidder did not want these items sent in tumblers [glasses with a sealed lid]. Galpin's were sent in this manner and leaked making "bad works of the trunk," according to Kidder. The eight, six, and four quart tin pails were to have "covers and stout ears and bails." These were to contain butter. He was adamant about this, reminding Harriet of it on two separate occasions. The enterprising captain was using butter as a trade item and in some instances sold it outright. A year later, he confessed to Harriet that he could have made a small fortune selling butter, for it was in such great demand.[39]

In addition to food, John S. Kidder asked for a large butcher knife, two empty flour sacks,

> made of heavy drills, and an axe—the lightest one he [Elisha Fisher] can find, put a helve in it. He can send it by notching the partition in the chest. I want him to put Capt J.S.K. 121NYV on it with a punch. We are troubled to get axes to use. I have but 2 in the Company and some days men are detailed to go over to the Brigade Headquarters, then they take all the axes, and we are troubled to get our wood [for cooking]. If I have one of my own I can keep it for my own use.[40]

As Harriet had the tins assembled, it must have appeared that she was outfitting an entire regiment rather than one hungry husband.

As well as sending material goods, Harriet kept John appraised as to the latest developments in the carriage shop. During the first months in the army, John kept up sporadic correspondence with his business partner. At first everything about the carriage business was his concern, from the largest account to the smallest detail. "Tell Fisher I have forgotten about the bands on Caswell's wagon, but I intended to have cushioned the seat with enameled cloth. Pope knows what I agreed to do. I think Pope was to trim it for $7. That is, do a cheap job."[41]

Eventually, time and distance from the business made him increasingly tolerant. On one occasion, Elisha Fisher sold a buggy, complete with a recently purchased colt. The deal soured when the horse abruptly died, and the owner demanded to be reimbursed for the loss. When news of this reached Kidder, he shrugged off the incident. "I certainly have no feeling on my part for we are all liable to be deceived in such matters and I am sure that I shall never whine or complain at the loss. I think," he admitted, "we have been remarkably fortunate in not losing any more than we have, considering the time that we have been in business."[42]

It would be weeks before John S. Kidder could expect to see the chest and its contents from home. At this time "home" was all he thought of. As Christmas passed through to the New Year, his thoughts returned to home and family. John and Harriet had been married for nine years and this was the first time he was away from home during the holiday season. "I send a holly branch in this," a letter he wrote in January. "I want you to send this letter to Father with that in it as he would like to see it. *There are mistletoe bows here*, one in an oak tree over my tent. Father knows what they are, you must not eat the berries as they are poisonous." He missed the simple joys that only a father could appreciate. "I am glad to hear that my Diamond can walk, bless her little heart. I would like to see her."[43]

Kidder's thoughts of Harriet and Clara quickly faded away. It was a pleasant diversion for him but the realities of camp life came back to him in the form of the Pattengills—both of them. He had enlisted Charles and Edward and knew them both before the war. Charles was problem number one. When he absented himself without leave by going down to Belle Plain Landing, Colonel Upton had him reduced to the rank of corporal. "He has been a stubborn *Corporal*," said Kidder. "I have had some thoughts of reducing him for disobedience of orders but the Colonel has saved me the trouble."[44]

Following on the heels of this problem was Edward Pattengill. By chance, Kidder had overheard an argument between Pattengill and another soldier. It appeared that Pattengill had two pieces of tent canvas. As soldiers were only issued one section of this half-lap material, Kidder asked him where he acquired the other section. Pattengill said he purchased it from George Teel. Obviously, Teel had no need for the canvas as he was in a hospital in Washington. Kidder couldn't argue that, except to point out that equipment issued by the government was not considered a sale item. Pattengill refused to yield the canvas and Kidder warned him of the consequences if he didn't.

That evening, when Kidder dropped off his report, Upton asked him what the problem with Pattengill was. Kidder told him what transpired, pointing out that the issue had not been resolved. Upton agreed that Teel had no right to sell the canvas to anyone, but that wasn't the problem. Pattengill's questioning the authority of an officer was the real issue. As far as the sale of the canvas was concerned, Upton instructed Kidder that Pattengill "must disabuse his mind on that point. . . . He told me to have Pattengill arrested immediately and tie him up to a tree if he had not given it up to the Orderly Sergeant."[45]

The entire episode seemed trivial to Kidder. He decided to reason with Pattengill one last time. "I thought I would give him a chance to escape, so I told Sergeant Colton to ask him for the tent once more and if he gave it up it would be all right, but if he was insolent to arrest him."[46] Pattengill resisted and suffered the consequences.

The way he handled this problem had the desired effect in two ways. First, Captain Kidder acted as a fair man, offering Pattengill a last chance to avoid disciplinary action. Second, Kidder emerged as a strict officer, willing to enforce discipline. Unsure of how this would be interpreted by his Company I men, he was relieved to discover that they approved of the way he dealt with Pattengill. "The boys were all glad of it," he said.[47]

Dealing with men in this manner was a different experience for Kidder. It wasn't the same businessman to customer relationship he enjoyed six months ago. To Harriet, he tried to explain the problem. "As our Colonel is a regular officer, we have to style a little and we are not permitted to be intimate with our men. I think this is a mistaken notion, but we must obey orders."[48] The differences between officers and enlisted men were clear. In time, Captain Kidder would not think twice about disciplining a soldier.

Eventually, stories of regimental discipline and Kidder's own treatment of Company I men reached Laurens. When Harriet informed him that the latest Laurens gossip had Company I men ready to desert due to his harsh discipline, Kidder sent a quick note.

> Tell Mr. Fields that I received his letter. I think his advice good and I have not let any such things trouble me as I wrote you that if you hear any yarns about me you must let them [go] in one ear and out the other. I do not care what folks say about me as I have a clear conscience, but the only thing that surprised me was that Wm. C. Fields, Rev. E. V. Wales, E. S. Fisher and Lewis Cronkite should believe such foolish yarns. I have always, before this, considered their opinions of more weight than old women gossip. Mr. Cronkite wrote to his son James saying that parents who had sons under my command felt very anxious to know the truth as they were afraid that I would abuse them and I think when he gets his son's letter, he will be able to quiet their fears. I do not wonder that parents have solicitude and [are] anxious about it when such men give cre-

dence to such lies that were only started to cover their [own] disgrace. If one that cowardly deserted his country's flag, I think that men who do so are no better than the originators of such stuff and any man that will justify a man's deserting is a poor miserable coward himself and the Country would go to ruin if we were all like them. There is one thing I believe, that my Company will stand up to the work like men. I do not believe there will be any sneaking out. I think they have got the backbone to do it. I like the service well, I think it is very doubtful if I [will] ever make any more carriages.[49]

This was tough talk and even Kidder knew that it was pretty shallow unless an opportunity presented itself on the battlefield. But when? The longer the 121st New York Volunteers remained at White Oak Church (they had been there for almost four weeks), the more likely they would stay there for the entire winter.

Then something happened to give John S. Kidder sufficient reason to believe the army might move soon. On January 7, he was ordered to General Bartlett's headquarters with twenty-five of his Company I men. As his men were not required to have arms, he correctly deduced that this was to be a small labor detail. When he arrived at headquarters, he was joined by seventy-five more men and told to proceed directly to General Brook's headquarters for further instructions.

When he arrived, he was met by one hundred men from a Jersey brigade. This was not to be a small work force. As Kidder was the highest ranking officer, he was ordered to take all the men down to the river road where they were to lay down pine logs for a "corduroy road." Marching his men back to camp at the end of the day, Kidder was astonished at the site of over one hundred wagons loaded with sixteen foot pine logs, each measuring between four to six inches in diameter. This sudden burst of road building confirmed his suspicions. Why build roads at this time of year unless you plan to use them? "I expect the next letter you get from me," he wrote to Harriet that night, "will be from the battlefield. I hope that if we cross the river we shall have better success than we did before."[50]

Hoping to salvage what little he could of his reputation following the debacle at Fredericksburg, General Burnside proposed yet another crossing of the Rappahannock River with his Grand Divisions. On January 19, the 121st broke camp and, with three days rations in their haversacks and sixty rounds of ammunition for each man, they moved toward Bank's Ford. The rain returned with a vengeance. For days it rained torrents, causing the roads to dissolve beneath their feet. Men struggled to higher ground as wagons pulled by teams of horses and mules sank in the mud. The wet, exhausted troops of the 121st New York reached the river's edge only to receive taunts and jeers from the Confederates on the other side. This movement toward the river would go down ingloriously as the campaign written in mud—not blood. John S. Kidder never offered any insight or comment on the "Mud March," as it was called, but used the experience as a measuring stick to describe Virginia weather. In the future, he looked upon mud as "not as bad" or "worse than" what he had encountered in January 1863.

On January 22, Burnside cancelled the campaign designed to vindicate himself; three days later he was removed from command of the army. Once again, what Kidder thought of this change remains a mystery. If he was typical of any soldier after the Mud March, he was probably more concerned about getting back to camp for the first time in days and warming up before a fire.

The 121st New York returned to White Oak Church, their winter camp, and soon heard that a new commander of the Army of the Potomac had been named—Maj. Gen. Joseph Hooker. A veteran of the Seminole Indian War and the Mexican War, where he received three brevets for gallantry, the forty-nine-year-old Hooker performed steadily as a division commander during the Peninsular and Antietam Campaigns. In command of the Center Grand Division (II and III Corps) at Fredericksburg, it was Hooker's men who made the suicidal attacks against the Confederate position before the stonewall at Mayre's Heights. Furious at Burnside's handling of this disaster, followed by another one with the Mud March, Hooker blasted his superior in the press and even went so far as to claim that the country needed a military dictatorship if it were to survive the rebellion.

What Hooker lobbied for, command of the army, is not what he inherited. There was not much of an army at the end of January 1863. It was beset with a multitude of problems; morale was at an all-time low. There was an increase in the sick list, and units lacked proper food and supplies. Some regiments, like the 121st, hadn't been paid in close to five months.

You didn't have to be a major general to come to the conclusion that the Army of the Potomac was in serious trouble. Even before the Mud March, Captain Kidder recognized major problems within his own regiment. One by one, officers were either resigning due to poor health, or were asked to leave by a demanding West Point colonel who had no patience with those who would not conform to his rigid standards. Kidder saw the list grow with each passing day.

Captain [Edwin] Clark of Company G has been dropped from the rolls on account of his health. Captain [Clinton] Moon of Company C has resigned. We have but 5 Captains that started with the Regiment. Lieutenant [Henry C.] Keith of Company B has resigned. This makes 11 officers that have left the Regiment since we came out.[51]

The total picture didn't look much better. In six months, the 121st New York lost seventeen out of thirty-nine officers. This rate of attrition was fairly high considering what little battlefield action the unit had encountered. Only two of the officers, Lt. Angus Cameron and Lt. George Davis had succumbed to disease. The others resigned their commissions and it looked as if more would do the same.[52]

Added to this was an alarming desertion rate that existed throughout the Army of the Potomac. As many as 81,964 enlisted men and 2,922 officers were absent from duty and presumed to have deserted.[53]

The 121st was typical of the regiments at the time. By the end of February 1863, Colonel Upton had a total of 101 men listed as deserters. When the problem first surfaced, Upton wrote to the local newspapers in Herkimer and Otsego counties and had the names of the deserters published in an effort, no doubt, to shame them into returning to the ranks. When the number increased, he had an updated list published with a scathing introductory by Lieutenant Colonel Charles H. Clark:

Sir: I forward you the following list of deserters from this Regiment, men who received nearly two hundred dollars to enlist and serve their country, and then disgracefully and cowardly deserted their comrades and the services of their Government. They are fit subjects to be published to the world and ought to be scorned by every honorable person. They have defrauded their friends at home, and cheated the Government of their services.[54]

The publication of this list caused a great deal of excitement in camp as well as at home. Kidder had nine men listed as deserters. This wasn't bad compared to other companies. His friend, Captain Nelson O. Wendell of Company F, had the fewest desertions with only three men listed. Company C had the same. Six companies were in double figures led by Company E with eighteen men officially listed as deserters.[55]

For John S. Kidder, a single soldier listed as a deserter was one too many. He looked upon desertion not only as unpatriotic, but also as a personal insult. He promised to stick by his men and he expected, in return, for his men to stand by him. Each deserter presented a special problem that demanded his immediate attention. Samuel Snediker, for instance, once a problem, wasn't any longer. He deserted in November 1862 shortly after Kidder returned from sick leave. Suspecting that Snediker was on his way home, Harriet was notified immediately. "Tell Mr. Fields to have Sam Snediker arrested if he comes home—this you can keep confidential as he might hear of it and run away."[56]

Snediker and the group he fled with were eventually caught and returned to the regiment in February 1863. Brought before a very angry Colonel Upton, justice was quickly meted out. Present at the court-martial, Kidder reported to his wife that the case against one soldier didn't look that good.

> They are trying one of my men that deserted the same time Samuel Snediker did. He plead guilty and as I have a letter which was sent him from his wife that I opened (as we are ordered to open all deserters' letters) stating that he must be more careful if he gets away again and not be caught the 2nd time. . . . I think that he will never desert again as he will be put where he can not run away.

"I am inclined to think," he added in an eerie postscript, "that they will have him shot."[57]

The prospects of having a soldier shot for desertion, no doubt, alarmed Harriet. Her fears were calmed when she received another letter from John on the subject. Snediker and the others were lucky.

> The deserters that were tried and sent away that I spoke of in my last letter were sentenced to forfeit all pay that was due them when tried and sent to the Rip-raps, some for one year and others for 18 months, to be confined to hard labor and forfeit $10 per month of their pay while there, then to return to their Regiment and serve out the balance of their time.[58]

Kidder was really concerned with three types of deserters. The first category included those that were sick in the army and through a mix-up of paperwork were listed as "absent without leave," and eventually, as "deserters." This was, of course, not their fault, and naturally got friends and relatives upset when word reached them. Kidder's good friend, Private Charles Dean, was in this category. Dean was convalescing in a hospital in Washington, D.C. However, he was listed as a deserter.

When the army failed to clear up the paperwork, parents and some-times relatives often got involved; they made matters worse. The most persistent of these letter writers was Mrs. Helen McIntyre. Her letters, and there were quite a few, were a constant source of irritation to the reg-iment. By the time she was finished, Kidder was so confused he didn't know what she wanted. Although it appeared as if Mrs. McIntyre wanted her husband, James, returned to the regiment, he was doing his best to convince the doctors to discharge him and send him home. As the McIn-tyres were neighbors of the Kidders, John tried to handle the matter the best he could.

> I rec'd a letter from Mrs. McIntyre. She feels very hard toward me about James but I cannot help it. I could write her an answer but as I told her, all that I knew about James or what was reported with the exception of some things which would not look well on paper. I think that I shall not reply. She asks why I do not get James back to the Regiment. I have written to the surgeons to send him back and for several others but I can get no an-swer from them and that is all that I can do. I have had the Colonel write but he gets no reply. I sent James a descriptive list while he was at Freder-ick supposing that he would be discharged but Doctor Bently, who arrived here some 2 weeks ago, says that they intended to discharge him but as he attempted to deceive them they would [neither] discharge him nor let him stay at Hagerstown Hospital. I have not written half what he says about James and I have no reason to dispute his word as he is a very fine man. I think the circumstances of the Doctors sending him away and not dis-charging him all go to corroborate the testimony of the other men that were with him as well as Doctor Bently's report.[59]

A month later, on April 11, 1863, James McIntyre was discharged for disability; he was able to return to his shoemaking in Laurens, much to the relief of Captain Kidder of Company I and his wife, Harriet.[60]

The second type of deserter that Kidder was concerned with was the soldier that was sick *of* the army and skedaddled home at the earliest op-portunity. The most troublesome as well as the most embarrassing soldier in this category was none other than his own brother-in-law, Delos Lewis. While everyone else packed three days' supply of rations to prepare for the Mud March, Delos Lewis packed up and headed home. When he eventu-ally showed up in Laurens, he had many adventurous stories to relate to the townspeople regarding his war experiences, none of which Kidder believed. Once more, Harriet was on the alert.

I wish that Damon Mead [he was the village blacksmith] would go over and arrest Delos Lewis and send him back here again. He pretends that he was taken prisoner that is all—as there was no Rebs on this side of the river and he could not have got outside of our lines without traveling 10 or 15 miles. . . . Tell Damon I will give him $5.00 if he will arrest Delos and send him along.[61]

John S. Kidder offered the same reward to other Laurens residents for the arrest of Delos Lewis but to no avail. Lewis managed to evade all his captors and eventually returned to the regiment on April 20, 1863 under the protection of a Presidential Proclamation. Under the terms of the Proclamation, or pardon, for in effect that is what it really was, Lewis had $30.37 deducted from his pay. This covered the loss of government equipment, such as his haversack, canteen, gun, and accoutrements, and also the train fare from Albany to Washington which amounted to $7.88.[62]

Finally, there were those deserters that seemed to be in a class of their own. Robinson Fox's case wasn't that unique, but he caused Captain Kidder a headache just the same. The twenty-two year old had obtained a leave of absence and returned to Laurens. When he failed to report back to the regiment, John S. Kidder made the proper inquiries. He contacted Harriet and soon a letter arrived in camp from Dr. Addison Strong, stating that Fox was, indeed, in Laurens but too ill to return to the regiment. Kidder wrote:

I am very sorry that Fox did not get back as he has been stricken from the books and is considered a deserter. The first morning after he should have been back, I ordered my Sergeant to report him as absent without leave, but the colonel sent the morning report back and ordered me to alter the report and drop Fox from the roll and report him as a deserter. . . . I showed the Colonel the Doctor's letter but I think, from what he said, that he should have him court-martialled.[63]

Kidder did his best to save Fox from the ignominy of a deserter's fate. The situation, however, grew worse, and he began receiving complaints from the Company I men. As it stood, no man from Company I could obtain a leave until the last one, Fox, returned to the regiment. "I have a great burden to bear," he confided to Harriet. "Many blame me for letting him go as many are waiting to visit their families and friends as another opportunity will not occur this season. I had all confidence in Fox that he would be up to time. I am very sorry he is not here as I had to certify to his promptness, etc. and that I thought he would be sure to return in time . . ."[64]

The situation continued to deteriorate. When Sergeant John Webber of Company D returned from leave, he reported to Colonel Upton: "Fox got very drunk and noisy while on the [train] car going home and, if he was sick, it was because of his own impudence."[65] This news distressed Kidder. He could only hope that the report wasn't true. As news circulated about Fox's antics on the train ride home, many thought that Dr. Strong had been influenced in some way to extend the leave. This was enough to cause the Kidder temper to show its face. When some chided him that the good doctor, "could be bought for a drink of whiskey or a shin plaster," Kidder retorted, "*Fox will be back. The Doctor is a reliable man.*" Still, others taunted Kidder, asking him if the doctor was a Democrat, or worse, a Vallandingham Copperhead.[66]

Despite the teasing, John J. Kidder held fast to his belief that Robinson Fox would return to Company I. Already a month had gone by when a letter arrived for Fox. Kidder held it aside and refused to open it, hoping to give it to him when he returned. "I hope to God that he will come back soon for I am tired of hearing complaints," said a thoroughly exasperated John S. Kidder.[67]

Cases like McIntyre's, Lewis's, and Fox's made life very difficult not only for the Captain of Company I, but also for his wife in Laurens. A day didn't pass that Harriet didn't encounter a sweetheart, family member, or friend who had someone in Company I. While her husband studied tactics, she became very adept in *tact* dealing with the people of Laurens.

As Captain Kidder concerned himself with Company I deserters, the army slowly came to life under the direction of Maj. Gen. Hooker. Many seemed to forget the good qualities Hooker possessed during his short tenure as commander of the Army of the Potomac, for he was haunted by rumors of hard drinking, womanizing, and a moniker he truly despised—"Fighting Joe." He had a solid three months to pull the army together and he did a good job of it. His reforms affected all aspects of the army. To the common soldier and line officer, like John S. Kidder, these changes came as a breath of fresh air.

Starting right at the top, Hooker did away with Burnside's "Grand Division" system and went back to the old corps style of army organization. Captain Kidder and the 121st New York were still part of the VI Corps but now they had a new boss. Criticized by Ambrose E. Burnside, which in itself was not very serious, and by the Congressional Committee on the Conduct of the War, which was *very* serious, Maj. Gen. William B.

Franklin was removed from command after the defeat at Fredericksburg. In the reshuffling of Union commanders that took place when Hooker assumed command, the VI Corps went to the very capable Maj. Gen. John Sedgwick. Like Hooker, Sedgwick was an 1837 graduate of West Point and had risen steadily in rank since the beginning of the Civil War.

In addition to corps appointments [Hooker had seven at his disposal], the corp patch or badge was introduced. Simplistic in their designs, the badges made it easier for officers and men to identify different groups of soldiers in the field. Their ultimate effect on the army was felt later on as a certain "Espirit de Corps" developed. Men were proud of their units and wore their corps patch as a symbol of honor. To the VI Corps went the Greek Cross. Since Captain Kidder and the 121st New York were part of the First Division, their cross was red. The Second Division wore white badges and the Third Division wore blue. As the VI Corps garnered honors throughout the war, men that were a part of it swelled with pride. Writing to Harriet during the closing months of the war, John instructed her to have her picture taken. "I want you to wear a plain red cross on your hat. Something like this . . ."[68]

Under Hooker, the quality of life of the common soldier took a turn for the better. While the roads of Virginia were impassable due to the mud, Hooker made sure the road home was a little more accessible to homesick boys in blue. Harriet knew that her husband had his hands full with Company I deserters and the problems that some presented by "extending" their leaves of absence, but she held fast to the hope that he, too, might obtain a short leave and return to Laurens. It wasn't that easy as the Captain explained, "Capt. Fish and Lieut. Gorton started on the 23rd [of February] for home. They have a leave of absence, 10 days, which is all that they could get. Only 2 officers of the line can be absent at the same time. I may possibly be one of the next 2, if not I shall have to wait another 10 days."[69]

Ten days passed only to see the next leave go to Captain Mather and Lieutenant Casler. Kidder and Lieutenant Ulysses Doubleday were scheduled to go home next. However, all leaves were cancelled as the second week of March grew near. It was rumored that the army was ready to move into another campaign. The rumor proved false but did nothing to change the leave situation. Kidder and Doubleday had to stay put for the time being.

For those unable to get home, at least the pangs of homesickness could be cured by the steady flow of mail that reached the camps. As for the pangs of hunger, there was a cure for that too. The food was good, there was plenty of it, and the results were obvious. "I think my men were never so healthy as they are at present," recorded Kidder in February 1863. "They grow so fat that they cannot button their pants and coats. . . . We have wheat bread and as good as I ever saw, in fact the men all agree that it is better than we got at home, generally. In fact, I never saw any better."[70]

As to the serious business of soldiering, Hooker stressed activity. There were frequent parades, reviews, inspections, drills, and target practice. The 121st New York had little time to familiarize themselves with any weapons when they were immediately rushed into the field at the dawn of the Antietam Campaign. While they were at Camp Schuyler, the very first order, "Special Order No. 1," covered the subject of firearms. It stated that no noncommissioned officer, musician, or private was to have in their possession any weapons "except those furnished by the government."[71] Any other weapons were to be confiscated.

The weapon eventually used by the 121st New York was the .57 caliber Enfield rifled musket. Weighing slightly more than nine pounds, it was capable of killing a man at eight hundred yards and could accurately reach distances of one thousand yards.[72] Unacquainted with their new weapons, the men of the 121st experienced their share of fumbling. Accidents occurred instantly. At Crampton Gap, Jacob Prame was attempting to load his weapon when it discharged. He had carelessly placed his hand over the top of the barrel when the rifle discharged. His hand was so badly mangled, it had to be amputated.[73]

When Colonel Upton assumed command, rifle practice became part of the daily routine. Consequently, when the men were not performing picket duty or actively engaged in a campaign, they practiced. In mid-March 1863, Kidder recorded the results of a regimental target practice, being careful, of course, to highlight the efforts and accomplishments of his own Company I.

> We have been out 3 times to practice target shooting. My company beat the regiment the first time. The 2nd time was 4th best, 3rd time 2nd best. . . . James Gardner was my best shot the 1st time. George Richardson the best shot the 2nd time. . . . We commenced firing at 20 rods [110 yards] the first time. The wind was very high, had three balls in the bull's eye and 20 within 10 inches of the centre. The second day, 30 rods [165 yards], wind very high. 40 rods [220 yards] the third day, had four balls in the bull's eye. Each man fired 3 rounds. It is quite [a] sport for the men.[74]

Captain Kidder never used an Enfield during the Civil War. Like other officers, he preferred the pistol and would use this weapon on several occasions in close order combat with deadly results.

In addition to firearms practice, Colonel Upton also stressed the basics. "The officers have been studying tactics the past months, shall continue to do so until we march. I think I am pretty well posted in the school of the *soldier, Company* and *Battalion,* also in *skirmishing.* I wish my Company was as large as when we started," said Kidder. "I have but 58 men present, shall have 60 when Dean and Colton return."[75] In another year, John S. Kidder would look upon fifty-eight men in a company as a large number, a luxury.

As Hooker made all sorts of staff changes, so, too, did Colonel Upton. There were many new additions to the staff of the 121st New York Volunteers. Upton secured a place for his brother, Henry, as a second lieutenant in Company G. This was quite a jump in rank for someone who had only recently been a private in the 104th Illinois.[76] This obvious display of nepotism didn't seem to bother Kidder. "He is a good officer," he later admitted.[77] In all likelihood, Kidder probably took this gesture in stride. There were *many* vacancies that were being filled at the time. In fact, there was wholesale reshuffling of staff officers. Seven sergeants were promoted to lieutenants and three more captains resigned their commissions. Upton took his time filling these vacancies, carefully screening each candidate to make sure they measured up to his standards. Delays did not go unnoticed in Albany. Letters arrived urging Colonel Upton to fill these positions with political appointments. Upton was quick to defend his position. In a letter to the Assistant Adjutant General of the State of New York, Upton tried to be tactful.

> There are about ten vacancies in the Regiment and the only reason they have not been filled is because I have not found men with the requisite energy, firmness and intelligence to make good officers. As fast as men have exhibited their qualities I have forwarded their names. I trust Gov. Seymour will allow me to fill the vacancies in the manner proposed and when filled, I will promise a Regt. which will be not only an honor to the State, but to the whole country.[78]

THREE

". . . a most terrible battle"

B y the last week of April 1863, the war in Virginia was under
way once again. The muddy roads which befuddled Burnside
were now sufficiently dry to warrant a move against the Confederate Army of Northern Virginia. Hooker was eager, and
quite confident, that his one hundred thirty-four thousand man army
could and would win the war with one decisive battle. It would then be
"on to Richmond!"

Despite having a vastly superior force at his disposal, Hooker did
not want to meet General Robert E. Lee in a head-on confrontation. A
veteran of both Antietam and Fredericksburg, Hooker saw for himself the
effects of frontal attacks on Lee's forces. Instead, Hooker devised one of
the most daring and imaginative plans of attack in the war thus far. The
V, XI, and XII Corps, roughly one third of the Federal Army, were to
break camp and move about twenty miles upstream from Fredericksburg
and cross the Rappahannock River at Kelly's Ford on April 29. While
this flanking maneuver was being performed, the VI and I Corps would
cross the Rappahannock just below Fredericksburg, in an effort to deceive
the Confederates.

For one brief moment, Hooker held the upper hand. The sudden
troop movements confused the Confederate commander. It didn't take
General Lee long, however, to come to the conclusion that the real threat
was not with the VI and I Corps to his left, but at a crossroads town
called "Chancellorsville." Carefully dividing his sixty thousand man
force, Lee placed a small number near Fredericksburg and moved the remainder toward Chancellorsville. In the end, Lee, too, could be quite daring and imaginative.

While the Battle of Chancellorsville raged, Maj. Gen. Sedgwick and the VI Corps maintained their position and awaited orders from Hooker. As of May 2, all of Hooker's Corps except the VI Corps were under attack. Around 11:00 P.M. that night, Sedgwick received orders to proceed immediately westward and join up with Hooker. The quickest way to do this was to move north on the Old Richmond Road toward Fredericksburg. Within an hour most of the VI Corps regiments had been awakened, and by 2:00 A.M., the Second Brigade, including the 121st New York, was ready to march. This moonlit march was made especially hazardous due to Confederate sharpshooters. They continually harassed Sedgwick's men as they traversed the Old Richmond Road.

Streaks of daylight outlined the ruins of Fredericksburg, a once beautiful city. The VI Corps positioned itself in much the same manner as the entire Grand Divisions of Hooker and Sumner the previous December. Before them stood the formidable stone wall at Mayre's Heights. During the Battle of Fredericksburg, most of Burnside's casualties had been inflicted here during a futile attempt to breach the Confederate line. The Heights had to be taken, for they blocked the most direct route to Hooker's beleaguered forces. It took four tries but Sedgwick finally broke through. Hours behind schedule, the VI Corps was at last moving west on the Orange Plank Road. The troops struggled under the weight of backpacks containing eight days' rations as they marched in the blazing sun toward Chancellorsville, twelve miles away.

The activity along the Orange Plank Road did not go unnoticed by nearby Confederate units. First to respond to this obvious rescue attempt was Confederate General Cadmus Marcellus Wilcox. The thirty-eight-year-old former tactics instructor at West Point was in command of a brigade of Alabama troops near Bank's Ford when Sedgwick reached Fredericksburg. By the time Mayre's Heights had been overrun, Wilcox was already moving his brigade toward the Orange Plank Road. Carefully placing his skirmishers ahead of the main force, Wilcox decided to make a defensive stand around a slightly wooded area near, as he called it, "a red church."[1]

Salem Church was a two-storied steepleless brick chapel built in 1844 to serve the needs of Baptist families along the Orange Plank Road. When the Civil War began, Salem Church had a congregation of forty-eight, twenty of whom were Negro.[2] The church, together with a schoolhouse situated on the same side of the road, proved to be an excellent location to position troops.

The buildings served a dual purpose. Not only did they warn Wilcox of the approaching Bluecoats, but they also effectively stalled the enemy's advance once they came within sharpshooter range.

By late afternoon, Wilcox had all five of his Alabama regiments in position. The 11th and 14th were on one side of the road and the 8th, 9th, and 10th took up position on the church and school side. Although outnumbered, Wilcox counted on the assistance of the nearby brigades of Generals Joseph B. Kershaw, Paul Jones Semmes, and William Mahone. He had to buy time, but he had several advantages over his foe. His men were already in position, were rested, and held the high ground. Union troops had to push through thick brush which offered little protection. As the day progressed, time was on his side. The later it became, the less chance of a prolonged conflict. Darkness would cut short any battle no matter how large or small. Confederate General Wilcox had only to sit, be patient, and let the Union forces meet him on his own terms.

The waiting was over by 4:00 P.M. as skirmishers on both sides made contact and exchanged rifle fire. A small artillery duel began and lasted a scant twenty minutes. The Confederates were forced to break off the engagement when their two rifled pieces ran out of ammunition.[3] It was close to 5:30 P.M. when the 5th Maine, 96th Pennsylvania, 121st New York, and 23rd New Jersey were poised to attack.

As the skirmishers traded shots with each other, Wilcox and his Alabama veterans braced themselves for the full weight of the Union attack. "Then," recalled Wilcox, "giving three cheers, they came with a rush, driving our skirmishers rapidly before them."[4] Pushing through the underbrush and cheering all the way, Colonel Upton's men advanced toward Salem Church. When they were within eighty yards of the Rebel lines, Wilcox ordered his men to fire. The first volley stunned the attackers and temporarily halted their advance. Men fell by the score. If they were not instantly killed, they were so seriously injured they were unable to move. Upton narrowly escaped death or possible capture when bullets wounded his horse and sliced the reins. Horse and rider bolted toward the Confederate position. Upton managed to leap from the animal and fought the rest of the battle on foot.

To Wilcox's surprise, the first volley he fired seemed to be nothing more than a minor setback for the Union troops. Instead of falling back, they advanced with renewed vigor. The 121st New York not only surrounded the schoolhouse, but also captured its inhabitants—members of the 9th Alabama.

As Upton's men neared Salem Church, Confederate resistance stiffened. Wilcox committed his reserves. During the ensuing melee, Captain Kidder left the ranks only once, when he saw young Fred Ford receive a painful wound to the thigh. Kidder went to his assistance and brought Ford to Salem Church. Here, lying against the brick church on a Sunday afternoon, the twenty-one-year-old former Fairfield student slowly bled to death. He had been wearing his second lieutenant shoulder straps for less than two weeks.[5]

Kidder didn't remain with Ford, probably not realizing how seriously he was injured. He returned immediately to Company I only to discover that the fortunes of the entire regiment had turned in a matter of minutes. Instead of being a part of a spirited advance, they were now actively engaged in a retreat. The schoolhouse had been retaken and the Union lines were steadily falling back.

An attempt was made to rally around the colors some 450 yards from the church. Here, the survivors of the 121st New York huddled; they were soon joined by other soldiers who had become separated from their units in the confusion of battle.[6]

The fighting was virtually over by 6:30 P.M. on May 3. Men were physically and mentally exhausted, to the point that even the pickets were too tired to shoot at each other. Together with the other regiments of the brigade, the 121st New York slowly made their way toward Bank's Ford, leaving their wounded comrades on the field. They remained there until midnight, and by 2:00 A.M., crossed the pontoon bridge over the Rappahannock River. The Second Brigade had been first in the fight at Salem Church and the last to leave the field and cross over the river.

During the early morning hours of May 4, the captains gathered to make their reports to Colonel Upton. It became painfully clear to him that his first real battle with the regiment was a slaughter. Of the 453 men he led down the Plank Road to Salem Church, 276 were missing. It was the highest reported loss of any infantry regiment at the Battle of Chancellorsville. Although the 121st had been seriously hurt, Upton closed his Official Report on an optimistic note. The regiment, he insisted, was "ready for any service that might be imposed upon it."[7]

John S. Kidder may not have agreed with Upton on this point, but it didn't matter, at least for now. He was exhausted. Like everyone else, he had been on his feet for over twenty-four hours. That morning he wrote to tell Harriet that he escaped harm in this, his first combat experience. Kidder feared that reports of his being wounded would get into the local papers. The fear was well-founded, as days later the *Little*

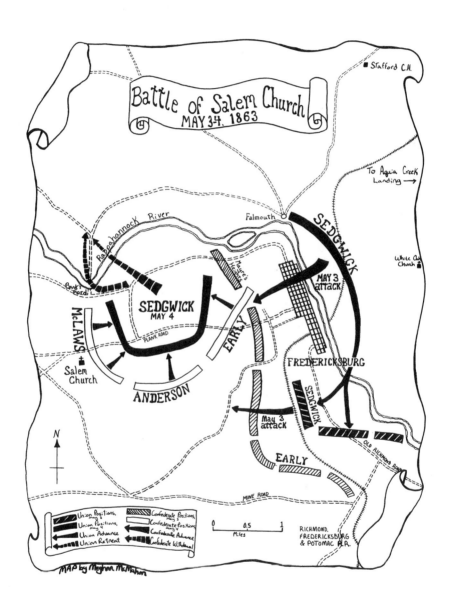

Battle of Salem Church
MAY 3-4, 1863

Stafford C.H.

To Aquia Creek Landing →

Rappahannock River

Falmouth

SEDGWICK

White Oak Church

Banks Ford

McLAWS

SEDGWICK
MAY 4

Marye's

MAY 3 attack

EARLY

PLANK ROAD

Salem Church

ANDERSON

FREDERICKSBURG

SEDGWICK

May 3 attack

Old Richmond Road

EARLY

N

MINE ROAD

Union Positions, may 3
Union Positions, may 4
Union Advance
Union Retreat

Confederate Positions, may 3
Confederate Positions, may 4
Confederate Advance
Confederate Withdrawl

0   0.5   1
Miles

RICHMOND, FREDERICKSBURG & POTOMAC R.R.

MAP by Meghan McMahon

Falls Journal and Courier erroneously reported that he had been wounded in the foot.

> Battlefield West of Fredericksburg
> Monday, May 4th, 1863
> Dear Wife,
>
> It is with a sad heart I pen you a few lines having been through a most terrible battle and lost many of my men although I have come out unharmed. [I] had my pistol shot off from my belt which I lost and [I had] one bullet [pass] through my blanket and one through my pants just above my foot.
>
> After we crossed over to Fredericksburg, we lay there to attract the attention of the Rebs until Saturday afternoon. About 6 o'clock we drove in their pickets, while Hooker was up north or west of them with five corps of the Army. What success he has had we do not know. On Saturday night we prepared to storm the heights above the city, started at 2 o'clock in the morning [on] Sunday. Our Regiment supported the left while some of the Vermont and New Jersey with the 43rd New York carried the heights and the U.S. flag was planted in their forts by eleven o'clock A.M.[8]
>
> Willis Hillsinger was shot dead while storming the heights. This I was told by one of his Co.[9]
>
> After we reached the top of the hill, our Brigade formed the front line of battle to pursue the Rebs. We marched about 2 miles and found them posted in a wood. We gave them battle. It was about 5 o'clock P.M. when we commenced the fight. We routed them at first and made a charge on them, and routed them until they came up to their 2nd line of battle. Then such a fire as we [Bartlett's Brigade] rec'd. has not been witnessed in this war, and is said by all the old soldiers and officers as being the very worst fire ever rec'd. from the rebels. The 23rd New Jersey joined us on our right but would not advance into the woods and after the fight commenced, [they] immediately turned and ran like sheep, such miserable cowards ought to be shot.[10] This caused the Rebels, who were in front of the Regt. to pour across [and] fire on our right wing. We were then ordered [after fighting 20 minutes] to retire to our 2nd line, and, as there were many tops of trees and limbs, we could not keep a good line and were somewhat scattered. A few cowards ran like sheep but most of the men retired without confusion. I am sorry to report that Zebulon Bowen ran about 11/2 miles and was stopped and arrested by the Provost Guard.[11] The boys say he is a coward, and I have 2 men from Worcester and one from Hartwick that acted cowardly. Otherwise, my men behaved splendidly and fought like tigers.

After we came out of the woods, we retreated about 200 rods then made a rally around the colors with our Col. (who is one of the best and bravest hero). There were about 75 men of our Regt. and the Major of the 96th Pennsylvania with 15 of his men that rallied around our colors and succeeded in driving back the Rebels into the woods. The 2nd line of battle that was back of us did not support us properly and, if it had not been for our Col. with his band of 75 men (for I think that there was not more than that number), it would of been a roust.[12]

I shall never forget the noble fellows who stood by at that moment and fought until dark and I am proud to say that. Co. I had 14 men of that number and 2 officers. I will send you a list of their names who stood by me like brothers and fought so nobly . . .

I had 7 killed, 19 wounded, and 5 missing besides both of my Lieuts. wounded. I had only 55 men go into the fight besides 2 Lieuts.[13] Is not this a terrible record? And our doctor went over to the ground which the Rebels held, and he says that they had many more killed and wounded than we had.[14]

Charles F. Pattengill and [Isaac] Peck of Milford were not in the fight, for they volunteered in the morning while we were about to leave the left, to take a very exposed and dangerous position on a knoll to watch the movements of the enemy where they were exposed to grape and canister from one [of] their batteries and also their sharpshooters and they are entitled to as much credit as any for performing their duty nobly and bravely. Leroy Hall and Sedate Foote were with the Doctor to help take care of the wounded. They are all safe and sound and all others are safe whose names I do not mention as I shall give you the names of all that we suppose are killed and all that we know are wounded and those that are missing.[15]

Killed
Corp. Reuben Card shot in the forehead
Corp. Samuel Fenton " " " "
Private Benjamin Fannin " " "
[Private] Fletcher Webb " " " "
[Private] [Julius] Henry Tracy shot in the head
[Private] Larry Hogaboom   " " " breast
[Private] George Pierson   " " " body

Wounded
Serg[eant] Leroy Terry shot in the leg, flesh wound [he later transferred
    to the Veteran Reserve Corps]

Corp[oral] Philip Potter in the arm, bad wound but the bone not broken [The wound proved to be very serious and Potter was discharged from the Army on August 1, 1863.]

Wounded and taken prisoner by the Rebs
Private H[arrison] Lattimer in the leg, was fighting like a good fellow afterwards [He died on May 11, 1863]
[Private] C[harles] Nichols in the foot and left on the field [He was later discharged on August 27, 1863.]
[Private] Matthew Rockefeller in the bowels, left on the field [He died of this wound on May 3, 1863.]
[Private] Wm. H. Coe in the head, left on the field
[Private] Austin Teel unknown was seen to fall, left on the field [*The Adjutant Generals Report*, 183, does not list him as wounded in this battle. Teel later transferred to the artillery on December 3, 1863.]

Wounded
Private Cyrus Westcott in the fingers
[Private] Richard Bennet flesh wound in the arm [Bennet survived this wound only to be killed a year later at Cold Harbor.]
[Private] Wm. Edward in the arm, thigh and privates, seriously [He was later transferred to the Veteran Reserve Corps.]
[Private] Albert Fuller ball went in the mouth and out of neck, bad wound, but not dangerously [Kidder obtained wrong information on Fuller and would later correct himself.]
[Private] David Marihue in the thigh but not dangerously [He recovered only to be wounded once more during the closing months of the war in the Petersburg Campaign.]
[Private] Gilbert Olds in the privates, a serious wound [This wound was serious enough for Olds to be transferred to the Veteran Reserve Corps.]
[Private] John P. Wilsey in the head slightly
[Private] Charles Wilsey in the wrist, probably lose his hand [He was also transferred to the Veteran Reserve Corps.]
[Private] Moses G. Wright bruised in the breast, not seriously
[Private] Henry Heniker, slight wound in the head, able to do duty
[Private] Joseph Edson bruised on the elbow but able to do duty
1st Lieut. [Charles A.] Butts on the leg with a spent ball, able to do duty
2nd Lieut. Delavan Bates was wounded and left in the woods. I am afraid he is dead.

You can see by the way and position of their wounds that the poor fellows were doing their duty like true patriots, never were men doing their duty more manfully than they were. Can their friends ask any more of them. I, for one, can testify that they were as noble and brave a set of men as ever lived. I am proud of such men and feel to weep with their friends over their loss. I feel also willing to stand or fall by the side of those that are left. I will give you the names of those that stood so manfully by their colors.[16] Col. Upton says that too much honor and credit cannot be given to these men and officers that rallied, for our 2nd line of battle, had commenced a general panic which would have continued and grown worse as the Rebs had cavalry to pursue us and we had none as Hooker had all of them with him.[17]

Capt. Mather was wounded in the shoulder but he stood by the colors until dark. I gave him the last of my brandy which I brought from home. I gave to 9 others that were wounded during the day.

Lieut. [Frank] Gorton of Butternuts did his whole duty and showed himself a brave and noble officer. The Colonel promoted him to Captain immediately. Lieut. Cronkite was as brave and noble also. I think he will be promoted to Captain.[18] Capt. [Henry] Galpin, Capt. [Cle[a]veland] Campbell, and Capt. Douw were equally brave and stood up manfully and fought like tigers also.

Lieut. [Jonathan] Burrell, Butts, [Lansing] Paine, [Thomas] Adams and [Silas] Pierce stood up manfully with us. In fact, the Colonel says that he is well satisfied with every one of the officers, thinks that they cannot be excelled and we know that a braver man than Col. Upton never lived.

Our Lieut. Col. [Egbert Olcott] was sick but he went into the fight and did his part most nobly. Sergt. Peter S. Perine, Sergt. Wm. Remmel and Corporals Treat D. Young, Mason S. Jenks, Privates Joseph Roberts, Joseph Edson, Edward Ostrander, Henry Snediker, James Gardner, Charles Downing, Ashbel Lamont, Peter Terrel and Norman Stone were the men of my company that stood by me like a band of brothers. Perine was as cool and deliberate as the Colonel. I hope he will be promoted as he is worthy. I have no doubt but he will be, also others of this list.[19]

Since writing the above, I have heard that the Rebels have retaken the forts and heights above the city and such works.[20] I hear that our General in command of this part of the army did not garrison them so that we are here 3 miles above the city and west with the Rebels on our rear and have one way to escape if attacked, that is by Bank's Ford about 4 miles above the city. We have got what ammunition we can carry and what other there is will be destroyed if we should retreat.[21]

In Laurens, Harriet was relieved to learn that her husband escaped his first combat experience unharmed. She couldn't help but notice that he did not close the letter with his customary, "Yours as ever." In fact, he didn't even sign the letter at all. She now faced the difficult task of seeking out friends and neighbors to tell them of the fearful losses at Salem Church.

By this time, mid-May 1863, the 121st New York had returned to their old camp grounds at White Oak Church. Here, Captain Kidder was continuously busy. The fate of those deemed "missing" was a primary concern. After interviewing several of the 121st who were near the schoolhouse, Kidder felt sure that Delavan Bates survived the battle. To the father of Delavan Bates, John S. Kidder wrote:

> *Dear Sir,*
>
> *It is with a sad heart that I pen a few lines to you to inform you of the painful intelligence of your son Delavan Bates. He is among the missing of our regiment. We went into a hard fought battle three miles west of Fredricksburg on Sunday last about 5:00 P.M. We were compelled to retreat and Delavan came out with me and we were rallying the men to resume the fight. I cannot find anyone who saw him fall and I think he was wounded and taken prisoner. My 1st Lieutenant Butts said he saw him limp as he was coming out of the woods so he may have been wounded in the leg. I have done all that I could [either] to find out where he is or whether anyone saw him but I am unable to learn anything concerning him. I will say that none feel more deeply his loss than I do as I have never met with a friend that I thought as much of as Delavan Bates.*[22]

"I expect," he later confided to Harriet "[that] Lieut. Bates [is a] servant down at Richmond."[23]

About a week later, Captain Kidder learned that Bates had, indeed, been captured and was interred at Libby Prison in Richmond. Kidder was now without the assistance of a lieutenant. Charles H. Butts, who had assisted him in an unofficial capacity at Salem Church [he was never posted to Company I], had been transferred to Company H to fill the position of slain Lieutenant Ulysses F. Doubleday.

With no lieutenants and one sergeant in the hospital, Kidder found it difficult to complain about his situation and simply got to work filling out Company I paperwork. There were daily reports and inventories to be completed. He noticed a dramatic increase in the amount of Descriptive Lists that required his attention. In the past, he had completed a few for those that were deemed too sick to serve and were released from the service. Added to this number were those that were wounded at Salem Church. And if this didn't give him enough to do, another form soon appeared, the "Equipment List." Kidder now had to list as "missing" every conceivable item an infantry soldier could lose. After the Battle of Salem Church, he listed as missing twenty-four Enfield rifles, cartridge boxes, and belt slings, right on down to the cap pouches.[24]

All of this military paperwork, handwritten, in duplicate and sometimes triplicate form, seemed a trivial aspect of the responsibility of command. Looking in on his wounded men whenever possible proved to be the serious side of soldiering to John S. Kidder. He found these visits anything but pleasant, for there was little he could do to ease their pain and suffering. "I was up at the hospital which is about 5 miles from here," he wrote to Harriet. "All of our wounded have been brought over. George Richardson has a flesh wound in the thigh, he can walk around, he will be well soon . . . Charles Nichols had his left arm amputated. [Corporal] Philip Potter's arm is doing well but he will have a stiff elbow."[25]

The sight of one soldier hit close to home. Brother Edward, a private in Company F, had just cleared the woods when he was struck. "Edward Kidder was wounded in the left arm, it is a very bad wound but I think he will not lose it."[26] The wound was indeed painful, the bullet having lodged itself just below the elbow, rendering the limb useless.[27]

In time, the wounded received what care could be provided to them and the dead were buried. As the Army of the Potomac licked its wounds following the defeat at Chancellorsville, the carriage maker from Laurens assessed the situation. He was shocked at the losses in his own regiment that were inflicted in a relatively short period of time.

> *Our Regiment lost more men than any other Regiment in the Army of the Potomac, 273 killed, wounded and missing and 19 of them were lost inside of 20 minutes. I think most of them (20) in less than 15 minutes. I think it was a great blunder of Generals of the 6 Corps in putting us into such a place without any support, especially at such a late hour in the day. There was 10 Regiments that formed a line of battle, 4 in our Brigade and 6 in the First or Jersey Brigade with only about 1500 of the Third Brigade for our support and they did not support us. The Rebs had 2 lines, their second line was behind a ditch while the other 6 brigades had gone down to the city after their knapsacks. We all think much of Hooker. He managed well for us to carry the heights but he has some poor generals under him that do not know how to fight. I think if Hooker had been with us we should have been over the river and probably near*

*Richmond by this time. The 11th Corps ran and did not fight or he
would have been able to have met us above the city. Hooker is not to
blame for the faults of his officers.*[28]

Captain Kidder still had confidence in Hooker's abilities to lead the
army to victory. It was a sentiment not shared by Lincoln.

While President Lincoln wrestled with the problem of Hooker,
Colonel Upton, too, had problems of his own to contend with. The loss
of so many officers and men at Salem Church presented the young colonel
with a serious replacement dilemma. It was now June; it was obvious that
many of his wounded could never be counted upon to resume their duties.
Some of them had already been discharged or transferred to the Veteran
Reserve Corps to perform light duty. He needed replacements to fill his
depleted ranks.

Fortunately for the 121st New York Volunteers, replacements were
close at hand. "We have got about 200 new men from the 32nd N.Y.," said
Kidder. "These are men whose time is not out but they expect to go home
with the Regiment when they want."[29]

In addition to the regiments Kidder named, there were also men
available from the 18th and 27th New York. These were all regiments
that were ending their two-year term of enlistment. Each contained men
that had not served a full two-year term and were now subject to being
transferred to other units. Many of these soldiers were under the impression that they could choose what regiment they wanted to be assigned to in order to meet their obligation of service. The 16th New
York, for instance, had 126 men who had the choice of joining the 1st
Massachusetts Battery, Battery D, 2nd U.S. Artillery, or the 121st New
York.[30] There was no choice, however, and all of the men were transferred into the ranks of the 121st. Naturally, there was quite a bit of
grumbling. John S. Kidder sensed that there would be problems with
these newcomers. "They are disposed to be mutinous. I am fearful we
shall see trouble with them as they say that they will not go into a fight.
About 20 of them refused to do [picket] duty last Monday . . . so we
marched them out under guard. They said that the men who recruited
them told them that they would not have to . . . they should be discharged with the others."[31]

Colonel Upton tried to smooth these hard feelings over by appealing to their patriotic duty, at the same time insisting that military discipline be enforced. He was only partially successful, for a few of the
protesters lodged formal complaints regarding this "Shanghai" with the

War Department.[32] For those that accepted their fate, Upton allowed them the choice of which company they would like to be assigned to for the duration of their enlistment. "To my surprise most of them wanted to come into my Company," said Kidder. "The Colonel had to disappoint many of them because I could not have only such a share. I have now the largest Company in the Regiment with the exception of Company D which is about as large as mine, and Capt. Fish commands [company] D."[33]

This minor insurrection was hardly out of the way when Upton was faced with a similar problem, this time with his officers. Before Salem Church, Colonel Upton had taken great pains to rid his staff of political opportunists or just plain incompetent officers and replace them with men from the ranks who measured up to his own set of standards. After Salem Church, Upton not only had to replace enlisted soldiers, but also had a large gap to fill in his officer corps. Captain Nelson Wendell, Lieutenants Ulysses F. Doubleday, and Fred Ford were killed in action on May 3. Captain Thomas S. Arnold was so seriously wounded that he died on May 18. Second Lieutenant Henry Upton was unable to resume his duties because his wounds were serious. Wounded Captain Mather was the only one able to return to duty. Delavan Bates was still listed as missing in action. It was reported that he now was a prisoner at Libby Prison in Richmond.

To fill these positions, Upton promoted from within the regiment. James W. Cronkite, Frank Gorton, and Marcus Casler were promoted to captain. "This is as it should be," said Kidder. "We are all glad to see such men promoted as they are worthy of it."[34]

Eyebrows were raised, however, when Upton countered this move by assigning Capt. H. Seymour Hall, Capt. Albert M. Tyler, and Lt. Lewis C. Bartlett of the 27th New York to positions in the 121st. For a brief period, this created quite a stir. Captain Kidder observed that many of the men felt such promotions should come from within the ranks of the regiment. In effect, there was nothing wrong with transferring needed men into the regiment, but not their officers.

All of this was forgotten when it was overshadowed by a larger crisis. In March 1863, Lt. Col. Charles H. Clark resigned and was replaced by Maj. Egbert Olcott. As Olcott moved up the pecking order of command, a vacancy existed. Captains who had been with the regiment since Camp Schuyler looked upon the position of major as a prize. Kidder knew that he wouldn't be considered for the promotion. His absence of two months due to illness (October and November 1862) hurt his seniority. When Harriet wrote and asked if there was even the slightest chance that he would be promoted, he reminded her: "It is very seldom that there is a chance for promotion above Captain."[35]

John S. Kidder made no secret of his choice for major. He enthusiastically supported Capt. Henry M. Galpin of Little Falls. "Galpin was a private in the 44th [New York] and was promoted for gallantry on the battlefield while in that Regiment to Orderly Sergeant," he wrote to Harriet. Later, Galpin was wounded and sent home. "When the call was made for more troops, he went to work and recruited a Company and had them all in the Camp at Mohawk by the 1st of August, and he has not been off from duty 1/2 day since the Regiment started and he is as brave a man as the Colonel."[36]

With Galpin's record of service, Kidder was shocked when Upton announced that his choice for the coveted position of major was to be Capt. Robert P. Wilson of the 16th New York. This sparked a firestorm of protest from the other officers. Galpin immediately sent his resignation to Colonel Upton, only to have it refused. Undaunted, he then sent it directly to Washington. John D. Fish also threatened to resign. With this, Upton called in all the line officers and told them, as Kidder recalled, "to smother their feelings or leave the service as he said that having Wilson for Major added another brave and good officer."[37]

Henry Galpin held fast. He told Upton that he was not going to resign from the service, for to quit wasn't his nature. He preferred, however, to be posted to a different command. It was about this same time that Robert P. Wilson arrived at the camp of the 121st New York to accept his promotion. Sensing that he had just entered a hornet's nest of controversy, he didn't stay long. He accepted and resigned his position almost immediately.[38]

John S. Kidder was more confident than ever that the well-qualified Galpin would get his just reward when Upton dropped another bombshell. He announced that Captain Andrew Mather was to be the new major of the 121st. Once again, there was a howl of protest. Granted, Mather was one of them, not an outsider like Wilson, but he had just recently been promoted to the rank of captain in January 1863. He didn't have the seniority of the other captains. This second attempt to fill the position of major was no longer gossip confined to the officer's mess. The entire camp was talking about it. Private John J. Ingraham was elated at the actions of the officers. "Capt. Mather has been promoted Major. Capt. Galpin ought to have been. Capt. Galpin, Lieut. Burrell, Capt. Fish, Capt. Kidder, I hear, have sent in their resignations. Bully for them. I would not be run over by a minor officer. Galpin was 1st Senior, Fish 2nd, Kidder 3rd, and Mather 4th and they jumped him over the whole of them up to Major."[39]

Once again, Colonel Upton called in his line officers to explain the situation. According to Kidder, "the Colonel told Galpin that the reason why he sent Mather's name was because Galpin was too familiar with his men."[40]

John S. Kidder chafed at this remark, since Upton had said it to him on another occasion. Of course Galpin was familiar with his men, so, too, was Kidder and Fish. This was a volunteer regiment in a volunteer army. Captains personally recruited and enlisted their neighbors and friends.

Feeling his friend, Galpin, had been slighted a second time, Kidder poured out his frustrations to Harriet.

> *Galpin is liked by everyone in the Regiment and he could lead 20 men into battle where Mather could not lead one, as Mather's Company perfectly hates him . . . but the Captain is a good officer and will do his duty, but men have no confidence in him because he is so overbearing and tyrannical. I think he is larger in his own estimation than General Hooker . . . I do not envy Mather his place. If I could be a general and have the feeling against me as there is against him, I should resign very quick. But Mather is not to blame for his promotion, because Galpin has been abused is no reason that he should be blamed for it . . .*[41]

Kidder continued in another letter.

> *The whole of the regiment, both men and officers, that is, the Captains and the Lieut. are very much displeased with the promotions as we think it is very unjust to Capt. Galpin. He is the Senior Captain and the best officer on the line but Mather can fill the office well as [he] is a good officer also, but Galpin was the man for Major and there is much feeling on the subject. Galpin has sent in his resignation and Capt. Fish also. The reason why Capt. Mather is not liked is because he is such a fop, all dress, that seems to be his style.*[42]

No one resigned over the issue, but with young men such as Emory Upton, Egbert Olcott and Andrew Mather holding onto the top regimental positions, advancement, from now on, seemed to be very remote. Kidder wondered if he would be haunted by his own words, that promotions above the rank of captain were, indeed, rare.

Slightly disillusioned by the outcome of the Galpin-Mather affair, it seemed as if the only good news Kidder received that June was that Delavan Bates was in Annapolis and would rejoin the regiment as soon as possible. This was just the beginning of the Bates luck. A prisoner of war for just over two weeks at Libby Prison, Bates was the very last prisoner to be exchanged. There wouldn't be another prisoner exchange for an entire year. The release of Bates was great news to Kidder. Delavan Bates was one of his best lieutenants; he was sorely needed to assist in the drilling and training of the new replacements in Company I. It was always exciting to have men return to the regiment from the hospital, or, in this rare case, from Rebel captivity. Sometimes they could provide information as to the condition or the fate of others. Such was the case with Leroy Hall.

After being held by the Rebels for ten days following the battle of Salem Church, Leroy Hall, Dr. Daniel M. Holt, members of the Drum Corps, and several hospital stewards were released. Perhaps Leroy Hall could shed a little light on the fate of fellow Company I members Robinson Fox and Larry Hogaboom. Kidder hoped that both were prisoners but was particularly worried about Fox. "None saw him fall," said Kidder, hoping that he had somehow survived the battle. He interviewed all that were released, including Dr. Holt. No one could vouch for the whereabouts of Fox. Still, Kidder held onto the chance that the fun loving Fox, who had made quite a name for himself on his extended drunken leave of absence, was indeed, alive. Listing him as missing in action, it wasn't until the very last days of the war that Kidder changed the official records to indicate that Fox had been killed at Salem Church.[43]

The second week of June 1863, found the 121st New York Volunteers still in the vicinity of Fredericksburg, engaged in a variety of duties. Like other regiments in the VI Corps, they split their time between picket duty and building fortifications. This included everything from trench work ("We have a rifle pit about 11/2 miles long") to the placement of artillery pieces.[44]

Captain Kidder's expertise in the field of artillery was limited to what his carriage maker's eye could see—the wheels. "The wheels that we used to draw it [the cannon] with were 8 feet high with 7 inch tires, rather a *large sulkey*. We swing it under the axle."[45] He also noted that placing these guns into position did not go unnoticed by his Confederate neighbors. Sharpshooter activity harassed the men to such an extent that Kidder preferred to work in the evening. Needless to say, it took a few days to mount the pair of 100 pound guns into position.

They were in place only a short while when the Confederates fired upon their position with their own cannon. The first shot sailed harmlessly overhead. "They were poor gunners," according to Kidder, but even he knew that in time they would improve their aim. He welcomed the sight of the 1st Connecticut Artillery. They sized up the situation, took careful aim, and fired one gun at the Confederate position. Men cheered wildly as the cannon boomed. A puff of smoke in the distance assured all that the Confederate battery had been hit. The recoil from the gun was so great that it tipped over onto its side.[46] Captain Kidder and his men worked until daylight to upright the artillery piece. After all the work was completed, he received word that it was to be moved to another location. This was a job made all the more difficult by a turn in the weather; a massive thunder and lightning storm left him and his men soaked.[47]

The cannon was on the move and so was the entire VI Corps. As soon as Kidder completed loading the cannon, he was told to rejoin his regiment at Stafford Court House. Picking forty good men to work with the gun, Kidder sent the remainder ahead to join Colonel Upton. Some of these men were walking wounded and would be of little use to him. Their presence in the ranks bothered him immensely. He was powerless to help these men and vented his frustrations to Harriet.

> Some of my wounded men are compelled to follow the Regiment and carry their rations. I think it is a most outrageous shame. I have one man, Willsey [John Wilsey] with a very bad wound in the head and Phillip Potter with his arm badly shattered with a ball and they have to march with us. Our Doctor cannot help it nor the Colonel as it is ordered by the Medical Directors. I think that such scoundrels ought to be shot, and I would as quick shoot them as I would Jeff Davis. It makes me feel terrible to think that such brave fellows should be so abused. I wish that the Northern Press would come down on those scoundrels of Doctors who are too lazy to take care of our poor wounded men and compel them to march with the Regiment for the purpose of having the Regimental Doctors take care of them. I have talked and said more than this, but I cannot get any redress. I really wish that some of their friends at the north would notify the War Department on their account as I will swear that this is a fact.[48]

With forty men in tow, Captain Kidder marched toward Stafford Court House, and along the way came across an abandoned Union campsite. In their apparent haste, the former inhabitants left behind all sorts of supplies and equipment including seven horses. Securing the horses as pack animals, Kidder and his men took whatever items they could use and set about destroying the rest. Kidder was determined to rid the camp of anything that could be of use to the Confederates. He later reported that he

> found 15 axes, 7 spades, 5 pickaxes, and a lot of camp kettles, and lots of
> bags, coats, blankets, pork, etc., etc. I immediately had my men burn all
> the clothing and we buried the tools. I think that I destroyed $3,000 worth
> of property on Monday as I burned up 3 wagons and 2 ambulances which
> were broken down and abandoned. I burned hundreds of blankets and
> coats that were thrown away by the men. Such a waste of property but I
> was determined that the Rebs should not have them.[49]

With the camp contents ablaze, Kidder resumed the march toward
Stafford Court House. Upon arriving, they were witness to a parade of activity. Two Divisions of the VI Corps had already passed by marching
north. Kidder was told that Bartlett's Brigade, which the 121st New York
was a part of, would not arrive until early the next morning. This news
brought smiles to Captain Kidder and his forty men. Hot, sweaty, and
dirty from their forced march, they could rest. "So we laid down as we
were very fatigued; we slept like pigs," said Kidder.[50]

Reunited with the regiment the next day, Colonel Upton pushed on
toward Fairfax Station, arriving there on June 17. It was here that the regiment heard that General Lee was in Pennsylvania. Stunned at first, Kidder
could only elicit a wry comment. "This accounts for our hard marching."[51]
It took awhile, but the reality of the situation finally got to him. The 121st
New York had been rushed onto the field on the eve of Antietam, Lee's
first invasion of the north. They were green troops in those days, harbor-
ing the mistaken notion that the war would be a glorious and short affair.
Salem Church ended all that. War was a hard affair and in the ten months
since Antietam, John S. Kidder had changed. "We are glad that Lee has
gone north as we shall not let him come back again," he wrote to Harriet.

> I feel confident that we can whip him now. He is out of his entrenchment.
> The news came to us about 6 P.M. yesterday. It seemed to electrify our men
> as much as the sound of the Russian guns did the French when they were
> retreating from Moscow. I have faith in the 6th Corps, can whip twice
> their number of Rebs. The Rebs told my Lieut. [this would be Delavan
> Bates] that they did not care for the rest of the army but that damn 6th
> Corps was rough on them.[52]

For the next few days, it was one long march after another in all sorts
of unpredictable weather. Crossing the Potomac River at Edwards Ferry,
the 121st New York and the VI Corps were greeted by violent thunder-
storms, after which the rain-soaked roads were quickly baked by the hot

June sun. Every eye scanned the horizon, for it was rumored that Rebel cavalry were nearby. Weary and footsore, with nerves on edge, the men welcomed the sight of Manchester, a small village. It was an oasis at the end of a twenty-eight mile march, which promised an entire day's rest. As men sought the shade trees, John S. Kidder relaxed. He had a few moments, and like Dr. Daniel M. Holt, put the time to good use, writing a quick letter home. Writing as if Harriet had a map before her, Kidder named every small town the VI Corps passed through. Some were so small, he admitted, they probably would not appear on any map. The beauty of these villages, however, did not escape him. Westminster was clearly his favorite. "Westminster is a splendid place, larger than Cooperstown. I think if ever I get through this war alive, I [shall] come down here and start a shop in this part of Maryland."[53]

The area was, indeed, a sharp contrast to the devastated countryside around Fredericksburg. It wasn't just the picturesque view that impressed him, but the people themselves were worthy of favorable comments. These were loyal Unionites who genuinely appreciated the efforts of the boys in blue. "The ladies were very kind to our men; called them their brave Yankee boys, etc., etc."[54] The appearance of a very excited Colonel Upton put an end to this idyllic daydream. Kidder dated his letter: July 1, 1863.

Upton assembled the captains and told them that each man was to be issued sixty rounds of ammunition and three days' rations. The combination of rounds and rations could only mean one thing—a battle! But where? Captain Kidder knew the Confederate Army was north of him but he really didn't have the slightest clue as to the exact location. "Where we are going I do not know," he confided to Harriet. "There is none but the VI Corps here."[55]

There were more surprises. This was the very first time that the 121st New York, and the rest of the VI Corps, heard that General Hooker was no longer in command of the army. There was no shortage of rumors. "Where Hooker is I do not know. We have heard that he was relieved and that General Mead commands, but some say that McClellan has been called to the command again, but I do not think there is any truth in the report as David Marihue has just come up to the Regiment."[56]

Twenty-year-old Private David Marihue, a farmer from Hartwick, had been recovering from a leg wound received at Salem Church and was returning to the regiment. He arrived with a variety of misinformation. He claimed to have just passed Hooker's headquarters the previous day and that there was no change. In fact, Hooker was off to their left with the III and V Corps. Marihue also claimed that there had been another fight at South

Mountain, just like the one previous to Antietam, and that the XI Corps had taken six hundred prisoners. Marihue was wrong on all accounts.

Hooker had been replaced. Disappointed with his performance at Chancellorsville, President Lincoln waited for an opportunity to remove Hooker. On June 28, while the 121st was marching toward Hyattstown, Maryland, Gen. George G. Meade became the new commander of the Army of the Potomac. Kidder was unfamiliar with Meade, and as an oversight, always omitted the "e" on the Pennsylvanian's name.

As for the rumor concerning the XI Corps, a victory, no matter how large or small in stature, would have pleased John S. Kidder. But the fact remained that the XI Corps was a hard luck outfit. Kidder never forgot how poorly they had done at Chancellorsville.

While Kidder tried to sort through the erroneous information given to him by Marihue, VI Corps commander Maj. Gen. John Sedgwick had no problem grasping the importance of the message he received from Chief of Staff, Daniel Butterfield. A large battle was underway at Gettysburg. The I and XI Corps had been pushed back to the high ground above the town and Gen. John F. Reynolds had been killed. The battle was expected to carry on into the next day. The VI Corps, at fourteen thousand strong, the largest Corps in the Army of the Potomac, was sorely needed. "We shall probably be largely outnumbered without your presence," wrote Butterfield.[57] As each new communiqué from Butterfield grew more and more urgent, Sedgwick sent word that he would be in Gettysburg at 4:00 P.M. the next day and would, as Butterfield suggested, "Force the march."[58]

Long marches were nothing new to the VI Corps. They had already been marching hard for several days. Each day on the road seemed to invigorate Captain Kidder. Days earlier he boasted to Harriet: "I am stout and healthy. I think I could march 30 miles a day and jump a seven rail fence at night." As usual, he had his own theory on the best way to march an army over long distances. He believed the best results could be achieved during the early morning and evening hours. Why not start the march at 3:00 A.M. and stop at 9:00 A.M. to rest, then march from 5:00 P.M. to 9:00 P.M., escaping the heat of the summer sun? By doing this, Kidder estimated that an army could move twenty miles, at a pace averaging about two miles per hour.[59]

What he proposed was not entirely original. Common sense dictated the best and worst times of the day to march. Marching the way Kidder suggested would take timing and coordination, and Sedgwick had neither. Pressing the men onward, "Uncle John," as the men called him, delivered as promised. Late in the afternoon of July 2, the first banners of the VI

Corps could be seen along the Baltimore Pike Road. The entire Corps had completed a thirty-two mile march, averaging about five miles per hour.

Even then, there was no time to rest. The Corps moved into the Union lines adding stability to the left side. The 121st New York moved onto the slope of Little Round Top and formed a defensive position. While doing this, Kidder noticed one of his men moving to the rear. It was Stephen Bolt. Limping, Bolt claimed that he had sprained his ankle when he was pushed aside by stretcher bearers. Kidder was not fooled.

> *I drew my pistol and told him he could march into the ranks or die. He walked up promptly as he knew I would have shot him. We were ordered to shoot any man that shows any cowardice and as sure as any of my men turn to run, I will shoot them. I have told them so and they know what to depend on . . . I shall not be troubled with cowards.*[60]

The 121st New York remained on the slope of Little Round Top for the duration of the Battle of Gettysburg. Here, in a supportive rather than combative position, they were afforded an excellent view of the battle. However, they still had to exercise caution as Rebel sharpshooters were just below them plying their deadly trade. Kidder granted them a quiet respect after being harassed by them at Fredericksburg. From this vantage point, the regiment watched the final phase of the battle. As the Confederate forces massed for their final assault on the center of the Union line, in what would forever be referred to as Pickett's Charge, Kidder wasted no time in writing home.

> *Battlefield near Gettysburg*
> *July 3rd, 1863*
> *Dear Wife,*
>   *I wrote you a letter on the 1st; we were then near Manchester. We started about 10 o'clock in the evening [of] the 1st. I stated that we might go to Hanover then to this place but as the road was not open we marched back to Westminster then up to Littleton. We did not stop marching to get anything to eat until yesterday about 2 o'clock P.M. We had then marched 29 miles. We halted about 3 miles back of the place for one hour to eat and cook our coffee. While there we heard that our 11th Corps had run again and that the 1st Corps was badly cut up.*[61] *We lay there about 1 1/2 hours. When the Rebs opened on our forces on the left we immediately started for the battlefield. Got here just in time to prevent Lee from turning [on] our left flank. The battle was raging very hot when we arrived*

and General Sykes Division was being driven by the Rebs. The Penn. Reserves were put in just in front of us and they drove the Rebs back again.[62]
We took a large number of prisoners. We did not fire [our weapons] any
but expected to go in every minute but darkness put an end to the conflict
that had raged with terrible fury for 3 hours. When the troops heard that
the 6th Corps had come to help them, it put the fight right into them and
the Reserves fought like tigers. It was very fortunate for the Army of the Potomac that we came up as we did, having marched a distance of 32 miles
and bringing all of our cannon and trains up with us. I think that there is
not such a march on record. How the battle will end I am not able to say
but if we had not got here just as we did our left flank would have been
turned and a general defeat would have followed. We lay on our arms all
night. While [in this position] we could hear some of the wounded cry for
help while the ambulances were busy taking them off from the field and
the place where we lay was so smokey and rough that it was impossible to
find a smooth place to lay down.

The Rebs opened at us about 11 o'clock this morning on our right
and having a most terrible artillery fight on our whole line set a terrible
fire I never before witnessed. There is a perfect shower of shell going over
our heads. We have lost no men in our Regiment up to this time, 3
o'clock P.M.[63]

I saw the Hospital Steward of [the] 76th N.Y. He says that this Regiment is very badly cut up. This was on the 1st [of July] and that Charley
Matteson was wounded in the right arm above the elbow halfway up between the elbow and shoulder. It broke and fractured the bone. He [the
Steward] dressed the wound and sent him into the village, said that
Charley had good pluck but as the 11th Corps ran, our side lost most of
the village and Charley is in their hands. The 76th had their Major killed
and most of their other officers were killed and wounded.[64]

I think that General Reynolds lost his life very foolishly as there was
bad management on his part. The 76th Regiment had not half of their
guns loaded when they were attacked by the Rebs.[65]

The Rebs are running on the centre and our men after them on double quick. Things look good. The Rebs have just formed a large hollow
square to resist one of our cavalry charges and a 12 pound battery of ours
that is here close where I am writing opened on them with grape and canister while 3 other batteries did the same thing, and the way they are mow-
ing them down is terrible. They have broken the square and what are not
killed are running back with greatest confusion. Our right has been attacked with a very heavy force and they have been repulsed with great

slaughter. We have an excellent view as we are posted high on a hill. I was much pleased with the way the battle was conducted.[66]

Last evening we had 6 lines of battle formed back of Sykes Division and that could have stopped any force that Lee could bring against us. Our side seem[ed] to act on the defensive. Why we do not take the offensive I do not know. The Rebel prisoners, after they were taken, when they passed through our lines, told me that Lee could clean us out, but as we were in the 3rd line, they did not think that we had so many troops, for when they were marched to the rear they were completely surprised and looked quite discouraged. They say that Lee had about 100,000 men when he started. They think that it would have been better if he had stayed at Fredericksburg.[67]

I hope and pray that we shall succeed. The Rebs have just made a desperate charge on our centre and right and have been again repulsed.

4 P.M. I must close for the present. If it should be my fate to fall do not regret that I came and did my duty.

Yours as ever
J. S. Kidder

July 4th, 8 o'clock A.M. Our forces made a charge last evening about 6 P.M.; drove the Rebs back. It was a victory for our side. Yesterday we took over 6,000 prisoners.[68] What the loss in killed and wounded is not known at present. The Bucktails and the Pennsylvania Reserves fought well yesterday. 3 companies of them were inhabitants of the town. I saw one man, he said that he charged right through his Father's dooryard and his Father and Mother saw him as he passed. They were looking out of the cellar window. Who could not fight under such circumstances. He said that they are determined to drive the Rebs back. He said that he would have died before they should have driven him back again.

It is reported for a fact that we captured General Longstreet yesterday. It is said also that the 11th [Corps] redeemed their name yesterday. We are under orders to move immediately. We got well paid for our march as we were in a position to witness all the grandeur of war and out of its danger, although we were within 1/4 of a mile of 2 of their batteries.

Tell Verona that I expect Charley is in our lines. I will see him as soon as I can.

Several days later, John S. Kidder found time to write another, more detailed account of his experience at Gettysburg. In one of the few letters to survive, written to someone other than his wife, Kidder does

not hesitate to editorialize on a variety of subjects while at the same time
trying to impress upon his neighbor the importance of this pivotal battle. "Friend Fields" was cotton manufacturer William Craig Fields. One
of the founders of the Republican Party in Laurens, Fields was quick to
feel the effects of the loss of southern cotton at his mill. Kidder, no
doubt, was trying to reassure his friend that the war was going well and
that victory would soon be in sight.

> Camp of the 121st N.Y.V.
> July 22, 1863
> 5 miles southeast of Snickers Gap
> Battle of Gettysburg
> Friend Fields,
>
> Having a little spare time, I thought to write a few lines to you.
>
> You have probably heard of our marches, etc., before this time. We
> started from the camp near Falmouth. We started in a very heavy thun-
> derstorm. I was left behind with 40 men to help Lieut. Cummings dis-
> mount a 100 pounder and load it on the cars, which we did, got through
> a[t] daylight. It cleared off [and got] very hot and the march from Falmouth
> to Fairfax Court House was very unpleasant, as the sun shone very hot and
> it was very dusty. We stayed at the Court House about one week. While
> there, it commenced to rain moderately and the sun did not shine again
> until we reached Pennsylvania. If the weather had continued as hot as it
> was when we were coming from Falmouth to Fairfax, we could not of made
> such long marches, but I never saw such excellent weather as we had to
> march in after we left the Court House. It did not rain so as to wet us, but
> kept very cloudy and misty about as it is in foggy mornings in Laurens. We
> marched from 15 to 32 miles a day and brought all of our artillery and
> trains along with us. We had any quantity of excellent cherries as the trees
> were loaded on each side of the road from Falmouth to Gettysburg.
>
> On the evening of the 1st of July, we started about 10 o'clock,
> marched back to Westminster, then up to Gettysburg. The morning of the
> 2nd it cleared off and the sun shone very hot. We did not stop to cook cof-
> fee not rest only 5 or 15 minutes at a time before we had marched 28 miles.
> We then halted for about 2 hours, while here we heard artillery open and
> saw the smoke of the guns. We immediately started for the field. The 3rd
> Division, being in the advance, (when we march we change positions every
> day; the Division that has the advance takes the rear the next day, and it
> is the same with each Brigade in each Division, and the same with each
> Regiment in the Brigade) was the first in line of battle. They were placed in

the front with the Pennsylvania Reserves. They got on the field just in time
to prevent our left [flank] being turned as the Regulars under Sykes had broken and were retreating. Our Division was immediately formed in line in
the rear of the 3rd. We had 6 lines of battle in a few minutes. The nature
and make of the land was such that the lines were within from 8 to 10 rods
of each other and none but the first and 2nd lines exposed to the enemy's
fire. I think our Regiment was in the 3rd line. We expected to go in every
moment, [we] had our guns primed and cocked. The men behaved well. I
had but one man that wanted to sneak out. All of the others faced the
music like men. That man was Bolt of Morris. I drew my pistol and told
him he could take his place in the ranks immediately or die. He did not
wait for to be told the second time as he knew that I should not have commanded him to do so but once. I should have shot him in a second if he had
refused to obey. While standing in line waiting, several prisoners and
wounded came up the road across which my Company were formed. Immediately in the rear of my Company were several Staff Officers of the Corps.
They stopped every man that came out with the wounded and sent them
back again, while the prisoners were compelled to help the drummers and
hospital attendants carry the wounded to the rear.

Night closed the conflict. The Rebs retired. We slept on our arms
(that is a part of us) in the same line and as quick as the break of day, we
were aroused by the firing of the pickets. Immediately, every man was on
his feet with gun in hand without any order from his Captain. It would
have done your soul good to see the poor fellows (who were so stiff and sore
footed that they looked like a lot of foundered men) so ready and willing to
meet the enemy. The value of such men cannot be over estimated. I can
assure you I felt proud of my command.

The Rebs opened their cannon on our right [flank] in the morning.
They must have had a hot fight on the right but it was out of our sight as
our lines were in this shape [Kidder included a simple line to indicate the
line of battle] so that it could not be flanked. In the afternoon the Rebs
attacked our centre with 150 cannon. Our cannon replied from the centre and from our extreme left and such a celebration I never before witnessed. Think of over 300 cannon blazing away at each other within 1/2
mile or at the furthest, 1 mile. Most of them were within 3/4 of a mile of
each other.

Our Regiment supported a brass 12 pounder smooth bored battery,
the 2nd battery from the left.[69] This battery did not fire a gun on the 3rd
[line] but had very sharp practice for 3 hours on the evening of the 2nd.
They were used so hard that they were quite warm the next morning. There

was a perfect shower of shot and shell thrown over our heads at the battery on our left, which was a very powerful rifled battery and it was on the top of a high hill some 40 or 60 feet above us.[70] We were quite safe as the shot generally went clear over the battery that they fired at. I went up near that battery so that I could see the Rebs when they made their infantry charge on the centre and while they were charging this battery did mow them down most terribly as it was in position to shoot parallel with their lines and as soon as their lines got up to engage our infantry, the Rebs' guns were turned toward this battery in order to silence it (as they could not fire at ours in the centre without hitting their own men) but strange as it may appear there was not a man killed from any of their shells, only 3 wounded out of the battery and one horse wounded. The reason was, it was such an excellent place. The place appeared to be made by nature for a battery. I do not believe that a better fort could be built with all the improvements of artillery. The only trouble that this battery experienced was from the sharpshooters that lay behind the rocks about 1/3 of a mile to the left of them. They lost 6 killed during the day. Here was where one of our Brigade Generals was killed on the 2nd by a sharpshooter, and while the 1st Lieutenant of the battery was listening to some words that the dying General wanted to communicate to his sister, the Lieutenant was shot dead through the head.[71]

The Rebs were repulsed twice and then they retired. If our Corps had not arrived just as it did on the 2nd, the Rebs would have come through our left [flank], and then they would have whipped us the next day. It was a great victory for our army as our men were badly whipped on the 1st. General Meade was not there until after the I Corps got repulsed. I think that any General that will lead his men in as Reynolds did and have not more judgment had better be out of the service. I think that the service is much better off without them. The I Corps got badly cut up through the mismanagement of their Generals. Poor fellow, he lost his life by it.

You hear much said of the XI Corps. I saw them pass and I think that the 2nd Division have as good men and officers as any other Division, but the Division commanded by Carl Schurz is the most miserable and abominable looking set that I ever saw—both officers and men. They were all the most miserable Dutch that I ever saw. Carl Schurz was about the only good man among them.[72] I saw but two divisions, the other was up at Hagerstown, but I am told that two out of the three Divisions have many excellent troops as they have many Ohio, New York and Massachusetts Regiments. They fought well on the 3rd.

I did think that we ought to have attacked them on the 4th, but I am not so sure but with the forces that we had it might have been a doubtful case as we were badly cut up. The VI Corps had lost but few men but our Corps has only about 10,000 fighting men while the I Corps has but 40,000 and the other Corps would not average anymore than the I and VI [Corps].[73] So you can see that on the morning of the 4th we had less than 50,000 men. Now if Lee had about the same number and had chosen his own position and fought on the defensive as we did on the 3rd, I think it is very doubtful if we should have succeeded. The Militia did not come to help us. I would like to know where Governor Seymour's troops were and the Pennsylvania Militia when we were pursuing them [the Rebs] while they were on retreat.[74] They had the advantage of position, for when they came to an excellent position where it would have cost us 4 or 5 lives to their one to have driven them out, they would halt until their trains, etc. moved on past another good position. Then, they would leave the first one and travel all night and halt when they got to the other position. So you see that a retreating army has a decided advantage when the numbers are about equal.[75]

Charley Dean thinks we ought to have fought them at Williamsport on Friday or Saturday. I think if we had we should have got badly whipped. I give my reasons for thinking so. It is said that Meade wanted to but that one half of his Generals thought it was not best. This I think is only news-paper gossip, for I think if Meade wanted to fight at this time he would have done so. I think the reason was because Lee was strongly fortified. He had a very strong rifle pit with positions for his artillery, and every man that he could bring to fight was moved back over the river as soon as we came up and it is well known that he had from 40 to 50 thousand men to defend those hills. Now, you people of the North may think that an Army of the same number ought to have taken them, but I am sure that one line of battle in those pits would repulse any 3 lines that can be brought against them, that is, if the troops in the pits are as good fighters.[76] If we could have known when the Rebs were moving over the river, and have known when the movement began there was the time for us to have fought them but this we could not find out until it was too late. If we had moved on them on Monday afternoon, we should have been al[l]right. We had some troops come up from the James River, got there on Tuesday the morning we moved.

The Rebs fight well, I think there is not much difference in the fight-ing qualities of either army.

When Hooker was removed, the McClellan men were very loud mouthed about wanting Little Mac to take command. All the sneaks and bummers, as we call them, said that Little Mac would not march them so and said that it was all wrong, an outrage, etc., etc., but since they have seen our 32 mile march on the 2nd saved the battle, McClellan's name had not been mentioned since. If he had been in command, Lee would have been in Baltimore before he got out of Virginia.

Some of the prisoners that I have talked with said that Lee told them that they were going to fight militia and after he had whipped the I and XI Corps on the 1st of July, he told them that they had only the militia to fight on the 2nd. But the men said it was the damnedest militia they ever met and they told me [this] when they saw the VI Corps flags. Where we were stationed on the 3rd, Lee said that he did not want to try to carry that point and the Rebs called that place hell. This probably was the reason why we were not attacked on the 3rd. Lee preferring to try the right and centre of our lines.

The day before we crossed the river at Berlin, I saw Phil Randle. He belongs to the 144th. They have been joined to the flying XI Corps as some of the XI call themselves.[77]

When the Rebs were in Pennsylvania, they stole all the horses, cattle, hens, sheep, and everything they could find, destroyed all the bees, stole all the honey and would strip many of the houses of everything. They had broken up their dishes and furniture in many cases.

There are Copperheads in Pennsylvania, you could easily tell who they were for they would charge the men from 1 to 2 dollars for a loaf of bread while the Union people would give them bread or charge only $.25 or $.10 for loaves of bread. But the boys are living high at this time, they say, as Pennsylvania flowed with milk and honey for the Rebs, Virginia flows with mutton and honey for them.

It is reported that Lee is going back into Maryland. I think we shall go back if he does. I do not think we shall take the offensive until we get the conscripts in. We have sent 3 officers and 6 men from each Regt. in this Brigade after the conscripts to fill our Regts. with.

I saw Charley Watkins while we were at Funkstown. He is looking quite thin but is well. He is acting Adjutant.

I saw the Doctor that amputated Charley Matteson's arm. He said that the bone was shattered, that he had to take it off at the shoulder joint. I asked him if he thought that he would recover. He said that he would bet $100 to $1 that he would get well and the other Doctors that were with him said they thought so also. The only difficulty they said was that he would not keep quiet but would walk around too soon, but they had told him of the danger of his blood being heated and that he must keep still or it would cause the ends of the blood vessels to break and bleed to death. This he promised them he would do. He told them that he was very *glad that they warned him as he should not have known the danger that he was exposing himself to.*

Your obedt. Servant
J. S. Kidder

Continuing the letter, John S. Kidder told his friend

You may ask why it was not as easy for Meade to have fought Lee at Williamsport as it was for McClellan to have fought him the next day after the Battle of Antietam. My answer is that while Lee was whipped at Antietam, his forces were in disorder; and he had no fortifications, and McClellan had 40,000 fresh troops to renew the fight with. Not so with Meade. Lee was strongly fortified and had as many men as Meade had while Meade's whole army was not much larger than McClellan's reserve was at Antietam.

You hear much said about fighting all day. This is all humbug! That there is firing by the pickets and some portions of the army the whole time during the day is true, but a charge where the rifles are used one side or the other gives away in a short time. I do not believe that any one Regiment ever fought more than one or two hours at one time. Most charges are either successful or are repulsed in 15 or 20 minutes and a majority are in less time than that. It is the opinion of most officers that Lee will concentrate all of [Braxton] Bragg's and what other forces he can collect and make a bold strike for the North before we get our army filled with more men.

In his letter to William Fields, Captain Kidder readily defended Meade's decision not to attack Lee after the battle. This was not always the case. "Why we did not fight on the 4th I am not able to say," he wrote to Harriet shortly after the battle. "I think we ought to have fought on the 4th as the Rebs were so badly whipped on the 3rd. I am one that believes in pushing a victory to a decided success. I think it can be done without going headlong as we did at Salem Chapel."[78]

It was only after this, as the army pursued Lee, that Kidder saw for the first time how terrible the three day conflict in Gettysburg had been. "We passed thousands of their wounded, whole barns and houses full, besides 4 fields full of tents that were filled with wounded."[79]

General Meade's losses of over twenty-three thousand men killed, wounded, and missing, represented almost one quarter of the army. This, together with the loss of many high-ranking officers (John F. Reynolds was killed, Winfield Scott Hancock and Daniel Sickles were wounded), and the fact that Meade had been in command of the army for only two days before the battle began, was enough to warrant a cautious pursuit of Lee.

After a brief skirmish along the Fairfield Road, in which none of the 121st New York were injured, it was on to Emmitsburg and then to Middletown. Years later, these marches would be forgotten, largely overshadowed by the heroic thirty-two mile march of July 2. To John S. Kidder, however, the march out of the Keystone State proved just as demanding as the march to the crossroads town. It was simply the most physically exhausting march he ever made.

Upon leaving Emmitsburg, the 121st New York Volunteers made their way to the base of Catoctin Mountain. Here, in a driving rainstorm, they attempted to climb the mountain. "It was about 4 miles up the mountain and most of the way as steep as Cooley's Hill," he said, comparing it to the hill near his carriage shop.[80] The road was so rough that he guessed that it probably had never been traversed by a wagon before. Making it to the top of the mountain in the company of Delavan Bates and two other enlisted men, Henry Heniker and Cornelius Chase, Kidder noticed that Colonel Upton was there, in the company of about forty others. By now, it was 1:00 A.M. and there was nothing the wet soldiers could do except pitch their tents and rest. Captain Kidder estimated that when he got to the top of the mountain there were only about five hundred men there. What upset him more than anything was the fact that he noticed some of his men had no shoes and most were out of rations. Nothing could be done about this until daylight. It was time to rest. "When I awoke I was wet completely through, not a dry thread on any of us," he said to Harriet.[81] Thoroughly exhausted, he hadn't realized that he had fallen asleep in a pool of water.

By midafternoon of July 8, the 121st arrived in Middletown for a much needed rest. As the companies assembled, the captains performed their usual head count to ascertain the damage from this difficult march. Stragglers were a moving army's worst nightmare and Kidder always positioned his "file closers" in key positions to ensure that no one slipped away. As intimidating as these file closers were (in some instances they were ordered to bayonet or shoot attempted deserters), some soldiers managed to escape. On the march to Gettysburg, Kidder lost two Company I men. This was upsetting to him not only because of the urgency of the situation, but also because one of these soldiers was, once more, his troublesome brother-in-law. "I expect that Delos Lewis is in Washington or somewhere else sick," he tersely reported to Harriet.[82]

Much to his surprise, stragglers were not a problem on this march to Middletown. All but two of his men reported for duty and he wasn't even worried about them. They were transfers from the 16th New York. Kidder considered them good men and they arrived later on July 9.

While in Middletown, the 121st New York not only collected their strength, but they also picked up the latest gossip. Word was out that they were waiting for the other corps to join up so they could attack Lee. "This Corps is the nearest to the Rebs. I expect we shall open the battle as we did [and] not do much fighting at Gettysburg."[83]

It was all rumor. There was to be no battle. By July 12, General Lee started moving his army across the Potomac River into Virginia. The Gettysburg Campaign was officially over. Although the VI Corps marched more than they fought in the campaign, the carriage maker from Laurens never lost confidence in his corps. "I think the old VI will fight like tigers."[84] In time, they would.

FOUR

"I do not wish to boast, but . . ."

AUGUST 1863–APRIL 1864

ugust 1863 was an anniversary month for the men of the 121st New York Volunteers. They had now been in the army for an entire year. During that time, John S. Kidder had seen, or experienced, just about everything and anything that could befall the common soldier. His feet had endured long marches ("It was the worst road I ever traveled . . ."), his stomach had survived his own cooking ("I have some squash for supper, also butter and an excellent ham . . ."), and he had waded through streams of army paperwork ("The longer a company stays in the field, the more work it is to make out the muster and paper rolls . . ."). He had also suffered from an occasional pang of homesickness ("How is my little girl? Did she know my picture?").[1]

Like many of the others in Upton's Regulars, Kidder considered himself a true veteran in every sense of the word. He had seen combat, served picket duty, participated in light skirmishing, observed and fought in great battles. In a year's time, he noticed that not only had the war changed him, but also changed the people. For the first time, he experienced open hostility on the part of the civilian population in the Virginia countryside. "Our Regiment," he wrote on August 12, 1863, "has been out after *guerillas* . . ."[2]

The guerilla leader in the vicinity of Loudoun County, Virginia, was the diminutive Col. John Singleton Mosby. Slight in stature (he probably weighed less than 125 pounds), Mosby was as daring as the men he led. Striking hard and fast, his Partisan Rangers built their reputation on harassing the supply trains, flanks, and rear guard of the Army of the Potomac. His ununiformed men easily blended into an already sympathetic populace. He was never captured, but Mosby was the subject of many an effort, including one led by Col. Emory Upton.[3]

It was when Mosby completed a daring night raid on the headquarters of Gen. Joseph Bartlett that Upton decided to act. Commanding the brigade since Gettysburg, Upton selected the 121st New York for this foray into Mosby country. Issuing only one day's rations, Upton divided the regiment into two battalion-sized wings. He would lead one wing and strike out toward Middleburg and Lt. Col. Egbert Olcott would take the other wing to the small village of Salem. Captain Kidder and his Company I men were to accompany Upton.

Employing Mosby's tactics, Upton and his men slipped out of camp about 3:00 A.M. Using the cover of darkness to mask their move, the men stumbled along the nine mile route to White Plains. Here, they rested and then proceeded to Middleburg. By the evening of the second day, the village was completely surrounded. The young colonel gave specific orders that every house was to be searched and all arms and horses confiscated. There was to be no violence or destruction of personal property unless provoked. "If we were fired upon from any house we were to order the inmates out and then burn it to the ground," said Kidder. "And if we came across any of Mosbies [sic] men, we were not to take them alive if we could help it."[4] These were harsh measures, but experience taught Upton's Regulars that the guerilla menace had to be stomped out once and for all. Too many times when soldiers had been sent to guard property at the request of an owner, they had either been captured or killed by Mosby's men. "Such scoundrels ought to be shot," growled Kidder, who always feared that one of his own men might be "gobbled" up in this way.

> There have been instances where men have gone to our Generals and obtained a guard and then had him gobbled by the Guerillas and at the same time [he] pretends to be very sorry about it. When they get guards now, they get them with the understanding that if the Guerillas take them they will forfeit all their property to the Government. The result is we have not had any gobbled lately.[5]

Parts of the countryside they passed through had already felt the hard hand of war. There were plenty of buildings in sad shape; there was an overall absence of livestock on some farms. The sight of all this made an impression on the man who left farming to become a carriage maker. "They are as poor as can be," John Kidder said.

> There is nothing here for them to eat but vegetables and milk. There was more sheep and grain near the Potomac, but this country is completely

stripped, every one of them hope[s] the war will soon end. . . . I do not see
how they can live through another winter. There is any quantity of hay and
grass but only a few cows to eat it. Destruction reigns in old Virginia.[6]

If the farms appeared to be poor, Kidder and the others soon discovered that the farmers were not poor in spirit. The Virginians he encountered loathed the presence of these blue-coated invaders. When a Middleburg inhabitant barred her gate and refused to let Kidder's men search her property, a shoving match ensued. She complained bitterly to Captain Kidder and demanded that the corporal in question be disciplined and for everyone else to leave her property. Her adamant plea made Kidder suspicious. She was, as he later recalled, a "spiteful secesh" woman. "I told her that the Corporal was acting under orders to search and, if she did not want to be pushed away, she should not show fight herself."[7] The house was searched and inside was her brother, reputed to be one of Mosby's men.

It wasn't just the poor who crossed swords with Colonel Upton's men on this raid. There were a few well-to-do farmers in the area who wasted few words on the Union. When Kidder's men saw a large farm with perhaps forty sheep, they approached the owner and offered to purchase one or two. The farmer refused to sell, so the soldiers went to the well to refill their canteens. Here they were met by the farmer's wife. She immediately began to curse these Yankee invaders and said she wished Lee had killed them all. "The boys immediately turned around and shot 3 sheep and 2 hens and went to dressing them. This made quite a fuss," said Kidder.[8]

Naturally, the farmer and his wife reported the incident at General Meade's headquarters. Kidder, who was responsible for the actions and conduct of his men, felt that he might be reprimanded for this incident, and he believed he would most likely have to make restitution. He was astonished at what happened next.

The impudent bitches did not deny but justified themselves in their abuse,
so the General [Meade] did not punish the boys. The time has passed in
protecting such people's property. There are but few such families and they
get used pretty rough. It serves them right. I tell the boys to take all they
want from such people, but the men are very good, as they do not injure
anyone that use them with respect and the men are always willing to pay
for anything that they get off them.[9]

The two day Middleburg-Salem raid was not a success in terms of captured men. Many suspected guerillas were rounded up, and all but one were released when their characters were vouched for. In terms of simple plunder, the raid was a wonderful first effort on the part of Colonel Upton. His group brought in over forty horses and Lt. Col. Olcott's group, about the same. There were also plenty of turkeys, chickens, and ducks which became "contraband of war."

There would be no more raids into Mosby country for the 121st New York that year. However, Mosby wouldn't be forgotten. He was always harassing them, a constant source of irritation to Captain Kidder and the others who worried about his style of fighting. To Harriet, Kidder gave the final word on the subject.

> There was an Englishman by the name of Green, a very sick man who has a splendid residence about 4 miles below here; [he] just passed through the lines. I had quite a talk with him. He showed me his pass from England. I told him that I was from Kent. He said a Kentish man was shot a few days ago and died at his house. He was left there with some of our wounded. He was one of Mosbies [sic] men. He came to Richmond and expected a commission but was disappointed and joined Mosby and [during] the first skirmish got shot through the lungs. I told him I was very glad that he got shot but was sorry that any Englishman should espouse their cause and fight for the South, especially as a Guerilla.[10]

Another peculiar thing occurred while on this raid. Straying off the main roads and in unfamiliar countryside, Colonel Upton secured the services of one of the locals. "We had a darky for our guide," said Kidder, noting that the escaped slave had, at one time, been a servant for a Confederate Colonel and was now assisting a Union Colonel.[11] What is most surprising about this comment is not the prejudicial term, "darky," which, in many respects, is much better than the often used "nigger," but that Kidder mentioned the incident at all. It was the first time he stated that he'd met a black man while in the army.

John S. Kidder had numerous opportunities to make contact with escaped slaves, opportunities he did not have at home.[12] "Contrabands," those escaped slaves who were not returned to their owners, were a common sight in almost every Union regiment. Some officers put them to work right away. Assistant Surgeon Daniel M. Holt used the services of his contraband, "Josh," in a variety of ways. He was cook, cleaner, and manservant to the doctor.[13] Kidder never saw the need to do this and still relied on Leroy Hall to provide these services. He may have also come under the spell of Colonel Upton, who was an ardent abolitionist since before his West Point days.

After the Mosby Raid, Kidder saw two, as he called them, "mulatto men" approaching the headquarters tent of General Bartlett, bearing gifts of eggs and chickens. "They were surprised when I told them that they were free," said Kidder. The Emancipation Proclamation had taken effect on January 1, 1863, freeing all those slaves in territory controlled by the Union Army.

> They were quite intelligent men but were kept in ignorance; [they] said that their masters had told them that we were fighting to get their slaves so as to sell them to Cuba. The men said that they should inform all their colored brethren and they would not stay with their masters for they were not going to work for nothing when they could get pay for their labor. One of them was 26 years old, the other, 24. They were both married. The youngest one had his wife sold away from him last summer and she was sent south.[14]

Perhaps little incidents like this helped change John S. Kidder. The war was much more than a conflict to preserve the Union. It was a war to help set people free. "Since we returned to Virginia after the Battle of Gettysburg, the soldiers have all got to be abolitionists. I never saw such a change in regard to the slavery question."[15]

For the most part, the incidents surrounding the Middleburg, or Mosby Raid, were about the only excitement experienced by Upton's Regulars following the Gettysburg Campaign. The next seven weeks would be spent in New Baltimore, Virginia. It was a needed rest for the hard marching veterans, but they were by no means idle or complacent. Discipline in the regiment did not waiver when Colonel Upton became brigade commander. There was always time for marching, target practice, and picket duty, as well as tactics classes for the officers.

Back home in Laurens, Harriet was delighted that the regiment was in camp. It didn't take her long to discover what all army wives knew; when the army was in camp, she received letters, when the army was on the move, it was time to worry. From New Baltimore, letters arrived. She eagerly looked forward to reading her husband's latest exploits. Thankful that he emerged from Gettysburg unscathed, she still worried about her brother, Charley. She expected him to be discharged from the army and sent home as soon as he sufficiently recovered from having his arm amputated.

The most recent letter detailed her husband's latest adventures in trying to capture the elusive Mosby. The biggest surprise in the letter, however, was a bank draft for $225.00. Not only had the 121st New York been resupplied in New Baltimore, they had been paid as well. Army pay was very good on the Kidder finances. The only problem was that Harriet could never depend upon it on a regular basis; it was notoriously late throughout the war. By mid-August 1863, the Kidder family finances seemed to be in good order. Still expecting the last installment of money from the state for his recruitment of Company I, John suggested to Harriet that they might want to consider paying off the mortgage, provided, of course, that her father agreed to accept the offer. Joshua declined the offer, thus enabling his daughter to have more cash in hand to meet household expenses.

Money never ceased to be a concern with John S. Kidder. In his numerous letters home on the subject, he carefully avoided telling Harriet exactly what bills to pay. Instead, he offered a large list of possibilities to choose from. He did remain firm on only one subject. "If you have got the money I sent you," he wrote, "you can keep it. I do not want you to put it into the company not buy any company notes with it until you have further instructions from me."[16]

Away from the shop for an entire year, John felt that the sale of a few wagons and carriages would keep the shop going at least until the winter months. He went as far as to suggest that Elisha Fisher might want to accept installment plan purchases from customers. Even Harriet knew this wasn't possible. A daily visitor to the carriage shop, she could see firsthand what was and wasn't being completed. As war made life on the battlefield uncertain, it had a similar effect on the life of the carriage business. With business on the wane, even Fisher had thoughts of moving on. The only recourse for Fisher seemed to be either joining the army or waiting until the draft and then make some sort of decision.

On March 3, 1863, Congress passed the much anticipated Enrollment Act or, as it was known to the common soldier, the Conscription Act. Captain Kidder, who could only count fifty-one rifles in Company I that summer after Gettysburg, hailed the measure.[17]

> *Every soldier is glad that the Conscription Bill has passed. . . . I will warrant you that if the draft is made, the men will have to come. I hope that some of those traitors will be drafted. I think that we will put down this rebellion if the draft is made. I feel much better about the war, as I think now that there will be a disposition among the northern people to return*

all deserters, as if they do not they will have to come down and fill up the ranks themselves.

Finally, he delivered a stinging rebuke to those who had enlisted in the 121st companies, accepted their commissions as captains and then resigned and gone home. He added, "I hope that all the officers that have resigned will have to come [in] as privates."[18]

On the surface, John S. Kidder liked what he saw of the Conscription Act. Men between the ages of twenty and forty-five could be drafted for three years service in the army and receive $300 bounty. The only difference was that drafted men had no choice as to their regiment and would be posted where needed.[19] Later, he learned that any soldier wishing to avoid the draft had only to provide a substitute or pay the Federal Government a $300 commutation fee.

The fact that men could *buy* their way out of the army made Captain Kidder furious. He now had a much different view of the piece of legislation he, at one time, thought could win the war.

> *We think the Conscription is a failure and I must confess that the prospects of the Rebels were never so bright as they are at present. I do not know what will become of our Country. How do the people of the North feel to think that our army is not to be filled? There is only one way that will prevent the success of the Rebels and that is for Congress to strike out the $300 clause of the Conscription Act and make the men come or furnish substitutes. . . . We have not received any conscripts in this Brigade and I do not believe that we have received 5 thousand in this whole army.*[20]

When Kidder wrote this in September 1863, he was partially correct. Conscripts were not filling the ranks as expected. In fact, only 21,331 men were drafted in the first ten months of the draft.[21]

By August 1863, the draft hit close to home. That month, Kidder received a letter from his business partner which made his blood boil. Fisher wrote and asked for money to pay for the commutation fee. An outraged Captain Kidder was quick to respond. "I do not think it is my duty to pay any man money to stay away when our country needs them as much as it does at present. I would prefer to give money to have men come and help whip the Rebs than to hire them to stay home."[22]

The only thing that upset Kidder more than the "$300" was the politicians who condemned the Conscription Act. Many of these politicians did not espouse the Union cause, therefore, Kidder had no use for them. Long before the Civil War began, John S. Kidder had been, as one newspaper recalled, "an old line Whig." Abandoning the fledgling Whig Party in 1854, Kidder was one of the founding members of the Republican Party in Otsego County. Although he had ample opportunity to run for elected office throughout his life, he never did. There were a variety of positions available at the village, town, and county level to choose from, but a growing family, time-consuming business, the ever present concern for money, and perhaps his own limited education, may have prompted him to steer clear of elected politics.[23]

Kidder supported the candidacy of Abraham Lincoln in 1860, but was somewhat dismayed when he saw President Lincoln in person two years later. While reviewing troops of the VI Corps on October 3, 1862, Lincoln passed by the soldiers of the 121st New York. For most of the men it was the first time in their lives they had seen *a* president, let alone Lincoln. Kidder was not impressed. "The President," he said, "is as homely as his photograph."[24]

Now, almost a year later, with the army stalled after the Gettysburg victory and discouraged about the eventual success of the Union cause, Kidder's faith and support of Lincoln remained steadfast. "You can begin to make up your mind," he wrote to Harriet.

> If you live with me or move to some other country, for I shall stick to the old ship until she is sinking and then I intend to sink with her (unless I am killed in trying to save it). I have the utmost confidence in Abraham Lincoln, but I have no confidence in the Northern People. I think they are a miserable cowardly set who will be finally subjugated by Lee's Army. I have no doubt you may not think so but I have every reason to believe that it will be the case. God knows I hope I am laboring under a wrong impression for I had hoped to see our army filled up and we be moving toward Richmond by the 1st of October.[25]

The "Northern People" Kidder expressed little confidence in were the Peace Democrats, or Copperheads, who favored a quick end to the war by means of a negotiated peace with the southern states. In effect, they wanted an end to the war as quickly as possible by whatever means necessary. The leading Copperhead was Ohio politician, Clement Vallandingham. His outspoken views on the war and the Conscription Act earned him national recognition. Arrested, he was later released by Lincoln, who banished him to the Confederacy. Not content to stay there, Vallandingham ran the Union naval blockade and made it all the way to Canada where he continued to be a critic of the Lincoln administration. In October 1863, he ran for the governorship of his native state in absentia, his competition being Democrat turned Republican, John Brough. The election results were stunning. "Yesterday morning . . . we heard that Vallandingham was beaten by over 50,000 majority," said Kidder. "That Curtin had 80,000 majority, and such rejoicing I never witnessed before."[26] When the official count was known, it was more than that. Brough won by a landslide, beating Vallandingham by 101,098 votes.[27]

In Pennsylvania, Governor Andrew Curtin fended off rival George Woodward, 269,506 to 254, 171.[28] Curtin, already a legend with the soldiers for his devotion to their health and well-being, had rightfully earned the sobriquet, The Soldier's Friend. Even Kidder recognized this when he said, "the soldiers know who are their friends."[29]

Unjustly maligned by John S. Kidder as being a Copperhead, was Democratic Governor Horatio Seymour of Kidder's own state of New York. Although the fifty-three-year-old Governor had been responsible for raising a tremendous amount of troops for the war effort, the former mayor of Utica incurred Kidder's wrath by publicly criticizing the Conscription Act. When the first names were drawn for the draft, New York City erupted in an orgy of violence. An uncontrollable mob took to the streets, burning and looting everything in sight. Over a million dollars in property damage was inflicted and dozens of deaths were attributed to these riots before federal troops were diverted to the area.

Governor Seymour, still reeling from the effects of the New York City Draft Riots (July 13–16, 1863), wrote a letter to President Lincoln claiming the draft was unjust and "is in itself a violation of supreme Constitutional law."[30] According to Seymour, some Republican Party districts were assessed fairly lightly while some Democratic Party areas faced harsher enrollment figures. He suggested to Lincoln that the draft be postponed until the courts could render a proper verdict on its constitutionality.

This was more than Captain Kidder could take. Still holding fast to the idea that the draft was necessary to fill the ranks of his beloved Company I, he exploded in anger in a letter to his wife.

I see by the papers that your Governor [Seymour] wants men raised by volunteering. I suppose that that would suit every Copperhead to have Republicans and loyal Democrats volunteer so that the Copperheads could control the state and get up a fire in our rear. . . . I think Gov. Seymour is a scoundrel—a real Copperhead. I think such men deserve to be shot more than the southern soldiers.[31]

It appeared as if conscription and Copperheads went hand in hand with a series of letters Kidder penned while in New Baltimore. He suspected that the Copperheads were at the root of the desertion problem that plagued the Army of the Potomac. These northern traitors were trying to pressure the soldiers into deserting the army while they were home on leave. Such was the case with the late Robinson Fox. While home on leave prior to the Chancellorsville Campaign, all but three of his friends urged him to desert and stay home. William Comstock insisted that he fulfill his obligation and return to the regiment. "Old William" Comstock, at sixty-one years old, was one of the wealthiest farmers in Laurens, and his gesture did not go unnoticed by John S. Kidder. "I am very thankful to Mr. Comstock for such advice," he wrote to Harriet, adding, "I wish everyone would advise so . . ."[32]

Rumors began to circulate that Leroy Hall, home on leave for the first time, was being influenced in the same way as Robinson Fox. Furious at this, John instructed Harriet to gather names.

> If you will send me the names of some that are advising Leroy to desert, I will have them taken care of. The Col. [Upton] and General [Horatio] Wright want I should obtain the names. I think they had better be in other business and they will think so before they get through with it. You need not say that I have written to you on the subject. We are bound to stop such Copperhead advice.[33]

Captain Kidder's only wish was that some of these Copperheads would be drafted and sent to his own Company I.

> I wish I had about 20 in my Company. My Sergeants and Corporals say that they would like to drill them. They would have to toe the mark and face the music and when we go into battle, they would be put into the front rank and if they showed any disposition to run, my file closers would bayonet them and if I saw one sneaking out I would shoot them if I could. You can send as many as you please, I will warrant that we would make fighting men of them in 4 weeks and all their talk about shooting their officers, etc., would not scare anyone.[34]

He was very serious in regard to the Copperhead activity in Laurens and with good reason. By the end of the war, the population of Laurens and the surrounding villages had decreased. The 1865 Census explained the cause. "The aggregate vote of the election district was much smaller last fall (1864), caused by absence of 'Canada Sneaks' who ran away from the draft, or deserted from the army."[35]

Deserters, either influenced by Copperheads or friends at home, were still a problem. In August, while in New Baltimore, Kidder noted that seven men had been returned to the regiment to answer to the charge of desertion. "Poor Robin Fox," lamented Kidder. Six months had passed since his return to the ranks of Company I under the provisions of a Presidential Pardon. He had escaped the stigma of being labeled a deserter, only to fall to Rebel bullets a short while later at Salem Church.[36] Deserters that were arrested did not have the luxury of a Presidential Pardon and sometimes the penalties could be quite severe.

John S. Kidder had serious thoughts as to the fates of the seven men who were returned to the regiment. Two of them, George Bull and Erastus Green, were Company I men and went before a Board of Court Martial. Bull had deserted the second day into Burnside's Mud March in January 1863. He eluded authorities, ignored the Presidential Pardon, only to be arrested by a fellow Company I man, who just happened to be home on furlough in May. Bull had no choice but to plead guilty to the charge of desertion.[37]

Green, on the other hand, wasted no time in leaving the 121st New York. He skipped out on September 12, 1862, as soon as the regiment entered the field, just one month after he enlisted. He was brought back to camp in irons on July 27, 1863.[38]

Both men appeared before the Board of Court Martial and the presiding Judge Advocate, Captain Cleaveland J. Campbell of Company C. Visiting Capitan Kidder in his tent, Campbell informed him that there would be an execution by firing squad in the near future, but it would not be a member of the 121st New York. This was a relief, for Kidder thought that Green stood, as he said, "A good chance to be shot."[39] Campbell then told him that the outcome of the investigation into both men was not yet completed, but the sentences would indeed be harsh ones. Bull was still under arrest when the regiment was mustered out of the service in 1865, and Green was sentenced to hard labor.[40]

George Bull and Erastus Green were indeed fortunate. As harsh as their punishments seemed, three days after their sentences were handed down, the firing squad that Campbell told Kidder about, occurred. On Friday, August 15, 1863, Kidder and his Company I men were performing picket duty. The remainder of the regiment reported to Warrenton, where they were joined by the First Division of the VI Corps to witness the execution of a deserter. "I would like to have gone with them," said Kidder in a half joking manner, "but someone had to stay."[41]

When the regiment returned from this somber task, Kidder was able to reconstruct the scene. The doomed prisoner was Thomas Jewett of the

5th Maine. He had deserted before the enemy at Salem Church and had been found guilty by a court-martial. If this wasn't in itself a cowardly act, it was discovered that he had also deserted from the English Army.[42] Jewett was seated on his own coffin as the brigade band played a funeral dirge and the chaplain of the 5th Maine offered a prayer. The Division formed a hollow three-sided square so all could witness the doomed prisoner. Kidder was later told he died instantly; six bullets found their mark.

Two months later, the entire scene was reenacted with the same chilling results, and this time, Captain Kidder was present. The 121st New York was ordered to report to the camp of the Jersey Brigade to witness the execution of Private Joseph Connelly of the 4th New Jersey. Kidder discovered that Connelly was also a two-time deserter. The first time, he was brought back, sentenced to hard labor, then released through the kindness of his captain. Ignoring this pardon, Connelly deserted again and boldly rejoined another regiment. Arrested a second time, Connelly was executed by a firing squad on October 9, 1863.[43] "11 balls hit him killing him instantly," noted Kidder.[44]

Once more, it had the same numbing effect on those that witnessed the event. Private John J. Ingraham of Company D, a witness to both executions, summed up the experience in a unique way. "When I am shot," he wrote, "I want to be shot by the Johnnies."[45] Kidder would have agreed with him.

By mid-October, the 121st New York broke camp in New Baltimore and moved to Centerville. Even though it was too early to think about moving into winter quarters, Kidder wasted very little time in making preparations. Once more, Harriet and Elisha Fisher busied themselves in gathering all the necessary items to be sent south. Fisher's job was to construct another box, similar to the one he sent the year before, but this time larger. It had to be a trunk big enough to pack food as well as winter clothes. In addition to an eight quart tin of butter, a ten pound box of honey, and a pint of brandy, Kidder listed his winter coat, three pair of socks, two pair of knit flannel drawers, four knit undershirts, and a new pair of boots.

> I want James Fuller to make me a good pair of hip boots. Make the legs long and large so that they will come nearly up to my knees and sufficiently large for me to put my pants into them. Make them of the best stock, especially the soles. Make wide heels as we are apt to run them over, make heavy soles, and put plates on the toes and heels.[46]

His request for the "wide heels" was a rare moment of levity for Kidder, but not one that was entirely out of character for him or any other

member of the regiment at the time. Denied their share of glory at Gettysburg, and increasingly confident in their abilities after chasing Mosby, the
121st New York Volunteers was once more anxious to prove their worth.
"The boys are all in good spirits, fight in every man's eye," he wrote. "I do
not wish to boast but I think you will hear a good account of the 121st."[47]

His prediction of a "good account" was, indeed, an understatement.
A short while later, the 121st New York, together with the 5th Maine, carried out one of the Civil War's rare night attacks at Rappahannock Station.
The attack was simply brilliant in its execution and John S. Kidder could
hardly contain his excitement.

> *Rappahannock Station*
> *November 8th, 1863 10 o'clock* A.M.
> *Dear Wife,*
> *I feel [I want] to rejoice that we have met the enemy and they are
> ours.*[48] *The 121st Regiment and the 5th Maine of our Brigade with the
> 6th Maine and 5th Wisconsin of the 3rd Brigade of our Division have as-
> tonished the whole Army of the Potomac. I do not wish to boast but I will
> tell you what we have done. Yesterday morning we started from Warrenton
> at daylight, marched down to within one mile of this place and to our sur-
> prise got within 500 yards of the Rebel pickets before we were aware we
> were anywhere [near] of it. We arrived about noon. We halted and put out
> 2 Companies, B and D as skirmishers with some of the other Companies
> of the Regiment in the Third Brigade. We put out 2 Batteries, also the V
> Corps were fighting on our left [flank]. About 4* P.M. *we formed a line of
> battle. The 5th Maine on our left and in line with the 121st, while the
> 95th and 96th Pennsylvania in line in the rear of us. We had to march
> about 1/2 a mile over a level flat under fire of 2 Rebel Batteries, one in a
> fort on this side of the river and one in a fort on the other side. As soon as
> we started, they opened on us and, although they were less than one mile
> from us when they opened, we did not lose a man. After we had marched
> 1/2 mile, we were covered by a small hill so that they could not see us.
> Here, we halted and General Sedgwick with General Wright rode out to
> within 1/4 of a mile of the Rebel fort and then came back. (They left their
> staff in the rear with us.) The 3rd Brigade then came up on our left and
> halted in line with us. The 6th Maine and 5th Wisconsin were immedi-
> ately moved out on our left [flank] and marched under a galling fire up to
> the fort, which they carried with the* Bayonet, *capturing 7 guns. There was
> a heavy line of rifle pits in 2 rows on the right of the fort and the Rebs re-
> treated into them, and the order came that our men had got a prize and*

wanted the 121st to come and help hold it, so we and the 5th Maine started on a double quick to the rescue, arriving to within 10 rods of the pits. We halted and lay down, unstrung knapsacks and fixed bayonets. Col. Upton had command of the Brigade as Gen. Bartlett was commanding a Division in the V Corps. Our Regiment was commanded by Major Mather as Olcott is sick in Washington, but Col. Upton then said that he would command the 121st to make the charge. He ordered us not to fire a gun but carry them at the point of Bayonet. He made a short speech, said that we were the 121st, and he was one of us and that we were all brave men fighting for a good cause and that some of us would fall but that we should all go to heaven and he was going with us. Then "Forward, March, double quick," and it was so dark that the Rebs did not see us until we were nearly on the pits. Then he shouted "On my brave boys, you have four lines of battle to support you," and in a second we were crossing swords and bayonets with the Rebs. He shouted after we got inside of the works for them to surrender and Company A, G, and I started into the 2nd line with some of the 5th Maine and it was all over with. The 121st captured 3 Colonels, 2 Majors, 17 Captains, 27 Lieutenants and 651 Privates and noncommissioned officers while the 5th Maine did equally as well capturing about the same number. The 121st took four stands of colors, the 5th Maine, four. Our loss was [that] the 121st had 4 killed and 22 wounded. I lost one man, killed, his name [Private] Asbel Lamont from Worcester. Norman Stone has a slight wound on his left ear. Capt. [Marcus] Casler wounded in the arm, not broken.[49] Company D had 3 killed. I must close as the mail is going out. My men all behaved splendidly, and [they] were into the pits as soon as I was, every one of them. [Zebulon] Bowen and [Charles A.] Butts did nobly, so did every one of them. We feel sorry to lose such a good fighter as Lamont, as he was one of my 13 who rallied at Salem Chapel. Company I captured a stand of colors and 7 swords. I took 4 and Lieut. Bates, 3. I took the Colonel of the 6th North Carolina; [I] have his sword. I took also, 2 Captain's swords of the 5th Louisiana Tigers.

I am well, so are all of my men. [Color Bearer Mason] Jenks is all sound, a brave soldier.

Yours as ever,

J. S. Kidder

The Rebs had the strongest works that I ever saw. I think we saved hundreds of lives in carrying of them in the night after dark. Silas Waterman of my Company captured the colors. They are pursuing the Rebs toward Culpepper.

The charge at Rappahannock Station stunned the defenders as well as the attackers. As Kidder said, the attack astonished the Army of the Potomac. In one quick dash, Colonel Upton's small force (he had only 314 men of the 121st and 254 men of the 5th Maine) managed to capture more than twice their number. In his official report of the battle, Upton stated that the Confederates, with their backs to the river, surrendered in droves. He counted 1,200 enlisted men and 103 officers, not to mention 1,255 stands of arms and six stands of colors.[50] It was a loss the Army of Northern Virginia could ill-afford.[51]

With the capture of so many men, there was no shortage of trophies. Captain Kidder wasted no time in collecting swords and neither did anyone else. Adjutant Francis Morse wasn't shy. He took six swords.[52] Entering the rifle pits, Lt. Delavan Bates grasped the uplifted sword of one Confederate officer while at the same time firing his revolver at another who threatened Colonel Upton.[53] Lt. Henry B. Walker of Company G was unimpressed with the sword he took but looked upon it as a souvenir all the same. "I took one officer's sword," Walker wrote in a letter home. "He surrendered and handed over his sword—It is a rusty old thing but I shall try to send it home."[54]

The real trophies, however, were the captured Rebel flags. Two days later, on November 9, a detail of forty men, including Upton, presented the flags to General George G. Meade at his headquarters. Meade graciously accepted the flags and complemented the men on the success of their daring assault. He then ordered that "Rappahannock Station" be inscribed on their regimental flag and added that they would have another opportunity to distinguish themselves in battle. Even though they were thankful for the honor and recognition bestowed upon them by their commander, some members of the 121st were worried that Colonel Upton would once more commit them to this running bayonet style of attack.

By mid-November, Kidder and many others were convinced that the war, at least for now, was over. He remembered all too well the hardships and weather conditions of the previous November. He thought that after Rappahannock Station the army would give up the chase and retire to winter quarters. He was a little surprised to receive orders to have his men draw eight days' rations.[55]

General Meade was aware of the weather too. He also knew that if a move was to be made against General Robert E. Lee, it had to be done quickly. His plan, to move five corps against Lee on the Rapidan River, would require speed, secrecy, and above all, coordination. When it was all over, all three of these vital elements would escape the victor of Gettysburg.

The 121st New York, still riding high from their Rappahannock Station exploits, broke camp on November 26 and marched toward Brandy Station, their destination being Jacob's Ford. From the start, the march was beset with problems. Sharing the same crossing with the VI Corps was the III Corps, commanded by Maj. Gen. William French. The almost fifty-year-old French, a native of Maryland, was a West Point graduate, in the same class as VI Corps commander, Maj. Gen. John Sedgwick. French had a steady, yet unspectacular Civil War record of service up to this point;[56] he had been in command of the III Corps since July 7, 1863. When French brought his Corps to Jacob's Ford, he discovered the terrain beyond the ford unsuitable for his artillery. He chose to reroute his cannon downstream, thus adding to the confusion of an already crowded road.

It was an unfortunate delay. The 121st New York and other elements of the VI Corps in that vicinity were halted in their tracks. They could do nothing but stand to one side and allow the guns to pass. The entire brigade that the 121st was a part of didn't reach the banks of the Rapidan River until dark;[57] it wasn't until the next day that both the III and VI Corps were united with their artillery and began the advance toward Payne's Farm.

Once again, there was a problem. "The III Corps marched out and took the wrong road," declared Kidder.[58] It was true. French's lead division was confused and inadvertently took the wrong fork in the road. With Rebel skirmishers before them, the blue-clad soldiers stood their ground and opened fire. Neither side yielded ground and, as Kidder said, probably surprised each other on the road. The Confederates thought they were fighting dismounted Union cavalry, while French thought he had stumbled on a large portion of the Confederate army. Both sides committed troops as quickly as possible. Sedgwick, about a mile and a half away, moved his VI Corps up to support French. As they drew near, the steady increase in the sound of gunfire indicated that a fairly large skirmish was underway. Some Confederate units exhausted their supply of ammunition in this exchange; French later reported that many of his troops had expended their forty rounds as the action seesawed across Payne's Farm.[59]

When the 121st arrived on the scene, Captain Kidder at first believed that a large battle was unfolding before the VI Corps. "The musketry firing," he recalled, "was about as heavy as it was at Gettysburg, but very small loss [of life] considering the amount of firing. I saw but very few wounded brought to the rear while we were marching."[60] Unable to get close enough to the real fighting, he had no way of knowing what really transpired at Payne's Farm, and once more fell victim to camp gossip. He heard that the 106th New York and the 87th Pennsylvania had been driven from the field. "Ran before they lost a man," he was told. The very hint of cowardice infuriated Kidder. He hoped General Meade would strip both units of their regimental colors for acting in such a cowardly fashion.[61]

When it came to cowards, Kidder felt that he had to look no further than his own brigade. He still harbored the utmost contempt for the 95th and 96th Pennsylvania. He put it bluntly. "They are cowardly Regiments."[62] When it looked as if the brigade might be committed to the fight at Payne's Farm, Kidder felt sure that the 121st and the 5th Maine would have to prod the Pennsylvania units into battle at point of bayonet.

The evening of November 27, the VI Corps camped on the field expecting to take a more active part in the contest at Payne's Farm the next day. At 11:00 P.M., however, Maj. Gen. Sedgwick received orders to move his entire Corps toward Robertson Tavern [near Locust Grove] on the Old Turnpike Road. This he was able to accomplish by daylight; he positioned his men on the right of the II Corps.[63]

The sight of the II Corps' flags caught the attention of Captain Kidder. Somewhere in the vast sea of blue uniforms was brother George. The two hadn't seen each other since October, and that was only for a brief visit over dinner. Still a sergeant in the 152nd New York, George experienced the same lack of advancement as his brother. But there was a real difference—John had seen combat. This move toward Mine Run was the first real field experience encountered by George Kidder and the rest of the 152nd New York. Most of the year and a half he had been in a blue uniform, he spent performing garrison duty at the nation's capitol. John Quinby of the 152nd, spoke for all when he said, "Who would have thought that I could be in the service more than fourteen months, on the Potomac, at Suffolk on the Nansemond on the Blackwater, on the Peninsula, the Pamunkey and famous Chickahominy and now the Rappahannock and Rapidan, in the most famous fighting division and corps of the Army of the Potomac, and yet never be able to get so much as a glimpse of a single Rebel in arms against the U.S.?"[64]

The elder Kidder worried about the 152nd's lack of experience and apparent lack of leadership. "I think if the 152nd had a Colonel like Upton, it would be under much better discipline in two months than it is at present."[65]

This was an observation shared by many in Upton's Regulars. "I tell you they are green enough," said Private John J. Ingraham. "Some of them curse the war. All sorts, they don't know how to cook and ain't got nothing to cook with. They make their coffee in their drinking cups and they don't like it. I tell you it is fun to hear these green horns talk and grumble and hear what hardships they have seen. They ain't seen nothing compared to us."[66] Ingraham was quick to point out that the 152nd New York would no longer be bystanders in the Civil War. They were attached to the II Corps, "a good fighting Corps."[67]

Captain Kidder didn't have his Company I men in place very long when orders were passed down the line to advance toward the enemy. The entire VI Corps began a snail's pace push through underbrush the likes of which few of the men had ever seen before. Briars tore at the men's clothing as they struggled onward under the weight of their knapsacks. "Of all the cursed wilderness to move in, I think this was the worst place that I was ever in," admitted Kidder.[68] It was all for nothing. Emerging from the dense thicket, the troops discovered that the enemy slipped away during the night.

Undaunted, with a gentle rain beginning to fall, Maj. Gen. Sedgwick pushed further on to Mine Run. In a relatively short period, the march slowed to a crawl. The rain became a steady downpour. The entire day was lost and the next, November 29, wasn't much better, as the rain gave way to freezing temperatures.[69] With precious time lost and nearly half their rations gone, the Army of the Potomac pushed onward.

Once more, the VI Corps made a night move. Breaking camp at 2:00 A.M. on November 30, Sedgwick made a two mile swing to the right to better his position opposite Mine Run.[70] With this move completed, Kidder was convinced that a battle was near at hand. At daylight, he ordered his men to remove the bullets from their rifles, clean, and reload them. After the rainstorm of the previous day, he was taking no chances with misfired weapons. In the distance, they could make out the camp fires of Rebel pickets. This afforded them little comfort. "We were not permitted to have any fire as the Rebs would fire on us," commented the Captain.[71]

As physically uncomfortable as it was that cold morning, mentally, Captain Kidder was ready to do battle. He still had the utmost confidence in the fighting ability of the VI Corps. Some of the brigades were well-known throughout the entire Army of the Potomac. There was the "Old Vermont Brigade," one of the few brigades in the entire army to maintain the same regiments throughout the entire war.[72] The 2nd, 3rd, 4th, 5th, and 6th Vermont were, as Kidder said, "considered the very best Brigade in the service of which I have no doubt, as every Regiment are good—no sneaks among them."[73] To their right was the "Jersey Brigade" consisting of the 1st, 2nd, 3rd, 4th, and 15th New Jersey. Kidder believed they were just as good as the Vermonters.

As soon as battle lines were formed (Kidder counted three lines, the 121st New York being in the third line), Colonel Upton passed word down that the brigade would make a Rappahannock-style bayonet attack once the order to advance was given. Kidder felt this would ensure success. "We were to charge without firing, as we have proven that that is the best way to carry rifle pits (in fact it is the only way)."[74]

Colonel Upton was so confident they would be successful, that Kidder overheard him say to General Alfred Torbert that his brigade would beat his Jerseymen into the Confederate rifle pits.[75] It really didn't matter who got there first, for Kidder felt that the fighting ability of both brigades was about evenly matched. Besides, he had other things to worry about.

This charge was going to be difficult. It was not going to be a repeat of the affair at Rappahannock Station. That assault was made under cover of darkness. This attack was scheduled for 9:00 A.M., in broad daylight against an enemy that was firmly entrenched. Every delay encountered by General Meade on this campaign was, in essence, a gift of time to General Lee. While Meade's men slogged along the muddy roads to new positions, Lee's men were busy building parapets, digging trenches, and felling trees. The results of their labor was an impressive line of earthworks strewn along a seven mile front. In some places, the Union forces would have to cross one thousand yards before they reached the first set of rifle pits. Others would have to ford swamps to reach the same objective.[76]

As the time to attack drew closer, John S. Kidder became impatient. "Every man," he recalled later, was "anxious to move forward for everyone wanted to go through the terrible ordeal of iron and lead without having to think about it. You could hear the brave boys say, 'Why don't we move?'"[77]

When Union cannons opened up on the enemy, every man shed his knapsack and held firm to his rifle. With bayonets fixed and hammers down, they waited for the signal to advance. At 8:45 A.M., Sedgwick received orders to suspend the attack. Word quickly spread up and down Union lines. In a short while, Kidder and the other line officers of the 121st New York discovered that it wasn't Meade who called off the attack. It was his thirty-three-year-old II Corps commander, Maj. Gen. Gouverneur Kemble Warren. Earlier that morning, Warren had taken it upon himself to reconnoiter the entrenched Confederate position. Impressed with what he saw, Warren advised against the attack. Meade, although upset at first, eventually concurred with his youthful subordinate. The Mine Run Campaign was officially over.[78]

The next day, December 1, the Army of the Potomac abandoned their lines and moved back to their previous position across the Rapidan River. This withdrawal, so complete and effective, was perhaps the only bright spot in the entire campaign for General Meade.

With the completion of this lackluster campaign, there came a great deal of finger pointing and name-calling. Gossip and accusations ran the gamut from inept colonels all the way to drunken generals. There was no better or ill-informed person to testify to this than John S. Kidder. In the case of the 10th Vermont, he heard that this regiment had been badly beaten at Payne's Farm due to the actions of an overzealous colonel. This officer, "had no experience," according to Kidder. "One of those with more courage than brains."[79] Part of this was true. The 10th Vermont had seen limited duty. Assigned to the defenses of Washington in the 'Corps of Observation,' the unit joined the III Corps as recently as August 16, 1863.[80] At Payne's Farm the regiment was under the command of Colonel Albert B. Jewett, and came into contact with the enemy immediately after clearing the woods. Jewett sent out skirmishers and then ordered a charge on the Confederates, which, according to his report, "drove the enemy, in much confusion and with great loss."[81] Holding onto his new position also resulted in great losses within his own troops. He reported that about a sixth of his command were casualties, with sixty-nine killed, wounded, or missing.[82]

Kidder erroneously heard that they lost a staggering 180 men. The entire brigade of which the 10th Vermont was a part, lost 183 men that day. This is where Kidder may have been confused.[83] Nonetheless, he had his final word on the subject.

> The other Colonels that had command of the Regiments on the right and left of them ordered their men to halt and lay down behind the fence and return the fire but their Colonel [Jewett] ordered every man over the fence and then halted them and ordered them to fire while they were a complete target all the time they stood there. I think if this is true such [a] Colonel ought to be shot. He should be dismissed [from] the service for incompetency.[84]

The most scandalous rumor to emerge from the campaign was a report that Maj. Gen. French was drunk on the day of the battle at Payne's Farm. Sedgwick categorically denied that French had been drinking, but rumors persisted. The *New York Tribune* seemed to reinforce these rumors by attributing a quote from General Meade that the failure of Mine Run was due, in part, to French, who "was probably too drunk to know or do his duty."[85] Meade denied that he made the remark. Kidder's reaction was typical. "I think Gen. French will and ought to be dismissed (ought to be shot) for getting drunk and taking the wrong road. We should have had a battle and I think a decided one but for his blunders."[86]

Mine Run marked the end of French's field career. Sharply criticized for his actions, he was removed from command of the III Corps.

Gen. George G. Meade thought his own career would come to an end in much the same way. "There will be a great howl," wrote Meade after his failure to bring about a decisive battle with General Lee.[87] The politicians may have grumbled, but the common soldier had nothing but praise for the Pennsylvanian for calling off the suicidal attack. "We are well pleased with Meade and Warren," wrote Kidder, adding that, they "could not suit us better."[88]

From Mine Run, Meade moved the Army of the Potomac to the vicinity of Culpepper, into winter quarters. "I do not know why we came back," remarked an exhausted John S. Kidder upon seeing his old campsite. "I expected that we should have gone back toward Fredericksburg."[89] The possibility of the VI Corps occupying the commanding heights above Fredericksburg for the winter had been suggested, but the idea was dropped when new orders from Washington were received. They would have to be content with winter quarters on the banks of the Hazel River, a tributary of the Rappahannock. Only about four miles north of Brandy Station, the 121st New York was essentially in the same familiar location they were in a month before the aborted Mine Run affair.[90]

Certain care was given to the selection of a site for winter quarters; fresh water had to be available and the surrounding countryside had to provide enough timber for firewood and the construction of winter huts. Since it met both of these needs, the area near Hazel River proved to be a perfect location. Muskets were quickly stacked and the sounds of axes filled the air as the men went to work making their new homes for this, their second winter of the war.

In no time, a variety of structures began to appear. Squads of men competed with each other in regard to the quality of their huts that shared a common style. Logs that were between eight to ten inches in diameter were split, notched, and stacked in a log house fashion to a height of about six feet. Stopping the cracks in the logs with mud, soldiers used their half-lap shelter tents as roofs, propping them up with makeshift rafters. With a door at one end, a fireplace at the other and bunks on the sides, the approximately 6 ft. × 12. ft. foot shanties were complete.

While these cabins were being constructed, a great deal of scavenging took place, for the men endeavored to furnish their new homes with certain creature comforts. Hardtack boxes quickly disappeared to be used as desks, tables, or chairs. Any type of scavenged plank lumber was used as flooring.[91]

The camp itself was laid out like a small village with five streets. About thirty feet wide and close to two hundred feet in length, the streets were appropriately christened "First Street," right on through "Fifth Street." The commissary and guard house were at the end of Fifth Street, while the drum corps situated itself near First Street. The officers' huts were located at the north end of each street. Kidder noted that little distinction could be made between the enlisted men's quarters and that of the officers, underscoring the fact that the camp was, as he said, "much better than we had last winter."[92]

Captain Kidder, for his part, was determined to be comfortable. As early as October, he began making preparations for moving into winter quarters by purchasing a small wood stove. Where he kept it during the Mine Run Campaign remains a mystery, but it was put to good use that winter. "I think it is worth its weight in gold," he said as he noted how quickly the other officers were drawn to his warm abode. "I have plenty of company from the Line Officers as my little stove feels very comfortable."[93]

By mid-December, the camp was completed and was visited by the Inspector General. With typical prejudice that any officer would feel toward his own regiment, Kidder proudly boasted that the inspection was a huge success. "He [the Inspector General] said that he never inspected so fine camps as we have, said that we [were] far ahead of anything in the whole army."[94]

Kidder was understandably upbeat about winter camp that year. It was a feeling that was shared by many in the 121st New York. The physical condition of the regiment was good. From the enlisted men to the officers, one could not help but notice the fact that the men were a lot healthier than they were the previous winter. Private John J. Ingraham said, "Last winter our Hospital was full. The dead beats are about played out now."[95]

Kidder echoed these sentiments in a letter written to his wife two days after Christmas. "I could [not help] but observe the contrast between this and last year. There was as much difference as between daylight and darkness. Last year the men were homesick and demoralized."[96] He was quick to point out that a lot of the credit was due to the medical staff for keeping the regiment healthy. A year in the field had reduced the original compliment of one thousand men to about five hundred, with sickness and disease thinning the ranks faster than bullets.

Through resignations and one dismissal, the medical staff of the 121st changed at the same rate as the officers' staff in a year's time. The ranking surgeon for the 121st New York was Dr. John O. Slocum, a forty-three-year-old general practitioner from Syracuse, New York, who had real army connections. His brother was a West Point graduate and XII Corps commander, Maj. Gen. Henry Warner Slocum. When Dr. Slocum was transferred and promoted to Surgeon of the 121st on July 1, 1863, Assistant Surgeon Dr. Daniel M. Holt, of Newport, New York, cried foul and protested. It took a little while, but Holt later forgave and forgot the incident. The two bearded doctors were no nonsense professionals who were constantly busy during this time of army inactivity, seeing to the needs of the men.

Captain Kidder was impressed with both these men. "Our Hospital," he noted, "is in a good place with a large fireplace and a good board floor. There are no beds in it for the reason that we have no sick men to occupy it. . . . The only use we have for the Hospital is for prayer meetings. Dr. Slocum has nothing to do, and he says that he does not mean to have anything to do for he sees that the men have good quarters and that their food is properly cooked."[97]

With such apparent good care, Kidder was stunned to learn that two men from Company E died of disease on the same day. Twenty-five-year-old Allen Matteson, a private, had been ill for several days and was being cared for by his friends when he died on January 4, 1864.[98] "It was a sad and dreary sight to see them borne out of camp just at dark—the ground covered with snow and still storming—the solemn dirge and muffled drums and escorts marching with reversed arms," remarked Lt. Henry B. Walker of the procession that tended to the lifeless forms of Matteson and thirty-one-year-old Isaac Whipple.[99]

As unfortunate as these incidents were, the men were in very good spirits that winter and John S. Kidder assured his wife that, "soldiers have many happy hours."[100] There were many lighthearted moments and amusing incidents that he casually mentioned from time to time throughout his correspondences.

The nicknames many of Kidder's Company I men had were a sign of the times. "I have one [man] by the name of Williams who the boys call 'General.'"[101] Sanford Williams, a transfer from the 32nd New York, earned this moniker in honor of Assistant Adjutant General Seth Williams. There were other famous names to go around. Cornelius Chase was often times called "Secretary" or "Governor," because of Lincoln's Treasury Secretary, Salmon P. Chase.

Camp life generally livened up a little when there was a dance. Captain Kidder noted that the 96th Pennsylvania had a dance almost every other night. "I think the Otsego girls would laugh to see them perform," he wrote to Harriet. "When we were at New Baltimore, they had girls to dance with but here they have to dance without them."[102]

They also had to make due with whatever musical instruments were available. "Allow me to tell you," wrote John J. Ingraham to a friend, "we had a little dance with Co. D a few nights ago. Our music consisted of one violin and triangle."[103]

There was a hilarious incident involving a visiting Russian Admiral. During the winter, Maj. Gen. Sedgwick reviewed the VI Corps with a Czarist Admiral and his staff. "The Admiral is what we call a 'Bully' looking old chap but some of his officers looked a little green," recalled Sergeant George W. Collins. Although it was mid-December, the Russians were in dress shoes with white stockings and black velvet coats. None were very much at home on horseback. "It was rather late when the review came off," said Collins,

> and when Gen[eral] Sedgwick rode down the line (which in a Corps Review is about 1/2 mile long and 4 of them and two ranks in each line), he went pretty fast. The Admiral who is a good rider kept up with him, but the others kept falling behind until they got back with the Cavalry Escort and there they were, bobbing up and down gripping the reins with one hand and holding on to the saddle for dear life with the other, and trying to take their caps of[f] to salute at the same time. Their pants had worked up most to their knees and to say the least of it they looked funny and I don't believe there was a straight face in the ranks.[104]

There was also a very serious side to winter quarters. This came in the form of honing one's military skills. Evenings for the officers were still spent studying tactics. Captain Kidder, who had at one time been a student of Colonel Upton's, now became the teacher. Holding classes every night save the Sabbath, his students included Lieutenants Jonathan Burrell, Henry Upton, Thomas Adams, Sheldon Redway, Francis Foot, Edward Johnson, Silas Pierce, Henry B. Walker, John Gray, and Daniel Jackson. By war's end, only three; Jackson, Gray, and Redway would escape unscathed. All the others would be killed or so seriously injured that they would be dismissed from the service.[105]

Perhaps the most serious problems confronting the 121st New York Volunteers that winter was not disease but boredom and alcohol. They were problems as old as the army. Then commander of the Army of the Potomac, George B. McClellan, summed it up best when he said, "No one evil agent so much obstructs this army as the degrading device of drunkenness."[106] Although a rigorous schedule was maintained to keep the men occupied, it proved almost impossible to keep spirits away from any of them, including officers. When it came to alcohol, the 121st was no different than any other regiment in the army. The regiment hadn't been in the field two months when Assistant Surgeon Daniel M. Holt recognized the problem.

> *We have plenty of company to help drink up the whiskey which stands in pails and whatever can hold a gallon. From the Colonel [Franchot] of the regiment down to the Officers' servants all stand ready to see that none of it is wasted. This one article is always sure of transportation let the other things go as they will. I think it would be hard to find much else than empty bottles after breaking camp.*[107]

The appearance of the paymaster, idle time, and the coincidental arrival of the camp sutler proved to be a deadly combination. Lt. Henry Walker discovered this during the post-Gettysburg days of inactivity in September 1863. "All was not quiet in camp last night as one of the sutlers got in yesterday with a lot of whiskey and brandy, ale, etc. And I am sorry to say that a good many men (mostly officers) were not men most of the night, but I am glad to say that none of Co. G in the least included that number." Walker, a prayer meeting teetotaler, was worried that this vice might overtake some of the friends he had made in the army. He was particularly worried about fellow Lt. Francis Foot, whom he said "would become a very fine fellow."[108]

One didn't have to wait for the sutler to arrive to supply alcohol; they just had it sent from home. Kidder did this on two separate occasions. Harriet sent him brandy for, as he said, "purely medicinal purposes." If Kidder drank, and he probably did, he was discreet, not like the episode recorded by Cassius Delavan in his diary on Thanksgiving Day 1862. "The Major was pretty tight in Battalion Drill."[109]

The major in question at that time was Egbert Olcott, a hard-drinking line officer who would be the subject of a very ugly incident involving alcohol.

"I enjoyed myself well on Christmas Day," wrote John S. Kidder to his wife, on this, his second Christmas away from home in 1863.

I accepted an invitation from Lieut. Col. Olcott to dine with him. We had the hospital fitted up and trimmed with evergreens, etc. [and] a large chandelier made of bayonets and evergreens decorated with fancy papers cut in various forms. At the head of the table was a large bow with the name of Olcott in the center. There were nine of us that dined, dinner at 6 P.M. I send the names Olcott, Doctor Slocum, Capts. Fish, Campbell, Gorton, Lieuts. Upton, Walker, and Lieut. Campbell from the 152nd New York. We had a splendid dinner, roast turkey, goose, chickens, potatoes, onions, cabbage, cranberry sauce, eggs, a variety of pickles, tarts, mince, apple, lemon, and chicken pies, butterbread, coffee, floating islands, and apples, also five varieties of cake.[110]

Lt. Col. Olcott, on sick leave from November 6 to December 19 (he missed the Mine Run Campaign), was in a very festive mood. When the dinner party broke up on Christmas Day, he continued to celebrate until well into the next day. After drinking heavily with the camp sutler, Olcott decided to share the Christmas "spirits" with other officers. He saw Officer of the Day Capt. Cleaveland J. Campbell and invited him to share a drink. Campbell agreed, stayed a while, and then attempted to leave. Olcott immediately became belligerent, demanding that Campbell stay and drink. Olcott then ordered the camp sutler to hold Campbell while whiskey was forced upon him. Campbell protested, freed himself from the grip of the sutler and returned to his own hut. Here the episode could have ended. A short while later, Olcott ordered Sergeant William Remmel of Company I to bring Campbell to his tent for being improperly attired as an Officer of the Day. "Sergeant," roared Olcott, "Captain Campbell is Officer of the Day and has got his sword and belt off. I authorize you to get ten men and bring Captain Campbell to my quarters. If ten men are not sufficient you may call out your whole company and if that is not enough I authorize you to call the whole regiment." As an extra incentive, Olcott told Remmel, if he did this, he would be promoted to orderly sergeant.[111] Remmel was a good soldier and knew that he had no authority to do any of this and went immediately to Captain Kidder.

Olcott, in the meantime, ordered Cpl. William Cady of Company A to do the same thing. Here, Olcott was more successful. Cady, with the help of Milton Snell, Benjamin Covell, and Brayton Priest, all of Company A, entered Campbell's quarters and were in the process of carrying the Officer of the Day to Olcott's quarters when Maj. Andrew Mather, Capt. John Douw, and Capt. John S. Kidder arrived. Mather wasted no time in preferring charges against Olcott for behaving, "in a misproper and disgraceful manner." Brought before Brigade Commander, Col. Emory Upton, Olcott was severely reprimanded but escaped a court-martial. In fact, the entire episoce was hushed up. The Regimental Day Books didn't mention the incident and, except for a letter written by Dr. Daniel M. Holt to his wife, the entire affair was forgotten. Kidder, who wrote a letter to his wife the day after, didn't mention it at all. He ignored the entire matter and assured Harriet that he was still very pleased with army life. "In fact," he wrote, "I think that if I ever leave the service, I shall have to serve an *apprenticeship* to become contented in civil life."[112]

From a military standpoint, the regiment remained relatively inactive for the remainder of the winter months. They were only under marching orders on two occasions and one of those turned out to be a false alarm. The first time, Confederates were rumored to be in the Shenandoah Valley; it looked as if the brigade might be involved in a winter campaign. Eight days' rations were drawn for each man but new orders cancelled any campaign.[113] The only other time the regiment moved was in February 1864, when the entire VI Corps was sent on a reconnaissance mission in support of Custer's Cavalry. This turned out to be a four day miserable march in the mud, reminiscent of the Burnside Mud March. All were happy to return to the comfort of their winter huts.[114]

During the first two months of 1864, John S. Kidder, when not seeing to his duties as company commander or Officer of the Day, seemed to concentrate all of his energies in one direction. He desperately wanted to obtain a leave of absence for the purpose of returning home and recruiting new members for his depleted company. All around him, regiments were actively recruiting. The Vermonters, whom he had been so impressed with during the Mine Run Campaign, had all enlisted. In the Third Brigade it was the same. Captain Kidder noted that the 43rd, 49th, and 77th New York men had signed on again, as had the 7th Maine and the 61st Pennsylvania. "They are all old Regiments and all but the 61st Pennsylvania are the best of fighting men," he said, being careful to add his disdain for any regiment from the Keystone State.[115]

Urging his friends to write to the War Department on his behalf, Kidder began a one man lobbying effort in hopes of getting home. "I could recruit much faster as being well acquainted with the people in the County," he explained to Colonel Upton.[116] It was difficult to fault his logic. Kidder helped organize Company I, drawing most of the men from his own village of Laurens. If given the opportunity to recruit, he could canvas the entire county of Otsego for men. He was optimistic about his chances and echoed those sentiments in a letter to Harriet.

I have talked with Col. Upton. He wishes I could get detached for that purpose. I dined with the Colonel the other day on a good fat turkey. I am going down to make him a visit this evening. . . . If I should succeed in get-ting an opportunity to come home and recruit, I think I could obtain many. David Winter wants to enlist as musician in our Brigade band. I think if the people of the North could see how well our soldiers feel and know what we do about war, they would not be afraid to enlist.[117]

The day after Kidder wrote this to Harriet, Lt. Col. Olcott forwarded a letter to Asst. Adj. Gen. Seth Williams requesting that both John S. Kidder and John D. Fish be sent to their respective counties for the pur-pose of recruiting more men for the regiment. Olcott received no satisfac-tion from this request; he sent another letter on January 3, 1864.[118]

Meanwhile, Kidder tried not to appear too anxious. After all, this was the army and he was familiar with the chain of command, army pa-perwork, and the often used quote, "request denied," that sometimes ac-companied letters from the War Department. He still felt that the leave was due him, since the last time he applied for a leave, the previous April, it was suddenly cancelled due to the Chancellorsville Campaign. As re-quest after request was ignored, however, it seemed a very real possibility that he might remain in Virginia for the entire winter. Gently, he tried to break the news to Harriet.

I think it is rather doubtful about our being sent [home], and as no fur-loughs or leaves of absence are granted, I do not know as I shall be able to get away this winter. I expect they will be granted when the veterans return as there has been so many [to] re-enlist that it has weakened our lines very much. They all get 30 days furlough when they get back.[119]

The thought of a month long furlough was very appealing to men who had been in the field for a long time. Even those who did not qualify for the re-enlistment bonus were envious of their comrades in arms; for ex-ample, John J. Ingraham, who, like Kidder, had been in Virginia for over a year and had yet to go home on leave. When one of his friends from an-other unit went home on a furlough, he wrote to his sister, "I guess I shall re-enlist. Then I'm sure of having a furlough."[120]

As January drew to a close and there was no word from the War De-partment, Captain Kidder accepted the fact that the possibility of a leave in any form looked doubtful. While Colonel Upton and Lt. Col. Olcott continued to press the issue, Kidder looked on hopelessly as members of the 152nd New York, relative newcomers to the war, sent their own recruiting parties back home. "I think that the 121st ought to be allowed an opportunity to fill up as well as those Regiments that have not been in the field to face the music," he wrote.[121]

At one point, when it looked as if he might be able to obtain a short leave of ten days, John suggested that Harriet meet him in New York City. Having already missed the Matteson family reunion during the holidays, at least he would be able to spend some time with his family. "I would like to see my little girl trotting around," he wrote. "I hope I shall before long."[122]

However, as mid-February approached, he suggested that Harriet might want to come to Virginia and stay at camp with him. Many of the officers' wives, as well as a few of the enlisted men's wives, were already in camp. Still, he cautioned her about rushing down to Virginia too quickly. "You must not come until I write for you, as I shall be on detached service by order of the War Department," he wrote on February 20.[123] Whatever this "detached service" was will never be known. Two days later, he received word that his leave was approved. Kidder and Fish rushed to Washington to take the earliest train northward.

Although recruiting for the regiment was foremost in Captain Kidder's mind, the status of his carriage business also weighed heavily. Absent from Laurens for almost a year and a half, he was soon face-to-face with his partner, Elisha Fisher. A quick review of the account ledger and a glance at the stock and unpaid bills, indicated the business was faltering. Fisher, who once worried about the draft to the point of asking Kidder to pay his commutation fee, now considered enlisting in the army to accept the state and federal bounties. There was little Kidder could do from discouraging Fisher from this avenue and he could hardly blame him. At this point, the money was far better in the army than in the shop. Fisher assured Kidder that he would enlist in Company I of the 121st New York and did so on September 1, 1864.[124]

Carefully dividing his time between family visits and touring the county in an effort to obtain recruits, Kidder still kept a pulse on the activities of the regiment. Periodic correspondences from Lt. Delavan Bates kept him abreast of all the latest news, with particular emphasis placed on any staff changes that might affect him. Before he left for home on leave, Kidder was aware of one staff change. Maj. Andrew Mather submitted his resignation to accept a position in a colored regiment. These new regiments were raised for the Union war effort shortly after the Emancipation Proclamation took effect. With typical nineteenth-century prejudice, all of the officers in these colored regiments were white. Mather discovered, as did others, that service in a colored regiment guaranteed advancement in rank. Mather accepted the position of colonel of the 20th U.S. Colored Troops.

With the departure of Mather, the coveted position of major was once more available. Kidder didn't even consider himself as competition. "Either Galpin or Fish," was his guess. "I hope Galpin will receive the appointment although Fish will make a good Major."[125] Both were his friends and he considered both to be very competent officers. Eventually, Bates forwarded the latest camp gossip. "Upton is in favor of Fish, I hear, and if he is, Fish may get it."[126] This would be a good reward for Fish, especially after how well he handled his men at the daring assault at Rappahannock Station. As the weeks dragged on, however, the position remained unfilled and Bates had no further news on the subject.

He did have another staff change to report, though. Kidder had to be a little surprised when he received a letter from Bates with a Washington, D.C. postmark. While on a short leave of absence, Bates was interviewed for a position in a colored regiment. "I went before the 'Nigger—' one day just for fun and what do you suppose they done?" he asked Kidder. "Recommended me for a Second Class Lieut. Col. So you see they raise Niggers enough and don't have enough 1st Class Lieut. Col., I am in for a fine thing; but don't expect much."[127] Two weeks later, Bates wrote to Kidder and told him that it was official. He was resigning to accept the position of colonel of the 30th U.S. Colored Troops.

Of all the companies in the 121st New York, Company I experienced the fewest changes. It had always been a Kidder and Bates combination. Now Bates was gone and Kidder could not fault him. Advancement was slow in the regiment and, as Kidder soon discovered, recruiting was also slow.

Recruiting in 1864 in Otsego County wasn't the same as it was two years earlier. Men no longer rushed to the colors the way they had in the past. It wasn't because of a lack of patriotism, but more due to the fact that there was an increase in the amount of available units to choose from. Saber-wielding cavalry units captured the hearts of young men who still held to the belief of a romanticized war. Kidder discovered that infantry units like his, that had been terribly thinned by battle, were not as popular as the new heavy artillery units that seldom suffered high casualties. In neighboring Herkimer County, the results were the same. "We must be contented with what we can glean from home territory. I hope you have some in your county," wrote Fish to Kidder of the poor results. "I shall have a few men whom I will take to Albany tomorrow and what you have, you must have here to the early train on Monday next if you can."[128]

John D. Fish did have some good news to relay to Kidder. Capt. Henry Galpin had been promoted to major and he, Fish, was offered and accepted a position on Colonel Upton's staff at the brigade level. Kidder was now the senior captain of the regiment. Both men were more eager than ever to return to Virginia.[129]

Packing his bags and saying goodbye to family and friends, Kidder boarded the train and headed north to Utica, arriving there on April 16. The next stop was Herkimer to pick up Fish and then it was on to Albany, New York City, Philadelphia, and Washington. Finally, reaching the camp of the 121st New York, the two reported to Upton and later received a warm welcome from the officers and enlisted men. "I thought the officers would shake me to pieces," said Kidder of the handshaking and backslapping that accompanied the impromptu welcoming committee. "They all appeared to feel glad to see me. My tent is full of them. The boys in the Company appeared the same."[130]

The next day, the senior captain was ready to assume his new duties. At the brigade inspection, he marched his Company I men to the extreme right of the line. It was, he later said, "the first post of honor in the regiment and Company I are proud of the position."[131] During this inspection, Kidder couldn't help but notice the absence of many familiar faces. Two of his tactics scholars, Lt. Henry Upton and Lt. Henry Walker, were gone. Both men resigned. Neither one sufficiently recovered from the wounds they received at Salem Church in May 1863; they were declared unfit for duty. In addition to Captain Mather and Bates, Capt. Seymour Hall resigned and accepted the position of lieutenant colonel of the 24th U.S. Colored Troops. It wasn't just the officers that were resigning. Sergeant Ward Rice became a first lieutenant in the 32nd and Nathan Garo, who had originally signed on as a musician, transferred and rose to the rank of lieutenant in the 25th U.S. Colored Troops.[132]

FIVE

"I rec'd a severe wound in the face."

MAY 1864

Perhaps the most important change to occur in the Army of the Potomac took place while John S. Kidder was home on leave. On March 11, 1864, Ulysses S. Grant was elevated to the rank of Lieutenant General and General-in-Chief of the Union Army. Leaving his subordinate, William T. Sherman, in the west to fight the war, Grant made his headquarters with General George G. Meade and fought General Robert E. Lee in the eastern theater of the war. Unlike other western generals, who were called to the east to fight, Grant had a string of victories to boast about but he never did. Quiet and unpretentious, he was unlike anything the Army of the Potomac had ever experienced.

One of the numerous problems facing Grant that spring was the size of the army. Re-enlistments were low and draft results didn't look all that promising. So few replacements arrived at the 121st New York that drummer boy Henry Hilton Wood recorded the dismal fact in his diary with a lone entry. "Kidder and Fish were ordered on recruiting service but had poor results."[1]

This was being kind. The recruiting party was a compete flop. They only returned with a handful of men. New recruits, draftees, or one year enlisted men would not arrive until January of the following year. Short on qualified officers as well (Company A was the only company that had a full complement of officers; Companies C, D, and F had only one officer present for duty), the 121st New York like most other regiments in the army, started the spring campaign with less than five hundred rifles.

Grant looked elsewhere for manpower. He didn't have to look too far, for the forts in and around Washington, D.C. were full of troops serving in heavy artillery units. These "Heavies," as they were called, led a charmed life in the army until this time. Cloistered in the confines of the nation's capitol, they wore pressed uniforms, ate regular meals, and slept in beds. Most of the units had neither seen the enemy nor fired a shot in anger. What's more, these units were large, far bigger than the standard infantry unit in the field in 1864. Their size was so great that when they were eventually armed with rifles and marched to the front, a Massachusetts soldier quipped, "What Division is this?"[2]

Captain Kidder was skeptical about these artillerymen turned infantry men. "We hear that Grant has many new men but I have not any confidence in them. If there is any person that the Infantry have the most *supreme contempt* for, it is that class calling themselves heavy artillery. They are hated and despised by the old Infantry Regiments."[3]

Not everyone shared this harsh assessment of these new replacements. Some, like John J. Ingraham, thought that any new men were a welcome addition to the army. "Our army is in good spirits," he wrote to his future wife. "Ready to take Richmond or some other good place. General Grant is sending the heavy Artillerymen out here to the front with their little muskets. They have been in the service 19 months and haven't been away from Washington."[4]

The addition of these troops bolstered Grant's army to about 122, 146. A river away toward the south, Lee had about half that many men.[5]

Grant had four corps at his disposal that spring. The ranks of the I and III Corps had been so badly thinned at Gettysburg that it proved almost impossible to reinforce them, so their troops were transferred to the other corps. The largest of these corps was still Sedgwick's VI Corps. Maj. Gen. Sedgwick, the fifty-one-year-old bachelor, was still a personal favorite with his men.

Still in command of the V Corps was former chief engineer, Maj. Gen. Gouverneur Kemble Warren. His day in the sun was at Gettysburg where he realized the importance of Little Round Top and moved troops into position to save the day for the Union.

Another Gettysburg hero returned to active duty was Maj. Gen. Winfield Scott Hancock. He was seriously wounded at Gettysburg when his troops helped fend off Pickett's Charge.

The last of the corps commanders, Maj. Gen. Ambrose E. Burnside, presented a particular problem to Grant. In command of the IX Corps, Burnside outranked George G. Meade. Returning to the Army of the Potomac, the Rhode Islander somewhat redeemed himself after a successful foray into Knoxville toward the end of 1863.

Rounding out this ensemble was the only western general, Philip Sheridan. He was personally chosen by Grant to take charge of the Union cavalry. Hot-headed and impetuous, his volatile temper matched his fighting spirit.

In the camp of the 121st New York, John S. Kidder witnessed these changes in the army and, like many others, anticipated a very spirited spring campaign. He was still upbeat and confident that the VI Corps would perform well on the battlefield. "Tell Clara," he wrote to Harriet, "that Papa will be home and see her again some day when we whip the Rebels."[6]

He also tried to ease Harriet's fears regarding his safety. Concern for her and his family was always on his mind. "You must keep up good courage as I hope and trust that I shall yet return from the war to live with my loving wife and little one."[7] A short while later, Harriet wrote and told him that she was expecting another child.

On Sunday, May 1, 1864, Kidder, in the company of Assistant Surgeon, Daniel M. Holt, and Hospital Steward, Newton Phelps, paid a short visit to the camp of the 152nd New York. With rumors already circulating regarding the start of the spring campaign, Kidder looked forward to seeing his brother George. The two hadn't seen each other in months and now had time to reminisce about family and friends. Eventually, the conversation turned to the serious business before them.[8] John expressed concern for the safety of his younger brother. The senior captain considered the fact that the 152nd New York saw little action at Mine Run, but was a part of Maj. Gen. Winfield Scott Hancock's hard fighting II Corps. He saw what Hancock's men were capable of as he viewed them from his vantage point on Little Round Top. If there was a fight, the II Corps would be there.

Looking at his brother, John S. Kidder tried to be realistic about their chances for survival. When we parted," he later recalled,

> *I shook hands with him and told him it was possible and very probable that we never should see each other again, but I thought that my chances were three to his one of being killed as officers generally suffer more in proportion to men. He replied that might be, but if it was his fate to fall he should fall in the way of doing his duty to the best of his ability.*[9]

With that, the two men parted.

For the next few days, Kidder and the rest of the officers were very busy. Orders to have the men supplied and armed were all too familiar. Each man was to be given eight days rations consisting of eight pounds of hardtack, twenty-four tablespoons of coffee, and a like amount of sugar.

Salt, pepper, and three pounds of pork were also added to their haversacks. In addition to their rations, each man was supplied with eighty rounds of ammunition.[10]

At 3:00 A.M. on May 4, reveille sounded for the 121st New York. Within an hour, most of the men had cooked their breakfast and struck their tents. By dawn, they assembled, checked their equipment and began the march toward the Rapidan River. Grant's plan was to cross the river at two fords and seek out Lee. Warren's V and Sedgwick's VI Corps crossed at Germanna Ford and six miles to the east, Hancock crossed his II Corps at Ely's Ford. Later on, Burnside's IX Corps also crossed at Germanna.

With the Old Wilderness Tavern as their destination, Colonel Upton marched his brigade on the Orange Plank Road about two miles beyond Germanna Ford. The next day, May 5, he resumed the march and was given new orders to march his men onto the Culpepper Mine Road for the purpose of protecting the flank of the advancing elements of the VI Corps. At 11:00 A.M., Upton was told to move his brigade forward and support Warren's V Corps. They were already engaged in a fight about two miles away from the Wilderness Tavern on the Orange Plank Road. It was probably at this time that Upton's men truly appreciated the term, "Wilderness." The young colonel later admitted that, "it was impossible to march in line of battle on account of the dense pine and nearly impenetrable thickets which met us on every hand."[11]

Eager to connect with the V Corps, especially with the sound of musketry before them, Colonel Upton pushed his men forward. The gunfire they heard was the exchange of fire between Warren's men and Confederate General, Richard Ewell's, II Corps. The 96th Pennsylvania, on the extreme left of Upton's line, was the first brigade unit to make contact with the enemy. Lt. Col. Edward Carroll, scouting ahead of his regiment, received one of the first volleys of the Confederates and was killed instantly. Seeing this, the nearby 95th Pennsylvania charged. Rushing the enemy, they not only gained ground, but also managed to capture thirty men. This impromptu advance connected the line to the V Corps and Upton decided to hold the position.[12]

By dusk, the rifle fire from the pickets became more and more scattered. Soon, the only sounds that pierced the night were those of the wounded crying out for help. Caught between the lines, these men were truly the most unfortunate victims of the battle. Their deaths were slow and agonizing as scattered fires began to develop in different parts of the forest. "The ground had previously been fought over and was strewn with wounded of both sides," wrote Upton in his official report of the day's events, adding that many men, "must have perished in the flames, as corpses were found partly consumed."[13] Having never encountered this situation before, Colonel Upton assumed that the Confederates purposely set the fires to slow the Union advance. In all likelihood, the fires were the result of sparks that flew from the hundreds of weapons that were discharged that day in the dry woods.

Upton ordered his men to sleep on their arms and be ready to move at a moment's notice. Officers made their way through the ranks to determine casualties and were surprised to discover that, as confusing as the day was, there were no men missing. All of the four hundred men and twenty officers who crossed the Rapidan were accounted for with the exception of a few stragglers.[14]

Roused before daylight, the brigade was held in readiness for an attack. For the better part of the day, they maintained the same position, continually dodging Rebel picket fire. It wasn't until about 7:00 P.M. that Upton was approached by Lt. Col. James Duffy of Maj. Gen. Horatio Wright's staff. Duffy needed two regiments to reinforce the right side of the line that was in danger of being flanked. An hour earlier, Confederate General John Brown Gordon had launched a flank attack on the right side of Maj. Gen. Sedgwick's line. With Union brigades caving in under the weight of this attack, it appeared as if the entire line might give way. Upton dispatched the 121st New York and 95th Pennsylvania immediately to meet this threat.

Once again, the terrain was as formidable as the unseen foe. Exposed to rifle fire throughout the move, Capt. Kidder and his Company I men, together with the rest of the regiment, were forced, some of the time, to march in single file through the dense brush. Lt. Col. Duffy eventually came into contact with his first blue-coated soldiers. These men were retreating instead of holding their position. Duffy managed to move the 121st New York and 95th Pennsylvania into position despite the interference of the straggling retreaters. While half of the men kept up a steady fire against the Confederates, the others busied themselves digging earthworks for protection. The repeated pounding by the Confederates, however, proved too much and Duffy was forced to pull his men back. Many of them fell back so quickly they didn't have time to collect their equipment. Captain Kidder later expressed astonishment at how much material his Company I men left behind. Lost were thirty-six knapsacks, forty haversacks full of food, fourteen canteens, along with five rifles and cartridge boxes, plus scores of other items that would, no doubt, assist the poorly equipped Confederates.[15]

As the rifle fire continued and intensified, Colonel Upton appeared on the scene and began to rally the men. Lt. Col. Olcott was trying to do the same when he was struck in the head, thrown from his horse, and captured. Darkness put an end to the day's fighting and those that didn't fall to the ground exhausted, took shovels and dug rifle pits in preparation for the next day's battle.

For Kidder, there was hardly time to mourn the dead let alone try to make some sense out of such a terribly confusing day. Company I lost four men, that he was sure of, and about as many were wounded. Among the dead was thirty-four-year-old Sergeant Chauncy Colton of Morris. A sergeant since the regiment was formed at Camp Schuyler, Colton's services would be sorely missed by Kidder. Another of his sergeants, Peter S. Perine, also of Morris, together with Sergeant Treat Young, became separated from the regiment and were captured.[16]

All that night, stragglers appeared in the camps, each with his own story of either how the fight went, or just eager to discover any new information. Some of these "News Walkers," as they became known, were surprisingly accurate with their information. Others, understandably, either fell victim to gossip, or just got the entire story wrong.[17]

When told that the 15th New York, one of those recently converted artillery to infantry units that he had no love for, fled, Kidder growled, "I would rather be without them as they are poor *miserable cowardly scoundrels*. . . . I would prefer old women with broom handles."[18]

In reality, the 15th New York did about as well as they could under the adverse conditions of the Wilderness. Their commander, Lt. Col. Michael Wiedrich, stated in his Official Report of the battle that his unit suffered eight killed and thirty-six wounded, making an issue of the fact that his men were, "carrying old Remington rifles with sword bayonets; and also that it [his regiment] never had been sufficiently drilled as infantry."[19]

When the 22nd New York Cavalry stampeded past the VI Corps the next day, it was more than Kidder could stand. "I would rather have 50 men out of any old regiment than five such Regiments as the 22nd [New York Cavalry]. Such rascally cowardly conduct I never before witness[ed]."[20] Perhaps he would have been more sympathetic to their plight had he known that a Rebel cannonade prompted this skedaddle.[21]

Unfortunately, the only story that had any solid truth to it was one that was personally devastating for Kidder. Far away on the opposite side of the field of battle, Hancock's II Corps was engaged in a fight just as John S. Kidder predicted. The 152nd New York, as part of the brigade commanded by Brig. Gen. Joshua Owens, was preparing for their first

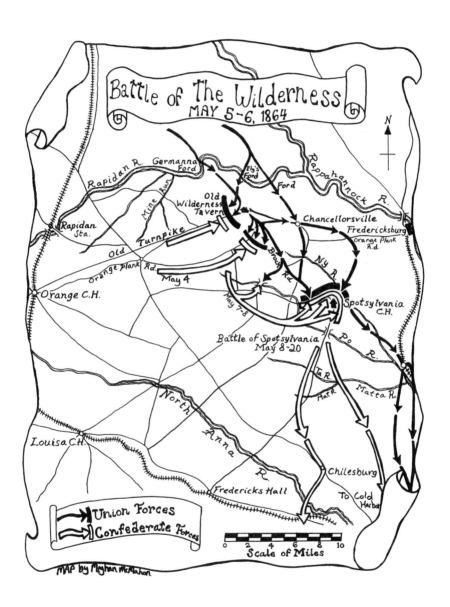

Battle of The Wilderness
MAY 5-6, 1864

N

Rapidan R. Germanna Ford

Rapidan R.

Mine Run

Rappahannock R.

Ely's Ford

Ford

Old Wilderness Tavern

Rapidan Sta.

Old Turnpike

Chancellorsville

Fredericksburg

Orange Plank Rd.

Orange Plank Rd.

May 4

Brock Rd.

Ny R.

Orange C.H.

May 7-8

Spotsylvania C.H.

Battle of Spotsylvania
May 8-20

Po R.

Ta R.

Math

Matta R.

North

Anna

R.

Louisa C.H.

Chilesburg

Fredericks Hall

To Cold Harbor

Union Forces
Confederate Forces

0 2 4 6 8 10
Scale of Miles

MAP by Meghan McMahon

taste of battle. Hampered by poor visibility, thickets, and rugged terrain, the men separated from each other as easily as had the other regiments in the Wilderness. While some sought refuge to the rear, others were simply lost or tried to move in any direction to link up with someone wearing a blue coat. In the confusion, Sergeant George Kidder and Sergeant George Manchester met.

Although his promotion to second lieutenant had finally been approved, George Kidder hadn't officially been mustered in at that rank; he was still wearing his sergeant's stripes. The two Georges fired their muskets and were in the process of reloading them for a second volley. Amidst the sound of a battle that raged around them, they had time to converse, a "passing remark," as Manchester later recalled. Then there was the "dull sickening thud" of a Confederate bullet that found its mark. George Kidder slowly slumped forward onto his side. The wound was serious and Manchester sent for the chaplain instead of the surgeon.[22]

Numbed by the terrible news of his brother's death, John S. Kidder could neither obtain any other information nor the location of his grave. There really wasn't time to do anything, as the army was once more on the move.

On the morning of May 7, Colonel Upton passed word to his regimental commanders to cease fortifying their positions and prepare to move. The entire VI Corps was to move toward Chancellorsville, a scant five miles to the east. With Upton's brigade in the lead, the march was soon underway. To many of the men, abandoning the line in this fashion seemed reminiscent of the old days. In the past, after a large scale battle with somewhat indecisive results, the army pulled back and retreated. Many thought that having General Grant as the new commander was the reason for the sudden move. When they reached the crossroads at Chancellorsville, however, Colonel Upton's troops veered off to the left toward the southwest. Instead of pulling back and licking their wounds, the army was moving forward to strike again. On May 9, the 121st New York was pulled out of line with the rest of the brigade and moved toward the Spotsylvania Road.[23]

Maj. Gen. Sedgwick arrived at the front line early that morning and, together with his chief of staff, was inspecting and directing the placement of regiments. Seated on a cracker box about 100 yards from the front, Sedgwick scoffed at the sharpshooter activity as balls whizzed past him. Observing one soldier lying prone on the ground in motionless fear and another scurrying past, Sedgwick chuckled, claiming that the Rebel sharpshooters couldn't hit a bull elephant at such a distance. In a cruel twist of fate, Sedgwick rose to his feet and was struck just below the eye and killed.[24]

Command of the VI Corps passed to Maj. Gen. Horatio Wright. The personal choice of John Sedgwick to be his successor, the forty-one-year-old Wright commanded a division at Gettysburg and would command the VI Corps until the end of the war in a capable yet inauspicious manner. He never attempted to, nor was able to, take the place of Uncle John in the hearts of the men.

For John S. Kidder, this was like Gettysburg all over again, with the loss of a popular corps' commander on the eve of a great contest. Still trying to cope with the loss of his brother just a few days earlier, he was bitter about the loss of Sedgwick. "Sedgwick threw his life away. He had no business out on the skirmish line."[25]

For the remainder of the day and most of the next, May 10, the Confederates strengthened their defensive lines at Spotsylvania. The unusual shape of their fortified position was of great concern to the new VI Corps' commander. In the shape of an upside down "U," the Confederate position was a mile long and half as wide. This salient was christened the "Mule Shoe" by both attackers and defenders. Breaking the Mule Shoe was the task before Wright; he believed that he had the perfect man for the job in Colonel Emory Upton.

Ever since Gettysburg, Upton commanded the Second Brigade, and ever since then, he had been frustrated with his lack of advancement in rank. The fact that he desired a promotion was no secret. Politicians had been contacted by family, friends, and admirers. High-ranking generals knew that he wished to advance, but it was all to no avail. His daring rush at Rappahannock Station the previous November earned him plaudits, but not the promotion he felt he deserved. He was still a colonel in command of a brigade. Summoned before General Wright, Colonel Upton was told that he was to crack the Mule Shoe with a handpicked force. "You will attack in four lines," he recalled Wright as saying. "The point of the attack will be indicated to you by Capt. MacKenzie of the Engineers. Mott's Division will support you."[26]

The four lines Wright spoke of would be made up of regiments drawn from the First and Second Divisions of the VI Corps. Brig. Gen. David A. Russel, himself a veteran of Rappahannock Station, personally selected the regiments that would be used in this daring assault. The first line would be composed of, from left to right; the 121st New York, 96th Pennsylvania, and the 5th Maine. Next in line was the 49th Pennsylvania, 6th Maine, and 5th Wisconsin. The 43rd New York, 77th

New York, and 119th Pennsylvania made up the third line and the last was all Vermont—the 2nd, 5th, and 6th regiments.[27] In all, Colonel Upton would be in command of approximately 4,500 to 5,000 men. "They are the best men in the army," he said of this, his first independent command.[28]

Aware of the general tone of the orders given to him verbally by Wright and confident in the fighting ability of those regiments entrusted to him (half were involved at Rappahannock Station), Colonel Upton quickly set about planning the assault. His past experiences showed him that, "assaults had failed for want of minute instruction . . ."[29] For this attack, Upton looked to every detail to ensure success.

First, he called all regimental commanders together and met with them at the edge of the woods. They carefully studied the gentle slope of the field and the Confederate breastworks that were about 200 to 250 yards in the distance. As speed and surprise were essential elements of the attack, Upton ordered the men to carry only rifles and cartridge boxes. Knapsacks, haversacks, canteens, and any other weighty or noisy items were to be left behind.[30] Once the order to advance was given, all company commanders were to constantly repeat the command, "Forward," to urge the men on to the Rebel works. If a soldier were to fall out of the ranks, wounded, he was to be left behind. This was not a heartless gesture but one that was necessary given the closeness of the attacking columns. If a soldier stopped to assist a comrade, he was in danger of holding up the entire line, or worse, causing the next soldier to fall over him, and the next, and so forth.

Upton further explained that the attack would be made in four lines with fixed bayonets. The first line would have loaded and capped weapons. This line, made up of the 121st New York, 96th Pennsylvania, and 5th Maine, was to break through the Confederate breastworks and swing toward the right to capture a battery of guns and silence it.[31] The remaining three lines were to charge with loaded weapons that were uncapped. For the same reason he didn't want his men stopping to assist a fallen comrade, Upton didn't want these remaining lines to fire their weapons on the run. Stopping to reload their weapons would cause just as much confusion as stopping to pick up or aid a fallen friend. Upton certainly didn't want to bring about a major engagement in an open field while the first line was trying to breach the enemy's works.

The second line was to advance toward the Rebel works with their weapons capped and ready to fire at will, thus supporting the first line who should have discharged their weapons by now. The third line would like-

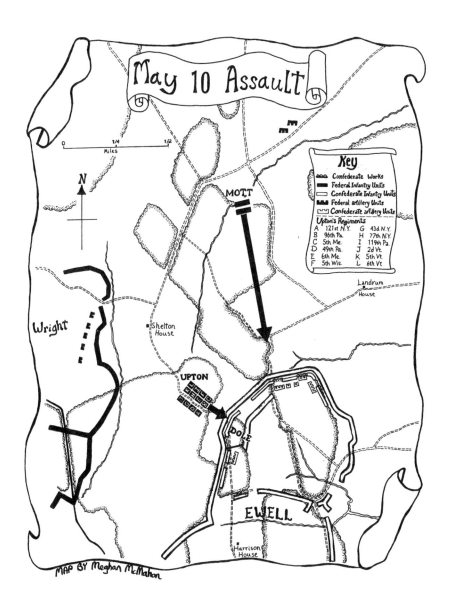

May 10 Assault

0   1/4   1/2
Miles

N

Key
- Confederate Works
- Federal Infantry Units
- Confederate Infantry Units
- Federal artillery Units
- Confederate artillery Units

Upton's Regiments

A	121st N.Y.	G	43d N.Y.
B	96th Pa.	H	77th N.Y.
C	5th Me.	I	119th Pa.
D	49th Pa.	J	2d Vt.
E	6th Me.	K	5th Vt.
F	5th Wis.	L	6th Vt.

MOTT

Landrum House

Wright

Shelton House

UPTON

DOLE

EWELL

Harrison House

MAP BY Meghan McMahon

wise support the second, while the fourth line of Vermonters would wait at the edge of the woods for orders to advance.[32] The entire assault was Rappahannock Station only on a grander scale. The only question on everyone's mind was, how long could the position be held until help arrived?

"My whole plan," Upton later recalled in a postwar letter, "was based on the supposition that I was to break the lines and make way for fresh troops, who would pass through the break."[33] These "fresh" troops would be from Maj. Gen. Gershom Mott's Division.

If Upton had a clear idea of what his mission was that day, Gershom Mott didn't. Throughout the day he received a series of confusing orders. First, he was to form a skirmish line to fill the gap between the corps of Burnside and Wright. Then he was told to support Burnside if the latter was attacked. Later, the orders were again revised and Mott's tiny division (he only had about one thousand men) was told to attack in front of Burnside if the Rhode Islander was attacked. These orders were also revised and Mott was instructed to support Wright. The lack of coordination between Mott and Upton doomed this daring assault on the Mule Shoe.

With nothing more to be said, or discussed, the meeting at the edge of the woods came to an end and each regimental commander returned to his respective regiment. Maj. Henry Galpin, representing the 121st New York, had been in command of his men for only four days since Lt. Col. Egbert Olcott's capture at the Wilderness. He called his company captains together. Like Upton, he briefly outlined the plan of attack. With rifles loaded and bayonets fixed, the regiment fell in line and joined the others on the march toward their position facing the Mule Shoe.

It was late afternoon and the cannonade scheduled to precede the attack began around 5:00 P.M. As the shells screamed overhead at the Mule Shoe, a lively exchange of picket fire began between the Confederates and the 65th New York. The cannonade was supposed to last a scant ten minutes. Through a mix-up in orders, it dragged on for a grueling hour. Throughout all of this, the men in Colonel Upton's command remained crouched down in their positions, motionless, in gut wrenching silence. All were terrified about the prospects of racing across the open ground toward the enemy position. "I felt my gorge rise," said Private Clinton Beckwith, "and my stomach and intestines shrink together in a knot, and a thousand things rushed through my mind. I fully realized the terrible peril I was to encounter."[34]

Finally, at 6:00 P.M., the big guns fell silent. Captain Kidder knew what this meant and turned toward Upton. "When the lines were all formed that afternoon," he wrote to Harriet, "Upton shook hands with

General Russell and his staff. . . . He then mounted his horse, rode out in front of the center of the front line and gave the command, 'Attention!' The men rose up, tightened the grip on their weapons, and waited for the next order. 'Forward, double quick march!'"[35] The 250 yard dash toward the Mule Shoe was on.

For the Confederates huddled inside the Mule Shoe, the abrupt ending of the cannonade was like a blessing, marking the end of the day's fighting. The shelling, together with the constant picket fire, prompted many of the defenders of the Mule Shoe to seek refuge in the rear. Those that remained were instructed by their commander, Georgian Brig. Gen. George Dole, to keep their weapons loaded and their bayonets fixed. It was well that they did. Soon the muffled sound of distant footsteps rapidly gave way to the whoops and hollers of Upton's advancing lines. Dole's men were caught completely off guard. Those that fired their weapons at the first blue coats they came in contact with soon found themselves unable to load their weapons; they had to fend for themselves at the point of bayonet. Others waited, and when the parapets were mounted, fired at the heads of their attackers. Colonel Upton noted that, after this, the remainder of the first line mounted the parapets with their weapons pointed downward.

Captain Kidder, armed with a revolver, killed four after crossing the parapet. Henry Henekir managed to kill two before blocking a bayonet thrust, the Rebel steel going completely through his hand. George Teel got off two shots, killing Confederate officers.[36]

Those of the first line that fired their weapons found they didn't have time to reload and therefore, used their bayonets to force the Rebels to surrender.[37] Meanwhile, the trickle of bluecoats that managed to pass over the parapet soon became an avalanche. The second line was over and not far behind was the third. "Numbers prevailed," said Upton of the scene. Soon after this, prisoners were rounded up and sent back across the open field.[38]

Well within the Mule Shoe, the first line leaned toward the right and raced toward the cannons they were assigned to capture. Colonel Upton, in front, urged the men of the 121st New York forward. "He jumped his horse over both pits and went down past the battery with us," recalled Kidder.[39]

The guns, part of Confederate Lt. Col. Robert Hardaway's Battalion, were still being fired and were abandoned at the last minute. Nearby, Confederate troops, seeing the danger this posed, rushed in to save them. Upton noticed this move and reacted swiftly. "He halted, turned around, saw that the Rebs were closing in on our left. He then commanded us to fall back on the first pits, which command was given and as such deliberately as though we were on the parade grounds drilling," said Kidder.[40] Amidst all this, the captured Confederate artillerymen were hustled to the rear.

Fighting raged inside the Mule Shoe. Colonel Upton's advance was soon checked by Confederate troops who managed to overcome the initial shock of the attack. Now fully recovered, they closed in on their attackers. Upton, fully aware of what was happening to his men, rode out to the field to bring up his fourth line of Vermonters. They had already joined in the fight and were assisted by the 65th New York.

Meanwhile, the 121st New York stubbornly held onto their prize, the cannon belonging to Hardaway's Battalion. As the Rebel gunfire intensified, it seemed they were being shot at from all directions. Bright flashes and the sound of screaming shells overhead meant that the Confederates were bringing up other field pieces to dislodge them. Upton reappeared on the scene and asked for volunteers to rush the new set of guns. When there was no response, he looked around and said, "Are there none of my old regiment here?"[41]

Scores of bodies littered the field and soldiers that were left standing were running dangerously low on ammunition. In the darkness, and with no prospects of receiving reinforcements, Colonel Upton was forced to withdraw. Men of the advanced regiments picked up what wounded men they could and slowly stumbled across the field toward the woods where it all started. The desperate struggle within the Mule Shoe must have seemed like an eternity. It was all over in thirty minutes.

Colonel Upton claimed to have taken about one thousand prisoners and suffered about the same amount in casualties. Some of his regiments were hit hard, notably the 49th Pennsylvania. Close to half of their 476 battle strength was listed as killed, wounded, or missing. In the 121st New York, forty-nine men were killed and 106 wounded.[42]

Maj. Henry Galpin, hit in the head near the eye during the attack, proved to have a minor wound. Momentarily stunned and blinded, he was soon patched up and ready to resume command.

Captain Kidder escaped unscathed but at least fourteen members of his Company I men were wounded. His chief concern was for the ugly side wound of Charles Pattengill. "I am told his was the worst," he said of the twenty-four-year-old Pattengill.[43] At one time, Pattengill gave Kidder fits as, "a most stubborn Corporal," but eventually he came around and developed into a good soldier. Promoted to the rank of Sergeant, Pattengill was waiting for his promotion to second lieutenant to become official. Two days later he was dead.[44]

Another soldier who gave Captain Kidder headaches earlier in the war was his deserting brother-in-law, Delos Lewis. He, too, did well that day, but the wound he suffered in the leg never healed properly, earning him a transfer to the Veteran Reserve Corps.[45]

Among the missing was James Gardner. Like Robinson Fox, who never appeared after the Battle of Salem Church, Kidder held out hope that he might learn the fate of James Gardner and Samuel Snediker. "I asked every man that night after the fight if they had seen anything of him and Samuel Snediker, but not one of them could tell me anything about them. I have my doubts. I do not believe that anyone knows that they are dead. It is possible they are and it is possible also that they were wounded and taken prisoners."[46] He never heard from either man again.

Kidder was almost through with his head count when John Fish appeared with a white flag and lantern. He had just returned from the Mule Shoe where he inquired as to the fate of fellow Captain Charles A. Butts of Company H. Fish was told that Butts was dead and that he had been given a proper burial. Butts enlisted as a private immediately following his graduation from Hamilton College and rose from the ranks having only recently been promoted to captain.[47]

That night while some men talked about the battle, others fell exhausted to the ground and some, like Clinton Beckwith, broke down and wept.[48]

Upton's attack was admired by friend and foe alike. Viewing the action from his vantage point near the Harrison House, General Robert E. Lee deemed it "the most obstinate, some of the enemy leaping over the breastworks."[49] Another witness, General Grant, praised the effort, while in the same breath condemned those of Maj. Gen. Gershom Mott. A combination of Confederate artillery and genuinely confusing orders prevented Mott from offering any real assistance to Colonel Upton that day. Mott's men, delayed by Confederate artillery, had to make five times the distance Upton's men had to make. Whatever the excuse, Grant neither forgave nor forgot the incident. Years later, in his *Memoirs*, he said, ". . . our success was decided, but the advantage lost by the feeble action of Mott." He added that Mott was ordered to assist, "but failed utterly."[50]

Upton was promised his general's stars if the attack succeeded. General Russell later presented him with the promotion with Grant's blessing. Upton's was a spectacular effort, one which Grant would try and duplicate on a much larger scale. He was reported to have said, "A brigade today; we'll try a Corps tomorrow."[51]

But it wasn't to be, at least not right away. The next day, May 11, turned rainy and miserably cold. While pickets kept up a lively exchange of fire, troops moved into position for an Upton-like assault scheduled for first light on the morning of May 12. This time, Hancock's entire II Corps was to strike at the very top of the Mule Shoe with Burnside's IX Corps in close support on the left. Wright's VI Corps was to offer immediate support to Hancock once the breakthrough was achieved and then Warren's V Corps was to join in.

There was still a light rain falling when the men of the 121st New York woke on the morning of May 12. Some found it difficult to boil water for coffee or even cook a little pork for breakfast. Through the fog and rain, the distant rattle of musketry told them that there was a fight underway. Some of the men stopped and stared at the staff officer who approached their camp on horseback. As the staff officer reached into his pocket to remove the set of orders, one soldier was heard to remark, "Damn those yellow paper orders. That means more fight."[52] It was announced that Hancock attacked at 4:30 A.M. and was successful. The VI Corps was to prepare to move in.

The next rider to appear was Upton, complete with the stars on his shoulders. Galpin knew what this meant. By 7:00 A.M., he had the 121st assembled and in line with the rest of the brigade.[53] The regiment now numbered less than two hundred rifles. Of the line officers, Galpin, Kidder, and Fish were all that remained of the original captains that had signed on two years earlier.

While Hancock's II Corps hammered at the Mule Shoe, the lead elements of the VI Corps advanced. The first to reach the western side of the Mule Shoe was the 95th Pennsylvania. They managed to get to a slightly elevated position only to receive a murderous volley from the entrenched Confederates. Upton saw this repulse and ordered them to lay down while the 5th Maine and the 121st rushed in to assist. Soon other brigades appeared on the field and the battle intensified. Visibility, which had been poor, grew worse as rain and fog mixed with the thick blue powder smoke that hung in the air. The Confederates, still huddled behind their makeshift breastwork of fallen trees, continued pouring volley after volley into General Upton's men. Frustrated at his lack of success, Upton ordered up two field pieces. The cannons brought in were Napoleon Cannons from Battery C of the 5th U.S. Artillery. Immediately filled with canister, these deadly buckshot like projectiles roared out at point-blank range into the Confederate position.

Cheering the efforts of the artillerymen, Capt. John D. Fish spurred his horse forward to assist the cannoneers. "Give it to them boys," he shouted. "I'll bring you the canister."[54] Turning his horse, he rode back and forth between the cassions and guns bringing up the needed ammunition. Struck in the head, the thirty-year-old Fish then fell, mortally wounded, from his horse.[55]

Eventually, the field pieces, the object of such intense rifle fire by the Confederates, had to be abandoned as bullets chipped away at the wooden wheels and ricocheted off the metal bands. Almost every artilleryman had either been killed or wounded. The fighting continued well into the morning hours as more and more infantry regiments were brought in. Major Galpin, still smarting from his eye wound, directed the rifle fire of the 121st New York. He felt numerous bullets whiz by and a few gently tug at his clothing. Suddenly he was struck in the shoulder and hurled to the ground. John S. Kidder was perhaps aware of Galpin's wounding and no doubt saw Fish fall from his horse. In all likelihood, this placed him, for a brief moment, in command of the regiment.

About noon, still directing the regiment from his side of the line, Captain Kidder was struck and instantly thrown to the ground.[56] Writhing in pain, he pressed his hat toward the incredible burning sensation that seemed to engulf the entire side of his face. A bullet had struck him just below the cheekbone and exited out his left ear, instantly deafening him. Miraculously, he never lost consciousness and managed, as he later recalled, "[to come] off the field alone." The wounded had to take care of themselves, the officers and men alike.[57] Those that were unable to fend for themselves, lay where they fell and bled to death, some even drowning in the thick mud.[58]

Captain Kidder made his way to the rear only to discover that there was no help available. Dr. Holt and Dr. Slocum were nowhere to be found. Still using his hat as a compress and determined to fine someone to properly dress his wound, Kidder began to wander aimlessly through the woods. He claimed, and could have been exaggerating, that he walked two miles before he reached an aid station. In all probability, he might have been turned away from several aid stations because they were overcrowded. Kidder, as a walking wounded, may not have been considered a serious case to the doctors who had to make life and death decisions that day.

The wounded were sorted into three categories, similar to the triage system of later wars. The least serious wounds were minor flesh wounds that required bandaging. The second group included those walking wounded that were able to sit upright in an ambulance. The last group the surgeons dealt with were those with the most serious wounds. This group of unfortunate soldiers suffered wounds either to the chest or abdominal regions, or had limbs that had been shattered by shot and shell waiting to be amputated.[59]

Once Kidder had been patched up, he had to wait his turn for the next available ambulance that would take him to the hospitals in Fredericksburg, a distant twelve miles away.

Shortly after General Grant assumed command, an Ambulance Corps was created for the Army of the Potomac.[60] Pressed into immediate service with the Wilderness Campaign, the Ambulance Corps had hardly enough time to recover from this battle when their services were in demand once more with the battle around Spotsylvania. Almost half of the available wagons were still being used to transport the Wilderness wounded to the hospitals when this new campaign began, leaving only three hundred wagons to do the job.[61]

No stranger to the wagon business, John S. Kidder probably approached his impending wagon ride with a certain degree of trepidation. He could see that these spring wagons offered little in the form of comfort to anyone who was seriously wounded. The makeshift bedding consisted of shelter tents and blankets covering straw and pine boughs. Those able to sit, like himself, had to balance themselves on empty hardtack boxes. His fears were well-justified. After Lt. Adam Clarke Rice was loaded into an ambulance the past September, Kidder never saw him again. "He was a noble officer," said Kidder of the twenty-three-year-old ex-Fairfield student. "We feel his loss very much."[62] Dr. Holt later admitted that the ambulance ride did little to improve Rice's rapidly failing condition.[63]

Captain Kidder's sojourn to Fredericksburg was a nightmare. About halfway to the city, the ambulance in which he was riding was forced to stop and make a detour. The rain soaked roads dissolved into a quagmire. "We got to within five miles of this place (Fredericksburg) but could not get further. The roads are far worse than they were on the mud march of Burnside's in January of '63."[64] The change in direction didn't make the trip any less painful. With each bounce of the wagon wheels his head throbbed and he became more and more nauseous. Finally, he could stand the pain no longer. "I got out of the ambulance and lay down by the side of the road and if I ever suffered, it was last night. I was so exhausted not withstanding the pain I was in. I slept about 1/2 hours. When I awoke, my left cheekbone was so swollen that I could not see out of my left eye."[65] Still wearing the same muddied and blood-soaked uniform he had on when the campaign began, the senior captain set out for Fredericksburg on foot. It was a less painful alternative to an ambulance ride, one he said, "all but killed me to ride on such rough roads."[66]

Kidder had been through Fredericksburg once before. A year earlier, the 121st New York passed through the city just before the Chancellorsville Campaign. In a year's time, the city's appearance changed very little. There were plenty of bombed out buildings but very few empty ones. Four days before Kidder was wounded, General Meade directed that all of the Wilderness wounded be brought to the city as systematically as possible.[67] The newly formed Ambulance Corps went to work and the city was soon divided up in a gridwork fashion, with each army corps being assigned a location in the city. Every available house, barn, church, or large building was commandeered for hospital use.[68] Eventually, over seven thousand wounded men would be brought to Fredericksburg. "The town was literally one immense hospital," recalled a VI Corps surgeon.[69]

The population of Fredericksburg swelled as a steady procession of ambulances brought wounded to a city that had seen enough of war. Added to this sudden increase in population was the unprecedented number of malingerers and stragglers that also made their way into the city. One estimate placed their number as high as five thousand. Some had minor flesh wounds that could have been easily dressed and cared for in the field, while others had wounds that were labeled as "suspicious," or self-inflicted wounds. Some showed up feigning an injury altogether, but they tried to look the part by wearing bloodstained bandages. For every man that was seriously wounded, it was said that at least two to four men left the ranks. These men just plain got in the way and wasted the valuable time of surgeons who were already overworked and desperately needed elsewhere.[70]

It was only after being treated at one of these hospitals that John S. Kidder was able to fully comprehend the effects of the Wilderness and Spotsylvania battles. The room he was in was filled with familiar faces.

Capts. Cronkite, Gorton, and myself are wounded but not dangerously. Capt. Paine is missing, Lieut. Kelly is a prisoner, Lieut. Jackson, Tucker, Adams, and Second Lieut. Johnson are wounded but all slightly. Lieut. Pierce is killed, was wounded in the right breast and brought to the hospital but died the next day.[71]

Thus far this campaign bled the 121st New York like no other campaign in the war. On May 13, 1864, Assistant Surgeon Daniel M. Holt sadly recorded in his diary that there were only 118 men left in the regiment. This number included only four line officers, none over the rank of captain.[72] Of the fifty-six men in Company A, who crossed the Rapidan in the beginning of May, there were only seven left.[73]

Captain Kidder had been unable to write to his wife since the overland campaign began. Ironically, his last letter home was full of concern for his wife's health. "If you think that you have not got entirely well . . . you must tell the Doctor and have him fix you something. I am afraid of the symptoms but you must not fail to have him examine that sore . . ."[74] At this time, Harriet was a delicate two months pregnant. He was quite worried about her as well as Clara. "Sorry to hear that my little Diamond was sick," he wrote.[75]

In a hospital in Fredericksburg, Kidder managed to procure some paper and set to work writing the most difficult letter he had to write during the entire Civil War. "Dear Wife," he began, and, in his own abrupt style, spilled it all out.

> It is with a sorrowful heart I pen a few lines. My brother George is no more. He was mortally wounded in the breast and died the next day. I have not seen any of his comrades to learn the particulars. I hear that he continued to fight after he rec'd his wound.

Then, almost as an afterthought, he broke the news to her about his own wound. "I have passed through 3 severe battles where our Regiment have been engaged in a hand to hand conflict with the enemy. At the last battle I rec'd a severe wound in the face. The ball entering just below the cheekbone and coming out through the ear. It is very painful . . ."[76] If all went well, he hoped to be sent home in a few weeks to recover.

He was partially correct. His stay in Fredericksburg was brief, just four days. As more and more wounded were brought to the city it became necessary to move the walking wounded elsewhere. Kidder and some of the other officers from the 121st New York were sent to the U.S. General Hospital No. 1 at Annapolis, Maryland. Any other enlisted men who were able to move were transferred to the hospitals in and around Washington, D.C. As Grant pushed further south, Fredericksburg's usefulness as a hospital depot diminished. By May 28, 1864, the entire wounded population had been evacuated.[77]

SIX

U.S. General Hospital, Annapolis, Maryland

May 1864–June 1864

The wounded were arriving in Annapolis at scattered intervals for days. On May 14, 1864, another collection of battered bodies arrived. Included in this number were three members of the 121st New York. They were registered as "H. M. Galpin, J. W. Coonkite, and J. S. Ridder."[1] The misspellings were an understandable mistake given the number of new patients, over two hundred fifty, that arrived that day. Captain Kidder and his entourage were escorted to the grounds of the U.S. Naval Academy. When the Civil War began, the faculty and midshipmen of the sixteen-year-old institution were transferred to Newport, Rhode Island for the duration of the conflict. The school was then converted into a hospital.[2] "The buildings are splendid ones and the grounds are beautifully ornamented with shrubs, etc.," observed Kidder. Impressed with the school and its grounds, he was nevertheless horrified at the city itself, calling it, "One of the most filthy holes I ever saw. They empty all of their swill and filth into the streets and let it remain there."[3]

Ushered into one of the buildings the men lined up, and one by one were stripped of their clothes. Most of the clothing was set aside to be disposed of, too filthy and bloodstained to be properly cleaned or too tattered to be repaired. Kidder did manage to cling to his hat, a souvenir of his scrape with death at the Bloody Angle.

The men were then brought before a barber who proceeded to trim their hair, beards included, with the efficiency of a farmer shearing sheep. For the thin-haired Kidder, there wasn't much to trim except for the stubble of his beard.

The next stop on this human assembly line brought the men into a room where they were greeted by attendants standing before huge tubs of hot soapy water armed with sponges. For many, it was their first bath in over a month and it was exhilarating. Said one soldier of this singular experience, "Now I feel as if I were a man again."[4]

It was only after completing this hygiene regimen that each man was brought to his room and met, for the first time, a member of the medical staff. Each patient gave his name, rank, and regiment and then described the nature of his wound to the attending physician. This typically led to a quick examination. Any recommendations the doctor had to offer while inspecting the wound or dressing was dutifully recorded by a notebook toting assistant. Two sets of records existed for each patient. One was kept in the notebook and the other hung from the foot of the bed. In this way, any doctor making rounds could quickly review the patient's progress.

Kidder was surprised, on one occasion, when a doctor recognized his "121 New York" identification and introduced himself as Dr. Lucius Comstock of the 155th New York. Comstock was a native of the village of Butternut in Otsego County. "I had a real visit," said Kidder. They spent some time together and reminisced about "all the old people of the County."[5]

Another card hanging from the end of the bed indicated the diet that was prescribed for each patient. Kidder brought a ravenous appetite with him to Annapolis. "We have beef, mutton, fresh fish, potatoes, strawberries, good bread, butter and cheese."[6] Although there was no cake for dessert, he happily reported that on the third day there was a choice between ice cream, pie, or pudding. With food like this being offered, it was easy for him to dismiss what he thought was very poor quality tea and coffee. He referred to them as, "miserable stuff, the poorest I ever saw." Of course, he passed up the coffee when he discovered that he could order a pint of port ale each day with his meal![7]

The only inconvenience suffered by Kidder was trying to eat all of this delicious food, since the least amount of jaw movement irritated his cheek wound. Except for this singular discomfort, this was probably the most comfortable time John S. Kidder spent in the army.

While Captain Kidder adjusted to the routine of hospital life at Annapolis, his surgeons were kept busy tending to his wounds. He had two wounds, one to the cheek and one to the ear, and he was quite honest as to his appearance. "I have a bad looking face," he said.[8]

When he arrived at Annapolis, both wounds were in danger of becoming infected. "It has mattered much and smelled very badly," said Kidder of the condition of the wounds and soiled bandages.⁹ Surgeons quickly went to work removing the sutures from his ear. This was a horribly painful procedure; it wasn't until later that he felt any gratitude for the efforts made by his doctors. Instead of stitches, they used plasters to reattach the bottom section of his ear. By the end of the month, however, he was pleased with the results. "It looks more than one hundred percent better than it did when I first came here. I expected at one time that I should have to lose the lower part of my ear but we patched it up with sticking plasters so that it has grown together again. I think it will look as well as it ever did."¹⁰

The damage to his inner ear took the longest to heal. The ear had to be continually flushed out as fluids saturated the bandages. This, too, was a painful procedure that he had to repeat several times a day.

> *When I dress my wound, I take a match and put a piece of lint on the end of it and insert it into my ear as far as I can get it and clean out the puss perfectly clean. Then I take a dry piece of lint and poke it into my ear as far as I can get it, fill the ear full, and, if I let it be there about one hour, it will be completely saturated with puss which comes from the inside of the head.*¹¹

Kidder performed this routine for five weeks until his ear stopped draining.

It was during this time that he tried to come to terms with his deafness. It was a different sensation; he didn't quite know what to make of it. "I went to the chapel yesterday. Heard a good sermon. They had good singing. It sounded very strange owing to my deafness of my left ear."¹² He tried to be optimistic about his hearing, believing that once his ear stopped draining, his hearing would be restored. The end result was that the damage proved to be irreversible. He rarely spoke of his deafness and in later years carefully sat for photographs, tilting his head to hide the injured ear.

At first, John S. Kidder wasn't lonely at Annapolis, for he had plenty of company in the form of fellow officers from the 121st New York—Maj. Henry Galpin, Capt. James W. Cronkite and Lt. Daniel Jackson. They were all recovering from wounds sustained in the spring campaign at Spotsylvania. Galpin was nursing the shoulder wound he received about the same time Kidder was wounded. He still sported the eye patch from the wound he received in the May 10 charge. Despite these injuries, he was the first of the group to leave the hospital. Galpin rejoined the regiment before the end of May with Cronkite not far behind. Lieutenant

Jackson did not fare as well. "His wound is a slight one," observed Kidder. "I think that as his health is poor is one reason that his wound does not heal quicker."[13]

Already in a weakened state, Kidder feared that Jackson, who had no appetite whatsoever, might run the risk of a fever. By the first week of June, however, Jackson rallied, appeared cheerful, and seemed optimistic about his own recovery. He was anxious to return to the regiment so he would not miss out on the capture of Lee's army and the triumphant march into Richmond. Such talk delighted Kidder. "Jackson is made of the right stuff, good pluck and ever ready to do his duty. He is a brave and noble officer. I hope the report is true that he has been promoted to Captain as he is worthy of it."[14] It was true. Jackson received word in the hospital that his promotion was, indeed, official. It was back dated to May 23, 1864.[15]

With his own wound healing slowly and little prospect in sight for his eventual return to the regiment, Captain Kidder literally had nothing but time on his hands. As his friends were discharged from Annapolis one by one, Kidder soon felt the onset of a very different type of ailment, boredom. To sit still was not in the Kidder nature. Fortunately, the staff at Annapolis was all too familiar with this type of individual. There were plenty of activities scheduled to keep the patients busy. The hospital boasted a good library which was open from 8:00 A.M. to 12 P.M., and from 2:00 P.M. to 8:00 P.M. Religious services were held twice every Sabbath, once at 2:00 P.M., and again at 7:00 P.M., with an additional service held each Wednesday. Bible classes were on Thursday.

Perhaps the most unique feature of hospital life at Annapolis was the hospital newspaper, not surprisingly entitled, *The Crutch*. With bold stars, striped block letters, and adorned with a patriotic eagle masthead, *The Crutch* contained all the latest hospital gossip, war news, names of those who were admitted and discharged, as well as poetry, and short stories written by the patients. When patients were through reading the paper, they could go outside and listen to music. The hospital had its own fourteen-piece brass band that played daily concerts for, as *The Crutch* said, "crowds of cripples, emaciated Belle Islanders and fair Annapolitians."[16]

The hospital endeavored to have its activities keep up with changing times. While the Republican National Convention in Baltimore attempted to nominate Abraham Lincoln for a second term, the hospital held their own mock elections. Those that were able to walk or move about in wheelchairs made their way from ward to ward campaigning and collecting ballots. Lincoln won by a landslide with 143 votes.[17] If John S.

Kidder voted (there is no record of the participants in this election), he most likely would have voted for Lincoln, as records show he later did in the November election.

Lectures presented another opportunity to while away the hours at Annapolis. One lecture Kidder attended was presented by Capt. A. R. Calhoun of the 1st Kentucky Cavalry entitled, "Prison Life in the Land of Chivalry." Calhoun had been a prisoner of war at Libby Prison in Richmond for seven months. Naturally, Kidder was interested in this lecture since his good friend, Delavan Bates, spent time there when he was captured after the Battle of Salem Church. He also was aware of the fact that the fate of Lt. Col. Olcott, wounded and taken captive after the Battle of the Wilderness, was still unknown. For all Kidder knew, Olcott was at Libby.

The highlight of Calhoun's lecture was his description of the daring tunnel escape that occurred on the night of February 9, 1864. Calhoun, in the company of 108 other Union officers, tunneled over fifty feet to make their break for freedom in the most successful prison escape of the Civil War.[18]

With all that Annapolis had to offer, Kidder's favorite pastime was good conversation. As an ambulatory patient, he freely roamed about the wards visiting wounded officers who hailed from almost every northern state. "We have Officers here from Ohio, Pennsylvania, New York, New Jersey and all the New England states," he reported to Harriet, being careful not to attempt to *spell* the names of any of the New England states. For the first time he met officers who came from the Border States. He admired these men for the difficult choice they had to make during this national crisis. Missouri, Kentucky, Maryland, and Delaware were all slaveholding states that sent officers and men to both the Union and Confederate armies. "The Kentucky and Delaware officers are splendid men of the right pluck. It would make Copperhead sneaks look ashamed to hear them talk."[19]

It was these sneaks, bummers, or cowards that were housed in the hospital that infuriated Captain Kidder. He estimated that the hospital housed approximately two hundred officers during that summer; the line was quickly drawn between those who had been wounded in battle and those who were feigning an injury. At a glance, observing the nature of the wound, it was fairly easy to tell what side of the line you were on. "We give the bummers the cold shoulder," Kidder said, "but unfortunately there are so many of them that they have plenty of company."[20] When the silent treatment and ostracizing didn't work, the verbal exchange turned into a barrage of insults. "We have several good officers here that are wounded. We make it quite uncomfortable for the sneaks. . . . When we can give them a rebuke, some of them look ashamed. Others have no shame."[21]

It was difficult for Kidder to tolerate these men when, at the same time, in the same ward, were men who had just been released from Libby Prison. Their emaciated appearance horrified Kidder. "There are several officers and men here that have been starving in Libby Prison for 9 months. Some of the poor fellows are nothing but skin and bones."[22]

The death rate of these recently released Libby prisoners shocked him. He noted that in one boat load of 163, more than seventy died while at Annapolis. He couldn't help but think that they reminded him of his sister, Salina, when she wasted away and died of tuberculosis.[23] It was even harder to accept sneaks when there were so many men around him that truly suffered. He was quick to point out that his own state of New York, along with Pennsylvania and Ohio, claimed the lion's share of sneaks. He went as far as to say that the Keystone State had more than all the others combined.[24]

Of all the sneaks and bummers he met at Annapolis, only one earned his particular disdain, Julius Townsend of the 152nd New York. Kidder felt it especially difficult to warm up to this individual who seemed to go out of his way to avoid his duty as a soldier. The fact that Kidder's own brother died in the service of the same regiment as Townsend didn't make the matter any easier. Townsend was, in Kidder's estimation, nothing more than a "Poor Cowardly Scamp."[25]

The Townsend boys, there were two of them, enlisted in the 152nd New York in the fall of 1862 rather than return to classes at Fairfield Seminary. Both were members of Company F, Edward as a Sergeant, and Julius as a Corporal. Edward, like many others, obtained a transfer in order to accept an officer's commission in the 23rd United States Colored Troops. Julius remained behind and slowly climbed the ladder of advancement. He made sergeant in April 1863 and second lieutenant three months later.[26]

The first real action any of the 152nd saw in the entire war was at The Wilderness. Townsend was probably at this battle but was listed as "missing in action" while the two armies grappled at Spotsylvania. On the sick and disabled list at Annapolis, his condition did not appear all that serious to Kidder. "I see that he is on hand every time to his meals and eats heartily as anyone," Kidder observed of the twenty-four-year-old Townsend.[27] He couldn't understand why Townsend was at Annapolis as there was no evidence of a wound. Townsend claimed that he was hit in the chest by a tree limb and was, "hurt inwardly." With this story, he managed to sneak past a few examining physicians. However, he was soon called before an examination board at Annapolis. Brazenly confident, he told Kidder that no matter what the outcome, he intended to seek a surgeon's certificate of disability. Needless to say, this attitude infuriated Kidder.[28]

A short while later, the examination board declared Townsend fit and he was ordered back to his regiment. Captain Kidder never forgot him and, in an effort to learn more details regarding his own brother's death, frequently asked other officers of the 152nd New York about Townsend. When Capt. Delavan Hewitt was admitted, "quite sick with diarrhea," according to Kidder, the conversation quickly turned to Townsend.[29] It seemed that his suspicions regarding Townsend were well-justified. Captain Hewitt claimed that Townsend never returned to the 152nd and that he was seen in civilian clothes at the Metropolitan Hotel in Washington, the first stop on his way home! "He ought to have been sent to the Old Capitol Prison," roared Kidder.[30]

Both men would have shaken their heads in disbelief if they knew the rest of the details. Townsend was arrested for being absent without leave and dismissed from the service on August 22, 1864.[31] He returned to New York and, after a short while, enlisted as a private in the 193rd New York and quickly rose to his old rank of second lieutenant.[32] Since this regiment was organized late in the war, January 21, 1865, it was never actively engaged in any battles. True to form, Townsend ended his military career by successfully avoiding any dangerous situation. His Civil War career was a sham. "Poor boy," Captain Hewitt later said. "I pity him."[33]

Aside from lectures, church services, visiting, or just gossiping with others, Captain Kidder remained preoccupied with his wound, changing the dressings as often as needed. At the same time, he anxiously awaited the latest news from back home in Laurens as well as news of the 121st New York Volunteers. To Harriet he wrote eight letters, some of which were uncharacteristically long, and three long letters were sent to his good friend Milton Gurney.

When Capt. James W. Cronkite returned to the 121st New York on June 5, 1864, the battles still raged around Cold Harbor. He wrote a letter to Kidder appraising him of the situation in Virginia. This was yet another attempt by Grant to turn Lee's flank. It proved costly for both sides. Cronkite reported to Kidder that the brigade had finally been reinforced by a regiment of heavy artillerymen turned infantrymen, the 2nd Connecticut. News of this sort probably upset Kidder, considering his low estimation of these ex-cannoneers, but Cronkite was quick to point out that these men were an asset to the brigade. "They made a noble charge," he said of their advance on the first day of the campaign, "and held their position after driving the enemy from a position of their pits which was more than any other brigade in the Corps accomplished. . . . They lost their Colonel, killed at the head of his column on foot."[34] They had indeed proven themselves. In his official report of the advance on June 1, General Upton reported that the 2nd Connecticut lost 53 killed, 187 wounded, and 146 missing.[35]

Cronkite told Kidder that Upton was out in front leading the men as usual and managed to survive having three horses shot from beneath him.

Losses were slight at Cold Harbor for the 121st New York, but unfortunately, not for Company I. Richard "Dick" Bennet was dead. The twenty-four-year-old farmer from Laurens was an unfortunate victim of friendly fire. Cronkite reported that Bennet had "his leg taken off *by our own* shell and died the next day." Sedate Foote was wounded in a similar manner and Joseph Edson was also wounded. Both men never fully recovered from their wounds and were later transferred to inactive duty with the Veteran Reserve Corps.[36] Cronkite also reported that in addition to himself, Hiram Van Scoy, Sheldon Redway, and Erastus Weaver were the only line officers present. The regiment could only muster 160 men.

In closing his letter, Cronkite described Cold Harbor as,

> *a dusty place to drive them [the Confederates] from and they make a desperate stand. Both armies recognized a flag of truce yesterday afternoon for a few hours to bury the dead. . . . Firing resumed as soon as the hour was up. Many have an idea we will swing around on the James River and not assault their position here. Charging is about played out for they eat up the men too fast. I hear this is Col. Upton's mind at present. But I must conclude. I hardly know where to direct [this letter] for I presume you are on your way home before this, or at least hope so. Write me very soon. I am truly your friend and able servant. My regards to all friends, J. W. C.[37]*

Home! The word struck a tender chord. With Harriet four months pregnant, home was all he hoped and dreamed for. Ever since his arrival at Annapolis, John S. Kidder was under the impression that he would eventually be sent home to recuperate. He was very optimistic, predicting that he would only be in the hospital two weeks or less. But as the weeks dragged on, he made a formal application to the office of the adjutant general in mid-May for a thirty day leave of absence. Hearing nothing from this department by the end of May, he decided to take another route; he

Twenty-four-year-old John Swain Kidder and seventeen-year-old Harriet Matteson Kidder sit for this early daguerreotype in what is believed to be their wedding picture in 1853.

(Jerry Reed Collection)

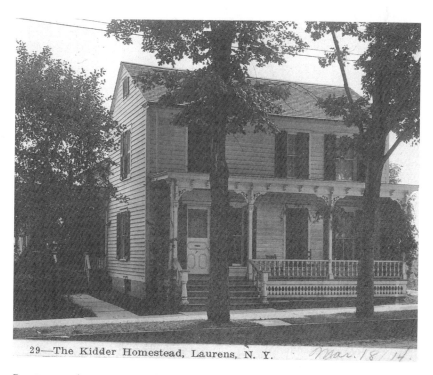

29—The Kidder Homestead, Laurens, N. Y.

By nineteenth century standards, the Kidder homestead on Main Street in Laurens, New York, was a comfortable dwelling. The large downstairs parlor was modestly furnished, complete with an ornate wood stove. This was home to John, Harriet, the children, Harriet's father, and an occasional boarder. In this post–Civil War view, the carriage shop can be seen in the rear of the house.

(Author's Collection)

Looking every bit the professional soldier, a very serious John S. Kidder sits for his first photograph as captain of Company I.

(Jerry Reed Collection)

Business partner and blacksmith Elisha Fisher remained in Laurens when Kidder joined the army in the summer of 1862. As wagon orders decreased and money became scarce, Fisher found it necessary to enlist and did so in late 1864.

(Jerry Reed Collection)

Ann Starr Kidder gave birth to her second child, Mary, on October 17, 1862. Four days later, her husband George left for Washington, D. C. with the 152nd New York Volunteers. His death at the Wilderness in 1864 was a devastating blow to Ann and the entire Kidder family.

(Jerry Reed Collection)

Far removed from the battlefields of Virginia was William Kidder. Seeking his fortune in the gold fields of California, William enlisted fairly late in the war and saw service with the 7th California Volunteers.

(Jerry Reed Collection)

Organizing the 121st New York Volunteers
and spending exactly one month in the field,
Colonel Richard Franchot resigned to return
to his true calling: politics. His resignation
was cheered by all, including John S. Kidder.
In this heavily retouched post-war photo,
Franchot is wearing the rank of a brigadier
general. He was promoted to this rank for
helping raise the 121st New York Volunteers.

(Author's Collection)

MAJOR GENERAL EMORY UPTON,

Batavia, New York native and West
Point graduate Emory Upton assumed command of the 121st New
York in October 1862. Stressing tactics and discipline, Upton weeded
out political opportunists and transformed the regiment into a real
fighting unit.

(USAMHI)

Denied a brevet or temporary promotion, perhaps due to a reputation as a hard drinker, Lieut. Col. Egbert Olcott was nonetheless fearless in battle. He was wounded and captured at the Battle of the Wilderness, but was released and joined the regiment for the closing months of the war.

(USAMHI)

The promotion of Andrew E. Mather to major caused an uproar in the officer ranks of the 121st New York. Captain Kidder was irritated by the promotion of Mather over the other captains, who had more seniority. Mather remained with the regiment until February 1864 when he resigned to accept the position of lieutenant colonel of the 20th U.S. Colored Troops.

(USAMHI)

Discipline as well as the appearance of the regiment improved with Upton in command. White gloves were required on the parade ground, and beards were shaved. This was Harriet's favorite picture.

(USAMHI)

When Laurens neighbor and friend Charles Dean took over all of the Company I paperwork, Kidder was pleased. As the war progressed, Dean was continually absent from the regiment for a variety of reasons. At one point Kidder wasn't sure if he should list Dean as a deserter, as being sick in the hospital, or as on detached service.

(USAMHI)

The fastest rise in rank of anyone in the 121st New York was James W. Cronkite. Mustered in as a sergeant, Cronkite finished the war a brevet lieutenant colonel. The friendship he and Kidder forged lasted well into the post-war years.

(USAMHI)

Assisting Kidder in filling the ranks of Company I was Worcester native and former store clerk Delevan Bates. Captured at the battle of Salem Church and briefly interred at Libby Prison, Kidder was overjoyed when Bates was released just prior to the Battle of Gettysburg. Bates remained with the regiment until March 1864 when he resigned to accept the rank of colonel in the 30th U.S. Colored Troops.

(USAMHI)

Kidder respected and admired Henry Galpin, of Little Falls, New York. Galpin was one of the few officers who had seen action in other regiments before joining the 121st New York Volunteers at Camp Schuyler. In the Shenandoah Valley Campaign of 1864, Galpin was seriously wounded and mustered out of the service.

(USAMHI)

Like Kidder, John D. Fish left a very young family behind when he helped raise Company D of the 121st New York. The former attorney from Frankfort, New York, was in the thick of the fighting at Rappahannock Station and was later killed in action at Spotsylvania.

(USAMHI)

U. S. GENERAL HOSPITAL, IDIV. N⚙I.

Dr B A VANDERKIEFT Surgeon in Charge

1 Tent of Medical Officer

2 Tent of Hospital Steward

(Jerry Reed Collection)

Kidder spent a miserable two months at Annapolis, Maryland, after having been seriously wounded at Spotsylvania.

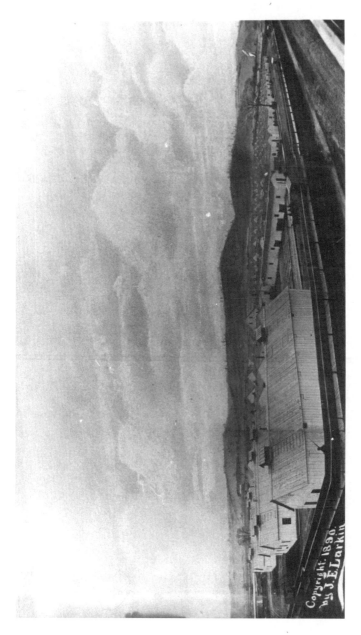

Kidder was ordered to Elmira Prison for 'light duty,' guarding Confederate prisoners of war after his release from Annapolis General Hospital. He managed to alleviate the boredom of this assignment by promoting and selling bone carved rings made by the Confederate prisoners.

(USAMHI)

LIEUTENANT COLONEL JOHN S. KIDDER

The strains of the last months of the Civil War are clearly evident as the recently promoted lieutenant colonel sits for one last portrait.

(History of the 121st New York, Chicago, 1921)

The Kidder family circa 1885. From left to right are John, Mary, George, Clara, and Harriet.

(Jerry Reed Collection)

On the 20th Anniversary of Upton's assault on the Mule Shoe at Spotsylvania, the 121st New York Veterans Association gathers at the edge of the woods for this reunion photograph. John and Harriet are in the back row.

(Jerry Reed Collection)

Kidder, in top hat and cane, gazes across the field where he was wounded twenty years earlier.

(Jerry Reed Collection)

The Port Warden of New York City always had time for his family. This 1898 picture was taken at the Kidder residence at 69 South Elliot Place, Brooklyn.

(Jerry Reed Collection)

On October 10, 1889, family, friends, and veterans met at Gettysburg for the dedication of the 121st New York monument. Kidder can be seen in the back row to the left of the monument, looking over the shoulder of James Cronkite.

(Jerry Reed Collection)

Kidder sits for this, perhaps his last photograph, at a veteran reunion in 1905. As with most photographs, Kidder sits in the back row.

The old soldier proudly displays his Grand Army of the Republic medals in this last formal photograph.

(Jerry Reed Collection)

Years after the passing of John and Harriet, family members erected this headstone to their memory at the Laurens cemetery. Harriet, who devoted much of her time to the upkeep and beautification of the cemetery, would probably have been amused to see that her name was misspelled.

(Joseph Scalise Photograph)

sent a letter to the Army Chief of Staff, General Henry Halleck. As an added precaution he fired off a letter to his Congressman, David Wilbur, after all, everyone who wanted a leave was writing to their congressman.[38]

By June he had heard nothing and was frustrated, annoyed, and now obsessed with getting out of the hospital. "I think when we have faced the music and received wounds and are not going to be fit for duty in several weeks, we ought to have the privilege to go home."[39] As this same privilege had been extended to enlisted men, Kidder saw no reason why it should not be made available to officers. "Why keep officers . . . shut up in a hospital away from their friends?" he asked.[40]

Kidder was fairly certain that this heel dragging on the subject of leaves of absence was the work of one man. "The Surgeon in charge here is a Dutchman and he appears to be determined to keep us here . . ."[41]

The "Dutchman" was Dr. Bernard Vanderkeift, a former surgeon with the 53rd and 102nd New York Volunteers, who at one time proposed an organized ambulance system for the Medical Corps, an idea that had so much merit it was later brought to the attention of the Medical Department.[42] Vanderkeift was a strict disciplinarian and a first-rate administrator. When not seeing to the paperwork of the hospital, he could be found making his rounds or performing surgery.

Vanderkeift knew what was right for his patients; he evidently didn't like patients going over his head to obtain leaves via congressional "influence" or any other type of army connection. Kidder claimed that when Vanderkeift discovered one of the patients obtained a leave in this way, he became "mad and abuses them when they come."[43] Kidder steeled himself as, he, too, had written to his congressman just as the others. "If I should get one [a leave] and if he should offer me the abuse that he has some officers, I would prefer charges against him, for I will not be abused by any doctor."[44]

Kidder was in the process of discovering what others before him knew about dealing with the medical profession during wartime. Doctors so desperately needed in time of war, were a breed apart, almost impossible to discipline. Hospitals were their fields of operations, and they ran them like generals. Vanderkeift, Kidder was to discover, usually had the final say in most matters.

When, by the first week of June, his original request for a leave of absence was returned with a flat denial, Kidder exploded in anger.

Vanderkeift lied like a scoundrel. He said that he was willing that all wounded officers should go home and that when he forwarded their applications for leave he did not approve or disapprove but made a statement how long it would probably be before they would be fit for duty and he said that he left it with the [War] Department to do as they thought best about it.[45]

Kidder came to this conclusion when he and several of the other officers who had applied for leave all had their applications rejected with the same "Disapproved" endorsement. The applications never got to Washington, having been rejected by Vanderkeift before they reached the Baltimore post offices.

Furious at the reversal, Kidder still had one application going through regular army channels. He hoped that a direct appeal to General Halleck would prove to be his trump card in this stubborn clash of wills. If this didn't work, he would plan a mutiny!

If that [application to General Halleck] should come back in the same way with the same endorsement as he put on the others, we are going to give old Vanderkeift fits. I shall charge him in the presence of all the officers of what he stated to me and I can prove it as the other officers heard him say the same thing. I will show what a mean lying scoundrel he is. The officers will help me.[46]

Blinded by his desire to return home, John S. Kidder didn't understand that Vanderkeift was only doing his job. From a medical standpoint, Kidder was not ready to be discharged. By the end of June, his cheek was partially healed but fluid still oozed from his ear. Even the ward surgeon warned him that in all likelihood it would be another four weeks before he would be ready to leave the hospital. Bored, depressed, and now sweltering in the heat and humidity of Annapolis, Kidder swallowed his pride and made a direct appeal to Vanderkeift.

By this time, Harriet was making plans to take the train to Baltimore and visit him at Annapolis. He certainly didn't want her to make this journey given her condition. Kidder argued that a cooler climate would do him good, and as for the ear, he was used to changing the dressing and cleaning the wound himself. In Laurens, Dr. Addison Strong was always available to assist him.[47]

Finally, on July 21, 1864, Kidder received word from the War Department that his coveted leave of absence was approved for a period of twenty days. He had been in the hospital for almost two months and was one of the last in his ward to receive a leave. He felt that it was long overdue.

The fact is, there has been more than 40 officers granted leaves of absence from this hospital since I have been here and about 2/3 of them have been those who have nothing apparently the matter with them but have obtained leaves through political influences and I think it is hard to see such sneaks get leaves while those who have faced danger in battle and been severely wounded in discharge of their duties have to be cooped up in a hospital . . .[48]

As anxious as he was to leave the hospital, he didn't depart right away. He wanted to make sure that all his paperwork was in order. Failure to complete or follow up on forms might lead to complications later on. Simple errors could ruin an officer. Captain Kidder saw this on more than one occasion.

It is a shame and disgrace to our Government to give a dishonorable discharge to some poor officers (as they have done to seven or eight in this hospital) who were badly wounded as to be unfit for service. They stated in their discharge that they had been absent from their Regiments without leave when the fact is the officers were sent by their Surgeons to Washington and then here, but their Surgeons at the Division Hospital have forgotten to record their names in their report (so much for red tape).[49]

Five days later, with bags packed and his goodbyes said, Captain Kidder was presented with another communiqué from the War Department. He was to report immediately to the commanding officer at Elmira, New York, for the purpose of performing "light duty guarding Confederate Prisoners of War.[50]

SEVEN

Elmira Prison

JULY 1864–DECEMBER 1864

T he residents of Laurens anxiously awaited news from the battlefields of Virginia as time drew near for the start of General Grant's spring campaign. Despite the invention of the telegraph, the village remained virtually isolated from the outside world and relied upon the stagecoach for mail delivery. The unmistakable sound of horses hoofs signaled all to stop work and make their way to the post office. People wandered over singly and in small groups. It was not unusual to have between seventy-five and one hundred people present when the stagecoach lurched to a halt. The mailbags were already in the possession of Postmaster Milton Gurney by the time the passengers, if any, disembarked. With the mail were days old copies of the *Utica Daily Herald*.

Whatever war news the papers contained was usually read aloud, with special emphasis on the casualty lists of the 121st and 152nd New York.[1] These were heart stopping moments for many present. When the last of the names had been read, the crowd quietly dispersed. Some wandered over to Gurney's Store, while the steady clanging of hammer on steel resumed at Damon Mead's Blacksmith Shop. It was as if nothing happened. Some, like Harriet Kidder, went home.

The big house was the center of Harriet Kidder's life. She ran it with the steady efficiency of a small hotel owner. It was a house that was rarely quiet. Her father, seventy-five-year-old Joshua, still lived with the Kidders, and at the other end of the age spectrum was Clara, a very active three year old. Harriet still rented out a room to carriage shop employee, James Cockett, and also assisted her sister-in-law by boarding her son, Charlie Adams. As time grew near for the birth of her second child, Harriet hired a domestic, Mary Secor, to live in the house and help her with daily chores.[2]

By mid-1864, Harriet had become quite adept at juggling accounts. Carefully she screened and determined what bills were to be paid and which ones could wait a while longer. Mindful of her husband's wishes not to interfere with the accounts of the carriage shop, she frequently bartered for services. Wagon repair bills were often times traded for overdue store accounts.

The fact remained that the carriage shop finances haunted the couple. John had not succeeded in directing the business from the battlefields of Virginia. This long distance effort proved futile. Two years having passed since he left, his concern for unpaid accounts and a backlog of bills gave way to anything in the line of a simple sale. "How does Fisher get along?" and "Does he sell any wagons?" were common questions he directed to Harriet from his hospital bed in Annapolis. In June 1864, he complained, "You never write anything about the business of the shop."[3] Harriet didn't write anything for the simple reason there was nothing to write about. Work was at a standstill. Elisha Fisher was preparing to join the army and apprentice James Cockett was left behind to perform minor repairs. The only thing that would save the business would be for the war to end quickly so John could return home to pick up the pieces.

Each day, including Sunday, was full of activity for Harriet Kidder. She continued to be active in the Baptist choir (she had been a member since she was fourteen years old), and she still taught Sunday school at the Methodist Church. When the Relief Corps of Oneonta formed, for the purpose of assembling food and clothing packages for the boys in blue, she quickly volunteered her services. These many acts of kindness on Harriet's part were thoughtfully recalled by Laurens' residents years later.

Another time-consuming activity for Harriet was reporting the latest news of the Kidder clan to her husband. In January 1864, Edward Kidder was finally discharged from the army. His left arm was permanently damaged from the gunshot wound he received at Salem Church. Crippled and with the responsibility of raising a family (he married Louise Thompson on March 28, 1858; a son, Rushton Edward, was born on March 5, 1860). Edward then returned to the family farm in Pittsfield.[4] His presence on the farm served as a constant reminder of the cruelties of war.

When the youngest Kidder, Major, or "H.P.," as he was known, announced his plans to enlist, his parents steadfastly refused to allow it.[5] With one son filling a grave on southern soil and another a whisker from death and yet another crippled, the elder Kidder was not about to have another son enlist in the army. There was nothing he could do, however, to change the way H.P. thought. As he neared his twentieth birthday, there was little his father could do to prevent him from enlisting.

Apparently a bargain was struck. Major could join the army provided he enlist in the 121st New York so that older brother, John, could look after him. So, on August 19, 1864, Major Henry Payne Kidder enlisted in the army and, through a mix-up in paperwork, found himself placed in the predominantly Irish-American 69th New York Volunteers.[6]

The most serious blow to the Kidder family in 1864 was learning of and accepting the death of George. "How does poor Anne feel about George?" John asked Harriet while at Annapolis. Harriet knew the answer to this question immediately—not well at all. Anne Kidder was devastated by the news and probably felt all the worse when she learned of the details from the Regimental Chaplain of the 152nd New York, Reverend Hiram V. Talbot. The day after George died, Talbot wrote to Anne.

> *Field Hospital*
> *May 7, 1864*
> *Dear Friend,*
>
> *It becomes my painful duty to inform you of your husband's death. He was wounded early in the morning of the 6th Inst. and died about 3 o'clock P.M. He was shot, the ball entering the fore part of the left shoulder and coming out the same side of the spinal column about midway. He suffered extremely. We have buried him and marked the place. I think it impossible to send him home. I asked him if he had any messages he wished to communicate to you. He said, "Tell her I die for my country, my family and my God." I pointed him to Jesus as his only hope. He said he trusted in Him and was not afraid to die. Let me commend you to the same Jesus that comforted him in his last hours.*
>
> *Our regiment is badly cut up. We are fighting desperately. So far we are victorious. If you cannot make out this note carry it to my wife. Tell her I am well. George said, "Tell my wife not to mourn for me, I die for my country."*
>
> *George was a brave soldier, after he was wounded he fought until he fell from loss of blood. He soon was taken to the rear and cared for [the] best we could. I remained with him most of the time till he died.*
>
> *I am*
> *Very respectfully*
> *Your Obt. Servant*
> *H. V. Talbot*
> *Chap. 152 NY*[7]

That summer, more frequent memorial services were held for the dead of the 121st and 152nd New York than were held the previous summer. When one such service took place for David Lewis of the 152nd who was killed at Cold Harbor on June 3, Anne Kidder had all she could do to get through it. Once more, she relived the pain and suffering of losing George. To Harriet she wrote,

> It brings all my trials fresh again and I'll assure you I'm feeling sad and lonely this evening. No one knows the utter dissolution of a widow's hurt except by sad experience. I wish I could feel more reconciled but it seems that every day adds to the heavy burden upon my heart. I feel surely that my last earthly friend is taken.[8]

Sadly, Anne noted that the day of the memorial service was the same day George left for the army eleven months earlier.

Harriet tried the best she could to console her grieving sister-in-law. Visiting helped but when she was alone, Anne could think of nothing but George. "Oh, Harriet," she wrote:

> "I find it very, very hard to be reconciled. George is in my mind day and night. I see him often in my dreams, but [I] awake to the sad reality that he has passed forever away from Earth. I shall never look upon that noble form again, never press those lips with the warm kiss of affection, never pen him another home message, nor receive one written by his own right hand. No. All hope, all anticipations of the future are swept away by this terrible besom[9] of destruction. War. Don't you think it hard to say "Oh Lord thy will be done." I sincerely hope you may never realize my feelings tonight. I received his diary last Saturday night all stained with his own life's current. Oh my God what a thought. I think sometimes if this war goes on much longer, it will make me about crazy. Still, I would see them fight till the last able-bodied man is in the field, and the last traitor slaughtered before I would have them submit to the murderers of our hearts dearest treasures. Many think I am rather an extreme, I can't help it. I feel that we must gain our cause, to be in the least compensated for the loss and sufferings of our friends.[10]

Anne Kidder never recovered from the loss of her husband and never remarried.

Toward the end of July 1864, the stagecoach made another scheduled appearance in Laurens. The townspeople gathered to receive their

mail and get the latest war news in a routine that had been continually re-
peating itself since the start of the war. This time, when the coach lurched
to a halt, a passenger emerged whom everyone recognized. Pounds lighter,
scarred and deaf in one ear, John S. Kidder was finally home. "Thank
God," he said. "It seems like [I'm] getting out of prison."[11] For nine weeks
he'd been a miserable patient at Annapolis and, even though he was
released, he was still not declared fit for duty.

When he left the hospital he had two sets of orders. One was his
twenty days leave of absence and the other, a set of orders directing him
to report immediately to Elmira Prison for "light duty." The dates on
both sets of orders were fairly close together and so Captain Kidder chose
to go to Elmira first, and then home. Boarding the train in Baltimore, he
proceeded via Harrisburg to Elmira and arrived there on July 22, 1864.
He hardly had time to familiarize himself with his new surroundings
when he was permitted to go home on leave. By now his leave orders were
almost a week old and, depending on the way they were interpreted, they
were either in effect when he received them, or, when he left Elmira. The
confusion caused by the mix-up in dates was trivial in comparison to the
real problems he faced when he finally arrived in Laurens. For most of his
leave, John S. Kidder was bedridden. Suffering frequent dizzy spells, due
in part to inner ear damage, he was further weakened by constant vomit-
ing. This proved that the tough old Dutchman, Surgeon Vanderkeift, was
right all along. Physically, Kidder was not ready to be released from
the hospital.

Realizing that his failure to report back to Elmira on time was a serious breach of military discipline, Kidder asked for and received a military tribunal to review his case. His only defense was a letter from his
attending physician, Dr. Addison Strong, detailing the extent of his illness. The case was immediately dismissed and no disciplinary action was
taken. Saved from the shame of a court-martial, the senior captain of
Company I of the 121st New York Volunteers was ready to assume his
new duties at Elmira.[12]

The idea for a prison camp at Elmira was first suggested on May 14,
1864.[13] As the war entered its fourth summer, the need for additional
prison space was more apparent as prisons became more overcrowded.
The site at Elmira looked perfect for two reasons: first, it was easily accessible by rail, and second, it was already constructed. The facilities on the
Chemung River had been used throughout the war as a gathering and
training center for troops from the western part of New York. Even with a
portion of this complex used as a prison, infantry, cavalry, and artillery

units continued to rendezvous here before being sent south. The last infantry regiment, the 194th New York, mustered at Elmira on March 29, 1865, less than two weeks before General Lee surrendered.[14]

The compound called "Barracks 3" that Kidder reported to contained thirty wood frame buildings. They were laid out in rows similar to the German-style stalags of World War II. Like those stalags, these were sealed off by a large stockade fence. Here, the similarities ended. If Elmira could be compared to any place, it probably resembled its southern counterpart, Andersonville. Both were unsanitary and both had high mortality rates.

One of Elmira's biggest problems was water. Andersonville had a lone stream that meandered through the camp inadequately providing for every need of the large prison in Georgia. Elmira had the exact opposite problem. At times there was too much water. Foster's Pond, located inside the camp, served as a garbage dump. The overwhelming stench that emanated from the stagnant pond, together with the odors from the nearby latrines, made the humid summer unbearable. When the rains came, and they did, the pond flooded and drained off, providing only a temporary relief to the problem. Excessive rain frequently caused the nearby Chemung River to overflow and flood the camp.[15]

Throughout July, Confederate prisoners arrived at Elmira and the wooden barracks filled quickly. Their journey had taken them from the battlefields to the prisons at Point Lookout, Maryland. From there they were loaded onto boats and sent to New York City where they boarded the prison trains to Elmira. By the time Kidder reported for duty, the population was already about 1,150 men. Placed in command of a small company of guards, Kidder was responsible for 232 prisoners whom he felt "behave[d] well."[16] However, as each week passed, more and more prisoners arrived. The barracks were completely full and the newest arrivals had to sleep on the open ground until blankets and tents could be issued. When Captain Kidder returned from leave that September, the prison population had soared to nine thousand, and he felt fortunate to "have only 1,000 Rebs" under his command.[17]

Most of the prisoners showed signs of their earlier confinement at Point Lookout Prison. Barefoot, with ill-fitting clothes, they were, by all accounts, a scruffy looking group. What surprised Kidder was how easily he was recognized by some of the prisoners. Two Confederates immediately approached him when they noticed the "121" on his hat and began asking questions about the May 10 charge at Spotsylvania. One prisoner claimed that he was standing next to a man Kidder shot during the battle. Another prisoner came forward and introduced himself as the soldier that captured Lt. Col. Olcott at the Wilderness. Kidder was at first suspicious about this claim until the prisoner accurately described Olcott's wound. "The ball," he told Kidder, "struck him in the upper part of the forehead but did not fracture the skull."[18]

This chance meeting helped Captain Kidder establish good rapport with the southern prisoners. Clearly remembering the emaciated prisoners who had been released from Libby Prison while he was at Annapolis, the captain was sympathetic to their situation. Food and adequate shelter were the immediate concerns of his charges; he tried to assist them in this regard. Tents would eventually be procured, but food was a constant problem.

The daily ration for a prisoner at Elmira, and at all other Union prisons, was suggested by Army Chief of Staff, General Henry Halleck, on May 19, 1864.[19] When Commissioner-General of Prisoners, Col. William Hoffman, suggested a reduction in the diet of Confederate prisoners, Halleck agreed and went one step further. "Why not," wrote Halleck to the Secretary of War, "dispense with tea, coffee and sugar, and reduce the ration to that issued by the Rebel government to their own troops?"[20] The policy was adopted with disastrous results. Bread and meat were strictly rationed and vegetables, for a time, were discontinued. By August 26, 1864, there were 793 cases of scurvy at Elmira. Despite the protests of the medical staff, including a letter signed by ten camp doctors, the diet remained.[21]

The scurvy epidemic could be easily remedied according to the camp commander at Elmira, Lt. Col. Seth Eastman. Vegetables were available and could be purchased by the prisoners from the various camp sutlers who frequented Elmira. "This will give great relief," wrote Eastman to Hoffman. "The prisoners have plenty of money and will purchase these vegetables for themselves if permitted."[22]

Opinions on sutlers varied, but one thing was generally agreed upon, that wherever there were soldiers, there was a traveling group of merchants plying their wares. At Elmira, the sutlers scoffed at the worthless confederate script many of the prisoners had and insisted on federal greenbacks. In no time, the prisoners began whittling away at soup bones making all sorts of trinkets to sell. Rings, chains, bracelets, and even horsehair macramé items began to appear.

When Captain Kidder discovered how easy it was to sell these souvenirs to the citizens of Elmira, he immediately sent for one-armed Charley Matteson. Harriet's brother had been discharged from the army on October 31, 1863, and John S. Kidder felt confident that his brother-in-law could make money at Elmira. "He can make money like fun," he told Harriet. "I can put him in a way of selling rings, as many want them, and I can furnish him all that he can sell. He can make a pile of money if he comes."[23]

Kidder's business mind soon slipped into high gear. This was a way to make quick money. Acting as a middleman for the artistic Rebels, who amazed him with their skill at using only "jack knives," Kidder placed orders and expanded the inventory. He sent rings to Harriet to sell in Laurens, complete with a price list. The "gents rings" sold for four dollars and other rings went for six dollars apiece. It didn't stop there. His father sold rings in Pittsfield and Elisha Fisher, also in the army now, was selling rings at Hart Island in New York City where he also guarded Confederate prisoners. Business was great and Kidder begged Harriet to have Charley get to Elmira as soon as possible. "I hope Charlie will come soon," he wrote her. "This you can keep to yourself. I have made over $200 since I came here in the ring trade."[24] Charley Matteson arrived in late September and in no time at all was busy selling rings.

Aside from the thriving ring business, Kidder's primary concern was guarding prisoners. His duties included supervising squads of guards, conducting daily patrols within the thirty-six acre compound, and overseeing an occasional work detail outside of the camp. These work details were a pleasant diversion from the crowded prison and the various odors associated with it.

Between the months of August and November, eight infantry units were assigned to Elmira in much the same way Captain Kidder was, on a temporary basis. Of those regiments, Kidder expressed a disappointment with the units from New York City. "I have no doubt," he said,

> but if we Vet[eran] officers had not been here, the prisoners would all been out before this time. We had more trouble with the militia than we have with the Rebs. We sometimes have some of the Rebs come out of the yard to work for us, cut wood or fix up our quarters. When they do so we have a guard with his musket for each prisoner but we never dare take any such guards from New York City Militia Regiments, as they were more likely to run away and leave their post than the Rebs were.[25]

It was a relief to Kidder when, in November, the 28th and 56th Brooklyn regiments and the 77th, 99th, and 102nd New York City regiments completed their one hundred day temporary duty and returned home.[26]

Only a few Rebs "ran away" from Elmira during the Civil War. Prison escapes were rare from any prison in the North or South at the time. It wasn't because there was a lack of desire on the part of the men. The fact was, that those who were incarcerated for long periods of time were too ill or weak to attempt an escape. There were always a determined few, however, who somehow defied the odds. The camp wasn't a month old when the first escape attempt was made. On July 7, 1864, two daring Confederates scaled the stockade wall near the east end of the camp and swam the Chemung River in their bid for freedom. One of the escapees was captured and the other was never heard from again.[27]

As more and more guards were brought to Elmira, security tightened and escapes over the stockade walls ceased altogether. The only way out was to dig. Toward the end of summer, wedge-shaped tents issued to those prisoners living in the open proved to be very useful to resourceful tunnelers. Tents placed closest to the stockade walls were the best places to dig. For five weeks a group of prisoners clawed their way through the dirt tunneling their way toward Hoffman Street. Using haversacks, they carefully deposited the dirt around the camp and in Foster's Pond. Around 4:00 A.M. on October 7, 1864, ten prisoners emerged from the sixty-six foot long tunnel in the largest prison escape from Elmira.[28]

Kidder was aware of the tunneling activity of some of the prisoners but did nothing about it. "We caught some of the Rebels digging out last night," he wrote to Harriet that November. He added, "We know of four different holes they are digging at. I expect one hole is about completed. We have a Sergeant that has just come from the front watching for the scoundrels to come out. The first who puts his head out of the hole will get shot."[29] This was a little bravado on Kidder's part, perhaps trying to impress his wife with the seriousness of the situation. In fact, there is no record of any prisoner shot while escaping from Elmira. It does seem cruel, though, to permit men to tunnel in their quest for freedom only to wait outside and recapture them. According to Sergeant Melvin M. Cotton of the 155th New York, it was an accepted practice. "My orders," recalled Cotton, "were to let the men dig."[30]

All in all, Elmira was about as exciting as Annapolis. Captain Kidder was bored, the possibility of escape attempts was the only real excitement the place had to offer. In his four months at Elmira, he wrote only eleven letters home and most of them were only four or five sentences long, and uninteresting at that. He longed for news from the 121st New York and begged Harriet in most of these letters to send him news clippings from the Utica and Oneonta papers. "I am afraid to hear," he confided to her, "as I think some of my noble boys are among the dead and wounded. I wish that I was with them to share in their honors."[31]

While John S. Kidder convalesced at Annapolis and performed his "light duty" at Elmira, the 121st never ceased to be active. From Spotsylvania, General Grant sidestepped the entire Army of the Potomac to Cold Harbor for yet another bloody encounter with General Lee. From this crossroads, he then moved toward the James River, crossed pontoon bridges at City Point and prepared to lay siege to Petersburg. The 121st New York Volunteers took an active part in the first assault of the Petersburg defenses and assisted in disrupting the lines of communication at the nearby Weldon Railroad. For many it appeared to be just a matter of time before the Confederates, trapped inside Petersburg and Richmond, would be forced to give up at least one of the cities.

In an effort to divert attention from this crisis, Confederate General Jubal A. Early took fourteen thousand men and launched his celebrated Washington Raid. Crossing the Potomac River on July 5, Early was able to defeat a small federal force at Monacacy four days later. With Early closing in on the nation's capitol, Grant ordered the entire VI Corps north to deal with this threat. While probing the defenses of Washington, Early learned of the arrival of the VI Corps and wisely called off the attack.[32]

Like the Confederate prisoners he guarded, Captain Kidder was now a bystander in a distant war. Relying on newspaper accounts that were days, sometimes weeks old, he tried to keep up with the latest events as the war shifted from the outskirts of Washington to the Shenandoah Valley. Kidder learned that the entire VI Corps had been placed under the command of fiery little General Philip Sheridan. The VI Corps, together with the XIX Corps and several divisions of cavalry made up the newly formed Army of the Shenandoah. Sheridan's mission was to rid the valley of Early's forces and render the area useless to the Confederate war effort.

On September 19, 1864, Sheridan struck Early at Opequon Creek (Winchester) driving the Confederates from their position. When news of this battle reached John S. Kidder, he was saddened to learn that Maj. Gen. David A. Russell was among those killed in action. "I am very sorry that we lost such a noble officer as General Russell," said Kidder of the general who led them successfully at Rappahannock Station the previous November. "He was one of my best friends and I think one of our best Generals."[33] Although wounded in the chest while leading his men, Russell concealed the wound and continued to direct his men. Then, an exploding shell killed him instantly.[34]

Another wounded officer who refused to leave the field was Gen. Emory Upton. When a shell ripped a chunk of flesh from his thigh, the young brigadier had a stretcher brought up to the front and continued to direct his men from a prone position. The wound wasn't dangerous, which pleased Kidder, but it did put Upton out of action for several months.[35]

Three days later, on September 22, Sheridan drove the Confederates from their defensive position at Fishers Hill. Confident with each of these victories, he continued to move his forces further down the valley and camped near Cedar Creek.

Despite his previous losses General Early was determined to take the initiative and, in a surprise move, struck Sheridan's forces at dawn on October 19. The blue-coated veterans were caught off guard. Some had their breakfast interrupted while others simply woke to the sound of guns. A general panic set in all along the Union line as officers desperately struggled to rally their men to meet the threat. Sheridan, who was absent from the field (he was returning from a conference with General Halleck and Secretary of War Edwin McMasters Stanton), heard the cannon fire fourteen miles away at Winchester. Unalarmed at first, he became concerned when the cannon fire increased with intensity two hours later. Convinced that a battle was under way, he spurred his horse quickly toward the sound of the guns. Arriving on the field about 10:30 A.M., Sheridan met with VI Corps commander, Horatio Wright, to assess the situation. The VI Corps had been pushed back but stubbornly held onto a defensive position and refused to yield. By 4:00 P.M., Sheridan ordered a general advance along the line. This counterattack with combined cavalry and infantry proved too much for Early's men. The Confederates were chased four miles beyond Cedar Creek and the Federals reoccupied their camps just as Sheridan had promised.[36] Captain Kidder didn't hear about the victory until October 21. "I hope that my boys came out well as in the other fights," he confided to his wife.[37]

Cedar Creek was the worst beating the 121st New York Volunteers endured since Spotsylvania. Ten men were killed outright and scores were wounded bringing the count to fifty-seven casualties. Among the dead officers were old friends like Lt. William Tucker. The native of Roseboom had risen from sergeant to first lieutenant and was killed in the last attack made by the Confederates. Lt. John D. P. Douw was also dead. He had been promoted to captain of Company K just before the Battle of Salem Church. His leg was so seriously mangled that a barefoot Confederate soldier, thinking that Douw was already dead, tried to strip off his boots. A passing Confederate officer, witnessing the scene, protested and then took the time to cover Douw's leg with straw. Douw later died of the effects of the wound on November 11.[38] Capt. Johnathan Burrell of Little Falls also suffered a serious leg wound. Kidder was pleased to hear that Burrell rallied after the leg was amputated and was on his way home to convalesce. Later, an Elmira Prison guard, returning home from a short leave in Little Falls, informed John S. Kidder that Jonathan Burrell was, indeed, home. He "was brought home in a coffin," said the guard.[39]

Cedar Creek was also the last battle for Little Falls native, Maj. Henry Galpin. Bearing a scar from a wound he received before joining the 121st New York, the popular officer was wounded twice at Spotsylvania. Lying on the field with gunshot wounds in both thighs and suffering from the onset of tuberculosis, Galpin was patched up and sent home.[40]

Of the dozen enlisted men reported killed, only one was a Company I man, Elijah Dingman, a farmer from Milford, New York. Another, Sergeant William Remmel, was reported killed in action, although his body was never recovered. It would be years before John S. Kidder would learn the fate of Remmel, who, like some others, had quit Fairfield Seminary to join the army in 1862. Wounded in the arm, Remmel had not been killed but captured and sent to Andersonville Prison where he lies in a grave marked "Unknown."[41]

George Teel and Parley McIntyre were wounded and so was the Color Bearer, Corporal Mason Jenks. "He has escaped well until this time," said Kidder of Jenks. "He is a brave noble fellow, always stuck to the Old Flag and carried it through many a hard fought battle. I trust he will recover."[42] Jenks did recover, but the bullet that shattered his arm caused such severe nerve damage that he was never able to close his hand again for the rest of his life.[43]

When informed that the wounded from Company I would be able to go home on leave, Kidder dashed off a quick note to his wife expressing his concerns that the townspeople of Laurens would give them, as he said, "a good reception, if they knew their worth as I do."[44] He didn't forget the fact that Jenks had been one of the "noble few" who had stood alone with him in the desperate struggle at Salem Church.

The most bizarre story Kidder heard from Cedar Creek was of the alleged cowardice of Private Moses Wright. Harriet had only sketchy details to relate and this seemed to confuse her husband. "I am sorry to hear such news," he wrote back, trying to make sense of the situation. "He was always prompt when I was with the Regiment. He never showed any cowardice. I am much surprised to hear such news."[45] Charged with "misbehavior before the enemy," Wright was court-martialed and later, dishonorably discharged.[46] In the past, Kidder would not, as he said, be troubled with cowards; he demanded that his men "face the music." Now, far removed from the sound of the guns, he showed a gentler side. His own brush with death and the loss of so many friends in each new battle, changed him. "I think it is very probable he was not very well," he later said of Wright. "When a man feels rather fatigued, he does not show pluck as when he is in good health." In August 1865, with the war long since over, Wright had his military record amended and received a pardon for the offense.[47]

The victory at Cedar Creek marked the end of the Shenandoah Valley Campaign for the 121st New York. The entire VI Corps was moved back to the siege operations around Petersburg and then into winter quarters. Despondent and lonely, Captain Kidder wrote, "You cannot have any idea how I have felt since I heard of those fights. I felt as though I should have been with them to share the glory they have so nobly won."[48] By November, he resigned himself to the fact that his winter quarters were to be at Elmira Prison and not in Petersburg with the regiment. Totally bored with Elmira, he made one more attempt to return home for a short leave; he used the pretext of returning to Laurens to vote in the national elections. What he really wanted was to be with Harriet for the birth of their second child. The ruse didn't work and the request was flatly denied. So, while sergeants and other officers traveled home to cast their votes, John S. Kidder remained behind and counted Confederate prisoners. If he had been able to go home, he would have been in for a grand time.

Political emotions were at an all-time high in Laurens. The village was not at a loss for speech making, torch lit parades, and rallies. Quite a few of the local townspeople ventured to the county seat in Cooperstown on hay wagons to attend the larger rallies. One such wagon was comprised of only women, each one representing a loyal state of the Union. Another, led by Henry Olin, was an anti-McClellan wagon, featuring a banner across the side that read, This is the wooden gun that scared Little Mac. The crudely constructed wooden cannon was in reference to the "Quaker Guns" or painted logs that caused McClellan to hesitate while on the Peninsula of Virginia in 1862.[49]

As one of the standard bearers of the Republican Party in Otsego County, John S. Kidder was a staunch Lincoln supporter. He felt Lincoln's chances of a victory in November were all the better after the success of Philip Sheridan in the Shenandoah Valley. He was quick to notice that his Confederate charges were nonvoting McClellan supporters.

"There only hope of obtaining their independence is in the election of McClellan," he said. "All of the real Rebels hope and pray for McClellan['s] election but I think they will be disappointed. Every one of the [Union] Officers here that have been to the front are for Lincoln."[50] When the ballots were counted and the official results were announced, it was just as John S. Kidder had predicted. "The Rebels mourn over the defeat of McClellan."[51]

The really good news during that November came to Kidder in a letter written by Verona, Charley Matteson's wife. It was the letter he had been anxiously awaiting. Harriet had given birth to a healthy baby girl on November 11. She was christened, Mary Salina, in memory of his oldest sister, Salina, who died of tuberculosis in 1856. The proud father wasted no time. He wrote to Harriet. "I am glad you are doing so well. I had expected a boy but as Verona says, there is time enough for that yet. I suppose Clara is delighted with a sister. Tell her Pa will come home to see it someday. I do not know when."[52]

With still no leave of absence forthcoming, a desperate Captain Kidder hit upon another plan. Noting that several of the officers at Elmira had their wives living with them at camp, he suggested that Harriet pack up the children and join him. He tried to assure her that the living quarters were comfortable; he could provide for their every need. He had come a long way as far as comfort was concerned since his arrival at Elmira. The officer's quarters, located just outside the main compound west of the camp, were very spartan. When Kidder arrived, he had to purchase blankets, a wash dish, pail, looking glass (mirror), and bedtick chairs.[53] By December, he had accumulated enough creature comforts to make the rooms quite inviting. "If you think that you could ride to Deposit [a small village 25 miles south of Laurens] with the baby without injury, I will come home and bring you. I have wood and coal furnished me, more than I can burn." The two stoves, one, a cookstove, kept the three rooms warm. He had a copper-bottom dish kettle, tea kettle, coffeepot, and spiders—traditional black cast iron frying pans. If that weren't enough, he could always employ his enterprising prisoners to make whatever was needed.

> I have a bedstead, could have the Rebs make me another and a cradle in half a day. I have one good mattress. We should have to bring only our bed and clothing, a few dishes. I have two tables. We could bring a rug carpet to cover the floor, etc. What do you think about it? My rooms are much warmer than our house.[54]

It certainly sounded inviting, however, Harriet had many things to consider. Who would care for her father and who would look after the carriage shop and their boarder, James Cockett? When she hesitated, John quickly suggested that she might want to bring along a hired girl to assist with the children. This was enough to win Harriet over and John quickly set the paperwork in motion to make the trip home. He was so excited that he already had a surprise gift for his Little Diamond, Clara, a kitten.

Suddenly, John S. Kidder came to his senses. Elmira was no place to bring a family. The death rate at the camp rose as the seasons changed. He estimated that the death rate in October alone was, as he said, between "8 to 30 per day."[55] While scurvy and exposure to the elements were to blame, December brought a new menace—smallpox. By Christmas, Elmira's physicians reported sixty-three cases, and by the end of the month, Kidder estimated that the number had risen horribly to one hundred.[56] Even though no cases of smallpox were reported outside of the compound, he was still concerned. "I hope there will not be but it is very probable as they have no matter to vaccinate with," he wrote on December 30. With this in mind, he wrote and told Harriet to remain in Laurens.[57]

In the end, this decision proved to be for the best. Harriet and the children were safe in Laurens. Dr. Strong was always near and a journey during the winter could have been harmful. Besides, far away in the trenches of Petersburg, forces were at work trying to get Captain Kidder out of Elmira and back into the ranks of the 121st New York Volunteers. Unbeknownst to Kidder, Capt. James W. Cronkite had written to the adjutant general's office requesting that there were but "few officers present" and that Kidder be returned to the regiment at the earliest opportunity.[58] Cronkite then dashed off a quick note to his friend telling him to expect new orders at any moment. They arrived in January, thus ending John S. Kidder's tenure guarding prisoners of war.

Captain Kidder's Elmira days were officially over, but the legacy of New York State's most famous prison was just beginning. The guns had fairly ceased firing when a great debate ensued regarding the reputation of Elmira Prison. Confederate prisoners of war wrote pamphlets and books condemning the prison they dubbed, "Hellmira," while a small cadre of northern writers tried to do exactly the same by writing horrific tales with regard to the notorious Andersonville. Finally, in 1912, Clay W. Holmes published *The Elmira Prison Camp*. This very sympathetic view of the prison was the best overall history of the institution that existed. Holmes, while admitting that Elmira had an appalling death rate (over 2,950 deaths were reported in the thirteen-month tenure of the camp), tried desperately to redeem the image of the camp by including excerpts of several letters written by ex-prisoners. Naturally, all were very favorable in their comments regarding their stay at Elmira.

One letter, written by M. T. Wade, a former member of Company B, 12th North Carolina, is particularly interesting in that it may provide some insight as to John S. Kidder's behavior while at the prison. Wade claims that after a confrontation with a guard, he was ordered to be punished, as he said, by being placed in a "small dungeon inside the guard house for ten days on bread and water, but thanks to Captain Kidd who was officer of the day, I only stayed in there two days, which was enough. I wish I knew that he was still alive, that I might write and thank him for releasing me from that dungeon."[59] There is good reason to suspect that the benefactor of Wade was, indeed, John S. Kidder. *New York State in the War of the Rebellion*, a massive five volume compilation of all the officers and regiments that served in the Civil War from the Empire State, includes no one by the name of "Kidd" who would have been at Elmira at this time.

However vague this reference is, there is another piece of direct evidence that suggests that Kidder was well-respected and liked by his prisoners. Among the collection of the Captain's memorabilia is a letter written by John A. Evans of the 9th Virginia Cavalry. Evans offered his services to the Confederate cause exactly one week after the fall of Fort Sumter on April 21, 1861. On September 13, 1862, shortly before the Antietam Campaign, he was captured near Culpeper, Virginia, and eventually found himself being shuttled from one prison to another, finally landing in Elmira. The thirty-two-year-old Evans was not exchanged from Elmira until the waning days of the Confederacy, on March 10, 1865.[60]

> *Stafford County, Va*
> *Sept. 5th, 1865*
> *Capt. John S. Kidder,*
> *My Dear Friend*
>
> These few lines will inform you that I am well and [so] also [is] my family. I left Elmira on the 11 of March. I arrived in Richmond on the 15th. I left Richmond on the 17th and arrived home on the 20th, found my family and friends all well and in a few days after I got home Richmond went up the spout. I was surprised at the prices of things when I got home, and [I] could not buy one thing only with the greenback as the Old South had returned back to the old flag. Well, Capt. Kidder you know when I was in [Elmira] Prison that I was all for the South. Though since I have gotten home I have returned, and now I am Union from top to bot-

tom. I do hope these lines may find you and your family in the enjoyment of good health. I often think of you and never shall forget your kindness to me while [I was] in Prison. I missed you after you left and so did all the boys. Well, Capt. I have Miss Hannah['s] likeness, she is a fine looking lady. I received a letter from her since I have been home and what was the best of all Mrs. E. got hold of the letter first. My wife often tells me that she knows that I was a bad boy while I was in Prison and that she will write to you to know about my bad habits. I tell her to write and you will tell her all about me. Capt. I do wish you would come to Va. and get you a far, I shall be glad to have you to come. You must come and look about and see how you like [it]. Capt., I think you could do well in Fredericksburg. You must write to me and write me a long letter and give me all the news. Have you seen Mr. and Mrs. Cooly. If so, let me know. Well Capt., as I have know [sic] news, I must close and [as] soon as I get a letter from you I then will give you all the news. I forgot to tell you that I have a stock of rings on hand. I am keeping them for you. Old Serg. Wager never paid me the 35 cts. for the rings I let him have. Now Capt. Kidder to be sure to write me a long letter, give my best respects to your family.

I am your true friend
John A. Evans

In the past, Upton severely criticized his senior captain for being too close or friendly with the men he commanded. At Elmira, he found it was possible to do his duty while at the same time forging a friendship under the most difficult of circumstances. After the war, Captain Kidder returned time after time to the fields of Virginia with the other aged veterans of the 121st New York. One can only hope that he took the time to visit his old friend, John A. Evans.[61]

EIGHT

"Victory is ours"

Whhile Captain Kidder went about selling his stoves and all the other furniture he accumulated during his stay at Elmira, the 121st New York Volunteers made steady progress southward toward Petersburg. The regiment arrived at City Point on December 4, 1864, and moved to their old camp on the Jerusalem Plank Road. Here, they settled down and prepared to wait out yet another (their third) Virginia winter of mud and snow. As miserable as this sounds, the men were well-fed and quite comfortable in their makeshift cabins. Packages and mail arrived from home on a regular basis, and the only real danger they faced was from an occasional shot or two exchanged by the men on picket duty. The boys in blue were aware of how fortunate they were compared to their southern counterparts who frequently deserted into their lines. "Their clothing," said Clinton Beckwith, "bore out the startling stories they told."[1]

John S. Kidder didn't get to Petersburg until January 29, 1865. As his orders did not appear to be of an urgent nature (Burnside's Mud March made it painfully clear that an army must not be moved during the winter months in Virginia), Kidder made a series of "side trips" before reporting back to the regiment. He stopped in Laurens to visit his family, then boarded the train for New York City. Here, he made his usual rounds visiting former Laurens' residents who made their homes in the city.

John also made a special trip out to Hart Island. Located in the Long Island Sound, Hart Island was used as a Confederate Prison Camp. It was here, on this one hundred acre island, that Senior Captain Kidder finally met his old business partner, Elisha Fisher. When Fisher enlisted in the 121st he decided, perhaps at the last minute, not to join Kidder's Company

161

I. Instead, he chose the company band. Since bandsmen were not needed, Fisher, for some unknown reason, only got as far as Hart Island. Here he remained for his entire enlistment, guarding Confederate prisoners of war. The two hadn't seen each other since Kidder was home on recruiting service the previous February. This was a social visit, however, business was foremost on John S. Kidder's mind.

Although he corresponded with Elisha from time to time, Captain Kidder still relied on Harriet for most of the details surrounding the carriage shop. Both men agreed that the hired man, James Cockett, would have to concentrate on simple repairs and smaller jobs. For an apprentice to take on new orders for wagons and carriages was out of the question. Any work that Cockett couldn't do, such as blacksmith work, would be sublet to Morris Mead. Hopefully, their creditors, who had been extremely patient with them, would continue to be for a while longer.

There was another matter to settle before the two parted. Kidder reminded Fisher that he still owed him money from the rings and trinkets produced by the prisoners at Elmira. Elisha Fisher came up with $125, leaving a balance still owed of $197.35.[2]

After leaving Fisher, Kidder boarded the train and headed south for the final time. At Annapolis Junction, he was greeted by James W. Cronkite, now wearing the shoulder straps of a major. Kidder noticed them right away. It was the rank both he and John D. Fish wished for. Fish was dead, and the promotion that eluded them now seemed even further from reach. Captain Kidder was noticeably depressed at seeing the rank but couldn't find any fault with his old friend for having received the promotion. Cronkite tried to reassure Kidder that promotions would be forthcoming *if* and only *if* the regiment got more men.

Having been away from the regiment for almost seven and a half months since being wounded at Spotsylvania, Kidder could see that the regiment was indeed small, the ranks having been thinned considerably. After the 121st returned from the Shenandoah Valley Campaign, it numbered only 175 men. When Captain Kidder called out Company I for its first inspection, he was shocked to count only twenty-seven men present for duty. Cronkite was right, unless more men were brought into the regiment, there would be no promotions. There was even a rumor circulating that the 121st New York might be dissolved, broken up; the men scattered throughout the division as replacements for other regiments.[3]

Recruiting officers sent to Herkimer and Otsego Counties met with the same dismal results Kidder and Fish had the previous year. As before, there were just too many units to choose from. Kidder heard that

Laurens residents, Henry Gardner, Horace Richmond and blacksmith Damon Mead, recently enlisted in Company E of the 2nd New York Heavy Artillery.[4]

Cronkite told Kidder that if enough men entered the regiment, Olcott would be promoted to colonel, thus filling the vacancy created when Upton resigned to accept his general's star. Released from Confederate captivity after three months, Olcott's head wound was sufficiently healed and, after a brief convalescence, he returned to the regiment. If Olcott moved up to colonel, the lieutenant colonel position would be open and Captain Kidder, the officer with the most seniority, would fill that position, skipping the rank of major altogether.

The prospect of this kind of promotion excited John S. Kidder immensely. He didn't waste any time sending a flurry of letters to officials in Albany and Washington, urging them to send more troops to the 121st New York. January turned into February and then March arrived without a single replacement. On March 4, 1865, a direct appeal was made to the War Department to fill the ranks of the 121st with four hundred short-term enlistees or drafted men.[5] Adding weight to this application were the signatures of Generals Ranald Slidell MacKenzie, Frank Wheaton, and Horatio Wright, the respective brigade, division and corps commanders for the 121st. Topping it off was the signature of General George G. Meade.[6] Unfortunately, the promised replacements didn't arrive until after Lee's surrender.

None of this helped explain how Cronkite got promoted to major. When Henry Galpin left Annapolis General Hospital, *he* was the major, *not* Cronkite. When Cronkite was wounded during the Shenandoah Valley Campaign, he resigned and the position remained unfilled until the end of December 1864. It was at this time that their former brigade commander, General Joseph Bartlett, attempted to get his brother, Lewis, appointed as the new major for the 121st New York.

Lewis Bartlett was no stranger to John S. Kidder. He transferred to the 121st in June 1863, having been a first lieutenant in the 27th New York. This regiment, coincidentally, was commanded by his brother Joseph.[7] As a first lieutenant in the 121st, he basically floated from one assignment to the next without ever accepting any permanent position with the regiment. He served in Company K and D with no specific dates of services, being at Brigade Headquarters most of the time. When Galpin's resignation was made official on December 21, 1864, General Bartlett submitted his brother's name as the next major for the 121st. Naturally, this caused a furor with the officer corps of the regiment.

Leading the insurrection was Captain Cronkite, the highest ranking officer in the regiment present for duty at the time.

Cronkite immediately rode over to Bartlett's headquarters, now at the V Corps, and personally confronted Bartlett. Dissatisfied with the results of this meeting, Cronkite returned to the regiment and quickly wrote a scathing letter. Brushing aside all military formalities, Cronkite got right to the point.

> I think there has been a growing feeling in the regiment since sixty-three that your brother had no further interest in the regiment than to maintain his present position—disclaiming rivalry by remaining absent from there since his transfer to it in the spring of 1863. However this conclusion may be; it is one which is firmly held by the officers and which gives tenacity to their purpose.

Then Cronkite drove the point home.

> The interest of the entire regiment is the first great principle which we as soldiers are bound to promote and with the present adverse feelings my convictions are that it would be greatly injurious to the general interests of the regiment if your Brother [were] to accept such a position as his commission would warrant in advance of those who claim legitimate right to demand the position by seniority and their continued connection with the regiment since its organization in August 1862.[8]

Two days later, Cronkite fired off another salvo, this time to New York State Governor, Reuben Fenton, protesting the promotion of Lewis Bartlett over the heads of "Six Captains and nearly as many Lieutenants."[9] Cronkite asked the Governor to help right this injustice and allow the position to be properly filled and approved by a brigade or division commander of the VI Corps. These efforts on the part of Cronkite paid off with unexpected dividends. Not only was Bartlett's commission immediately revoked but Cronkite, by reason of seniority, became the new major. If John S. Kidder had returned a few weeks earlier from Elmira, and had not gone to Laurens or New York City, perhaps the promotion could have been his.

This turn of events didn't dampen Captain Kidder's spirits. In fact, the ever present rumors of replacements and new promotions made him all the more optimistic. Kidder, Cronkite, and Olcott, were indeed, the "old men" of the regiment, each wanting to rise in rank before the war ended. "I think the Regiment will be filled," he wrote to Harriet. "If so, all the officers want I should be the Lieut[enant] Col[onel] of our Regiment."[10] Only time and a cruel twist of fate would make his dream a reality.

Setting dreams of advancement aside, Kidder returned to the reality of army life. He was still the senior captain and this meant an endless parade of paperwork and other duties. There were still the daily inspections, monthly and quarterly reports, not to mention clothing and supply reports to be completed. Some of these reports were long overdue. One, "Voucher No. 5," an equipment voucher for weapons and haversacks lost by Company I at the battle of Cold Harbor, had to be completed with the assistance of Sergeant James Taft. Captain Kidder was at Annapolis when this battle was fought and had to rely on others, like Taft, to complete the report.[11]

The paperwork routine was the same. The only thing that appeared to be different with the regiment was the lack of familiar faces. Old friends were gone, some dead, others so seriously wounded they were sent home.

There was only one new member of the staff, the new Regimental Chaplain, Reverend John Adams. He was new to the regiment, but he was no stranger to the brigade. Reverend Adams served throughout the Peninsular Campaign as chaplain of the 5th Maine. He saw General Ambrose E. Burnside and General Joseph Hooker come and go, was present at Gettysburg and had been to the Wilderness. When the term of service for the 5th Maine ended, Reverend Adams was approached by officers of the 121st New York and asked to accept the recently vacated chaplaincy. About a month shy of his sixty-third birthday, when Captain Kidder first met him, Adams was tireless in his efforts seeing to the needs of the men. When not visiting the sick and wounded at the division hospital, he was usually leading prayer meetings or trying to wrestle supplies from the Christian Commission.[12]

The love and respect the men felt for Adams was clearly evident. On Sunday evening, February 5, his chapel was filled to capacity the same way it was that morning. A delighted Adams had just announced the subject of his sermon when he was interrupted by the steady drum roll calling the men to assembly. Soon, shouts of, "Pack up! Pack up!" could be heard. The congregation was stunned. John S. Kidder had just finished a letter home telling his wife not to worry. "I am well, we are in good quarters. Perfectly safe. I think the Rebs will not try to break through here," he wrote. "They would get a warm reception if they should try."[13]

The prayer meeting came to an abrupt end. Everyone ran to their huts to gather up their equipment. Adams closed his Bible, tucked it into his haversack and soon appeared on the parade ground with the first companies of men.

By 8:00 P.M., the regiment was assembled and ready to march. The entire First Division of the VI Corps was under marching orders to move toward Hatcher's Run. General Grant, encouraged by the mild weather, wanted to continue his strangle hold on Petersburg. Suspecting that Confederate wagon trains were supplying the starving city by use of the Boydton Plank Road, he dispatched a cavalry division and two corps of infantry to take possession of the road.[14]

A cavalry division led by Gettysburg veteran, General David Gregg, was on the move toward Dinwiddie Court House with Maj. Gen. Gouverneur Kemble Warren's V Corps and the II Corps of Maj. Gen. Andrew Humphrey closing in fast. Assisting these two corps was the First Division of the VI Corps which acted as a reserve unit. In command of the division was yet another unfamiliar face to Captain Kidder. Thirty-two year old Maj. Gen. Frank Wheaton was the only non-West Pointer at the division level of command in the VI Corps. Previously, the respected and reliable Rhode Islander served in the regular army on the frontier, fighting Indians. Wheaton was ordered to report to Humphrey's II Corps on the night of February 5 by 8:00 P.M.[15] He not only made contact, but had his men dig a series of rifle pits just in case they were attacked at dawn.

Last to arrive in position was the 121st New York. Forced to backtrack when they took the wrong road, they didn't get into position until around 1:00 A.M., and this was only possible, because they saw the lights of the other first division campfires.[16]

The next day began quietly for Wheaton's men. Abandoning their rifle pits, they moved closer to the V Corps, which, by now, was in the vicinity of Gravely Run and Dabney's Mills. By midafternoon, the crackling of rifle fire became incessant. Wheaton rode out to take stock of the situation. Initially, Warren's men were successful, attacking and driving the enemy before them. This attack soon ran out of steam, however, and the Confederates recovered to launch not one, but two counterattacks, forcing Warren's men to fall back. Maj. Gen. Wheaton formed a defensive line with his division as the first of Warren's stragglers appeared. Soon, more and more arrived. "Squads, companies and regiments went rapidly to the rear despite our greatest efforts to halt them," said Wheaton in his official report.[17]

These "fugitives," for that is what they were and what Wheaton called them, began running through his lines as he was trying to hold his position. In the confusion, Lieutenant Colonel Olcott grasped the regimental colors and rode forward to rally the 121st New York. A skirmish line formed and soon other regiments fell in behind them. With the line now reestablished, Wheaton slowly withdrew three hundred yards to a better position.[18] Darkness put an end to the affair, and the calm weather, which everyone depended on so heavily to ensure success, turned sour. Men huddled together next to smoky fires without the shelter of tents as rain, sleet, and snow pelted them. For Captain Kidder, shivering in a rain soaked uniform, it proved to be an instant reminder of the hardships of a soldier's life.[19]

The affair at Hatcher's Run, or Dabney's Mills, was a minor battle; however, it wasn't fought without cost. Union losses went as high as 1,539, and Confederate losses were estimated at about 1,000.[20] In his official report, Wheaton had nothing but praise for his division and made a special point of mentioning Olcott's bravery while leading the 121st. The division suffered twenty-seven casualties of which three belonged to the 121st. Even these figures were too high for a regiment that had so few active members.[21]

Returning to the Petersburg defenses, the men of the 121st found themselves occupying winter quarters previously used by the Third Division of the VI Corps. These quarters weren't quite as comfortable as the ones they vacated and this naturally caused some grumbling in the ranks. Cold wind swept through the cracks of the poorly constructed shanties. Some filled with smoke due to inadequate chimneys and others didn't have floors.[22] Once again, the men set about scavenging everything that could be of the least amount of use to them. By mid-February and early March, the Union forces laying siege to Petersburg had just about picked the countryside clean. Sutlers supplied what they could, and, some enterprising individuals seeing the need, went into the lumber business.

It was about this time that one-armed Charley Matteson appeared on the Petersburg scene. The last time John S. Kidder saw his brother-in-law was at Elmira where John introduced him to the "ring trade," After leaving Elmira, Charley hired on as a boatman, a two month stint that earned him $80. This was fairly good money for someone in his position.

Once more, Kidder sent for Charley and furnished him with a cash advance to put him back in business. Purchasing small amounts of lumber at City Point, Charley sought out Laurens residents he knew from the army as potential customers. James Blatchely and Henry Gardner of the 2nd New York Heavy Artillery were his first ones. Lumber was in such high demand that both men had their wood planks immediately stolen while in camp and had to reorder more from Charley Matteson. Kidder was pleased that Charley had work and wrote home to Harriet that her brother was doing just fine. "We do what we can for such boys," he wrote.[23] Charley and his covered wagon of lumber (Capt. Daniel Jackson had secured for him a large section of canvas) soon became a familiar sight in the Petersburg defenses.

Those soldiers that were not fixing up their huts were busy filling out paperwork during February and March 1865. Several leaves of absence were approved, for many of the men and a lot of the officers were anxious to return home before the spring. John S. Kidder had already been home so he didn't qualify for any of these furloughs. As senior captain, he reveled in his position as company commander after Olcott and Cronkite went on leave at the same time. When told that General Ranald Slidell Mackenzie was going to hold an inspection, Kidder made every effort to have the regiment in good order. The discipline and efficiency instilled by Upton and carried on by Olcott was still there, and Kidder was determined not to have it falter. "He [Mackenzie] complimented the Regiment very highly and reported it at Division Headquarters as being the best inspection of any Regiment in the Brigade," boasted Kidder.[24]

A week later, the entire division was brought out and reviewed by a cadre of high-ranking officers, and still the 121st continued to elicit compliments. As General Meade, General Horatio Wright of the VI Corps, and Admiral David Porter rode by, one of them was heard to remark, "Is not that regiment one of the regulars?" "No, sir," replied another. "It is the One Hundred Twenty-First New York, General Upton's old regiment." This would have been enough of a compliment had not General Meade added, "Yes sir, there is not a better regiment in the whole army."[25]

Reverend Adams, who heard this exchange and recorded it in his diary, felt that the praise was well-deserved. "It is a well-drilled regiment and has received a good name for its valorous deeds."[26]

Other than inspections and regular drill work, the only other activity that seemed to occupy the 121st's time that winter was the gathering up of Rebel deserters. By March there was a steady parade of these poor souls into the Union lines as General Grant's viselike grip on Petersburg tightened. As the "no man's land" that separated the opposing forces was quite narrow in some places, pickets could clearly see each other and a constant banter between them continued throughout the siege of Petersburg. Time was running out for the Confederacy. One hundred gun salutes shook the lines in celebration of Sherman's victory at Columbia on February 2, and another salute was fired three days later to celebrate the fall of Wilmington. For good measure, another hundred guns were fired for Washington's birthday.[27]

The pickets of the 121st New York devised their own system of escorting deserting Rebels to safety. "They hit upon a plan like this," explained John J. Ingraham. "Our boys took off their overcoats and threw them over their—the Johnnies—shoulders. The Reb pickets would see the blue overcoat, of course, and think they were our men [and] would not fire."[28] Even if they did shoot, the shots were fired well over their heads.

Georgia soldiers seemed the most anxious to desert, perhaps because they were concerned about their homes and worried as to the fate of their loved ones upon hearing the news of Sherman's devastating march. Virginia soldiers remained steadfast defenders of their native soil. Reverend Adams thought it odd that loyalty to one's state was still a concern to the Confederate soldier even at this late stage in the war.[29]

"Five deserters came in our lines yesterday," observed John S. Kidder. "It is not a good time for them to come in at present. Too moonlit at night. We expect another swarm again when the darkness of the night will permit them to come with more safety."[30]

And swarm they did, all across the VI Corps lines. Hardly a night passed without deserters entering the lines. "They come in squads of 5-10-15-20-30 and 40," said John J. Ingraham, noting that they brought their guns and what little equipment they had with them.[31]

It wasn't just the enlisted men who deserted. Chaplain Adams casually remarked that one morning, half of the forty-seven Rebel deserters who filed past his tent were armed and led by their own officers![32]

Other than collecting deserters, the waiting game and sheer boredom during March echoed in the official report of VI Corps Commander, Horatio Wright. "March 1 to 25. Remained in camp near Petersburg, nothing unusual or worthy of record taking place," he wrote, "until the morning of March 25th."[33]

In the early morning hours of March 25, the Confederates, under the command of General John Brown Gordon, made a daring assault on Fort Stedman. Of the forty-one Union fortifications on the Petersburg line, Fort Stedman was the closest, at about 150 yards from Confederate lines. Gordon's axe wielding frontline chopped through or moved a variety of wooden obstructions before them. Some were the fearsome looking "*chevaux-de-frise*," (wooden spiked logs), while others were simply felled trees. Gordon's men made short work of this job and attacked Fort Stedman at 3:00 A.M. It didn't take long for the alarm to spread. Federal units were quickly called into the area to restore the kink in the Union line.

Those soldiers in the 121st New York that didn't wake to the sound of distant musketry, certainly shot bolt upright at the sound of cannons. Many were dressed and in line before the order to assemble was given.[34]

By 8:00 A.M., the division was marching toward the sound of the guns. Even before they arrived, the Confederate attack turned into a retreat. The IX Corps, which General Gordon attacked, recovered and now launched their own attack. "The affair was over before our arrival," noted one VI Corps general.[35] Even so, the Second Brigade managed to form a skirmish line near Fort Fisher.

Major Cronkite, in command of the 121st this day (Olcott was still absent on leave), had a horse shot from beneath him and except for a few bruises, escaped unscathed. Three enlisted men were slightly wounded in the affair and one officer was killed.

First Lt. Horatio Duroe, who Private Clinton Beckwith considered, "the largest man in the regiment," was killed in the attack.[36] Duroe, who rose from the ranks and had only been a first lieutenant since October 29, 1864, was struck in the head by the bullet of a Confederate soldier; he was killed instantly. Sergeant Simeon Smith remained with the body and then helped escort it from the field where they were met by Chaplain Adams. In the prayer service that followed, Reverend Adams eulogized Duroe as, "a worthy officer, a noble man."[37] Later, the officers and men took up a collection to have the body embalmed and sent home.[38]

A few days later, there was more action. Despite a heavy rainstorm on March 30, the men of the 121st New York could hear musketry and cannon fire on their left. General Sheridan's Cavalry, fresh from their devastating tour of the Shenandoah Valley, and Maj. Gen. Warren's V Corps were presently engaging the enemy on White Oak Road and Dinwiddie Courthouse. Sheridan's success at "Five Forks," as it was called, prompted General Grant to issue orders for an assault all along the Petersburg lines for April 2. Four corps, a total of 63,299 men, descended upon the beleaguered city.[39]

This was exactly the moment General Horatio Wright was waiting for. Wright personally inspected the lines before him and also interviewed several of his regimental and brigade commanders. His plan was to concentrate his entire VI Corps, almost seventeen thousand men, into a wedge like design for the attack. "If the Corps does half as well as I expect," he said, "we will have broken through the Rebel line in fifteen minutes from the word 'go.' The Corps will go in solid and I am sure will make the fur fly."[40]

When Lt. Col. Olcott, just returned from leave, was told the position the 121st would occupy in the assault, he, in turn, called his own officers and told them to make the necessary preparations. Frontal attacks, especially against breastworks were nothing new to the men of the 121st. These veterans knew what to expect. Chaplain Adams went about the somber task of collecting letters and personal effects from the men. John S. Kidder noticed that the chaplain had an armful of letters and silently turned to Regimental Quartermaster Theodore Sternberg and pressed a small white envelope into his hands. It was a letter he hoped that Harriet would never receive.

> *Camp of the 121st Regt. N.Y.*
> *March 30, 1865 9* P.M.
> *Dear Wife,*
>
> *I have a few words to write as we have rec'd orders this hour from [Lt.] Col. Olcott that we shall have to storm the enemies works tomorrow morning by daylight. We shall probably move out of our camp about midnight. I think from the plan of battle we shall not have the worst place in the line. I shall leave this letter in the hands of our Quartermaster who will, if I fall, forward it to you. I hope to survive the contest but God only knows. I feel in good spirits. If I should fall do not mourn for me. I leave you and my little girls in much better circumstances than many fathers do. I feel that it is not any more for me to die for my country than it was for poor Brother George or thousands of others. . . . I do not know of anything more to write. Kiss my little Girls for me and bring them up, educate them well. I hope to come home and see them.*
>
> > *Yours truly,*
> > *J. S. Kidder*

That evening Kidder inspected the men he was to command. Noisy items such as canteens, cups, or cumbersome shoulder packs and haversacks, were to be left behind. As in previous assaults, all weapons were to be loaded and capped. He had about half of the 121st New York under his command, a total of 148 men and four lieutenants. Cronkite commanded the other half of the regiment. Under cover of darkness, Captain Kidder advanced his men to the front and assumed the position of the forward picket line. His orders were clear. "We were ordered to hold the line at all hazard."[41]

Kidder didn't have his men in position all that long when a fierce artillery duel began and lit up the night sky. Startled at first, he saw the cannonade extend down the line. "Such a sight I never witnessed before," he said of the fireworks. As shot and shell rang overhead, he and his men hugged the ground and waited. At dawn, a lone signal gun was to fire to commence the attack.[42]

The attack General Wright planned was scheduled to begin at 4:00 A.M. The entire VI Corps was assembled in front of Fort Fisher and Fort Welch in the form of a triangular wedge. At the point of this flying wedge was the division commanded by General George Getty, to the left, General Thomas Seymour's division, to the right, the division of General Frank Wheaton.

Captain Kidder, as part of Wheaton's division, was probably right in his estimation of the placement of the 121st. It didn't really look all that bad. There was only one problem and, unfortunately, he didn't realize it until dawn. While moving forward into position in the darkness, he drew his men out too far and they became separated from the rest of the regiment. When the signal for the attack was given, he was on his own.

At 4:00 A.M. there was silence. The hour to attack had arrived and now the minutes seemed to drag. General Wright hesitated and with good reason. He wanted to wait for the morning fog to dissipate. Thirty minutes later a lone gun boomed from Fort Fisher and the attack was on. A wave of blue coats rose up and traversed the muddy landscape that was void of trees and vegetation. They advanced as quickly and as quietly as possible, however, the Rebel pickets were soon alerted as to their presence.

With the sound of the first rifle shots, Kidder and Cronkite moved their men toward the Rebel trenches. Kidder was, by this time, almost two hundred yards from the trenches and lost sight of Cronkite. Entering the Rebel works with his men, he moved in the direction of two field pieces. The first to seize the guns was Sergeant Redfield Dustin of Company F. Recalling his days as a former artilleryman with a Massachusetts battery, Dustin wasted no time in turning the guns around and firing several shots at the fleeing Confederates.[43]

Inside the Confederate works, the boys from the 121st New York rounded up prisoners by the score. Those Rebels that fired their weapons had no time to reload and were at the mercy of the blue-coated invaders. Some dropped their weapons immediately, others ran, and others had to be flushed out of huts and caves. In about fifteen minutes, it was over. John S. Kidder tried to make a headcount of prisoners and was busy getting receipts for the guns his men captured. It wasn't until later that he was told the attack had been a success and that the lines were broken.

James W. Cronkite's portion of the 121st continued the advance with Kidder not far behind. The lead elements that reached the Boydton Plank Road stopped and twisted the telegraph wires with their bayonets.[44]

Moving toward Hatcher's Run, the entire corps made an abrupt about face and turned toward the city itself, hoping to trap a large number of Confederates. As they neared the outskirts of Petersburg, the exhausted troopers halted.

Wright estimated that his men had been under arms and in a running fight for about eighteen hours. His weary troops simply ran out of steam before they entered the city.[45] Despite this, General Wright was far from being disappointed. The VI Corps assault was a huge success.

Captain Kidder was elated, amazed, and shocked at the day's events. What the 121st New York accomplished was nothing short of a miracle. With only 243 men, the regiment managed to capture two field pieces, complete with cassion and carriages, along with 202 prisoners.[46]

Always fearing the worst in casualties from frontal assaults, Kidder was told that most of the dozen wounds suffered by the regiment were slight. Private Timothy Dasey had a ball from a Rebel's rifle strike him on the forefinger. The nineteen-year-old native of Little Falls managed to fight in many battles escaping harm until this day. The wound proved serious enough to warrant his being discharged and sent home.[47] Only one casualty was fatal and it was, indeed, horrific. Private James Hendrix of Company A was instantly killed when a shell from a Rebel's canon tore him in half.[48]

The following day, April 3, at 4:30 A.M., the skirmish line that the 121st was a part of, moved forward and entered the city of Petersburg. The siege that lasted for over ten months was finally over. Brigade Commander General Joseph Hamblin, of the 121st New York, proclaimed that his units were, as he stated later, the "first organized force in the city."[49] As the brigade advanced into the city, they gathered up prisoners. The 121st made a special effort to raise the stars and stripes over the first public building they came upon. With several other regiments also vying for this singular honor, this would become the subject of many a conversation at 121st reunions after the war.[50]

Their stay in Petersburg was brief. After collecting prisoners and stuffing their pockets full of worthless Confederate money for souvenirs, the VI Corps moved out of the city. With the fall of Petersburg there also came the fall of Richmond. General Lee marched his hungry legions westward in the hopes of reaching vital railroad junctions that could take him south to join the forces of Confederate General, Joseph Johnston. But as Lee moved, so did General Grant. On April 4, a disappointed Lee arrived at Amelia Courthouse only to find that there were no provisions for his starving army. He had no choice but to let his men forage the countryside for food. It was a costly delay. The life of the Confederacy was no longer measured in terms of years and months, but in days and hours. The gap between Lee and Grant was closing.

Two days later, Lee was at Rice's Station with Longstreet's Corps where he waited for the rest of his army to join him. Times had indeed changed. They were no longer the quick marching greys that had bewildered a succession of Union army commanders. The Army of Northern Virginia was weak and tired, stretching out along a road from Rice's Station to Amelia Springs. They were constantly harassed by Sheridan's Cavalry and only steps ahead of the infantry.

On April 6, the 121st and the VI Corps were on the road at 6:00 A.M. Traversing swamps, ravines, through thickets, and fording small streams, the men pressed on never complaining. All seemed anxious to catch the fleeing Confederates. "I never saw troops pass on more eagerly or show greater desire to meet the enemy," said Division Commander, Gen. Frank Wheaton, of this spirited pursuit.[51]

By 10:00 A.M., the 121st arrived at the Smithy House, near Jetersville, on the Richmond-Danville railroad line. The increasing sound of musketry alerted all units that the Confederates were before them. Pushing ahead, the 121st emerged from the rough countryside to see the ground before them wide open. The first elements of the VI Corps could plainly see the Confederates partially entrenched a short distance away. A division had already been deployed on the right side of the Rice Station Road and Frank Wheaton was busy placing his division on the left side. On the extreme left of Wheaton's line was General Hamblin's brigade with the 121st New York.

The Confederates in the distance were the rear guard General Lee had been waiting for. It was Ewell's Corps plus a wagon train that belonged to Confederate General Richard Anderson. Attacks on Anderson's wagon train were so severe that morning that the entire corps halted to enable the wagons to move ahead. By the time Anderson was ready to move, it was discovered that Sheridan's Cavalry blocked the way. Meanwhile, Confederate General Ewell saw Union General Wright's entire VI Corps closing in fast. Ewell and Anderson were trapped, caught in a nutcracker vise of Wright on one side and Sheridan's Cavalry on the other.

As the Confederates made preparations to deal with this threat, Wright saw to the placement of his divisions. Since the Confederates had no field pieces, they opened up a one-sided artillery barrage.

At 5:00 P.M., Wright ordered his divisions forward toward Sayler's Creek. Descending from an open field, it didn't take the 121st long to discover that Sayler's Creek wasn't a creek at all. The section they crossed was a swamp that varied in width from forty to one hundred yards. Some men were able to slosh through water that was knee deep. Others were less fortunate, carrying rifles and cartridge belts above their heads in water that was shoulder deep.

When the men reached the other side of the creek, there was no time to arrange themselves in brigades one behind the other. The order to advance was given immediately. Ascending a steep hill, they came under the constant rifle fire of the Confederates. All across the Rebel line, Ewell's men held, and even attempted to counterattack, but their line buckled under the sheer weight of the blue wave before them. As the Union forces closed in, Lt. Col. Olcott saw the ground before him wide open and the enemy to his right. Seizing this opportunity to flank the Rebels, he immediately shifted the 121st toward the right and drove into the Confederate flank. The enemy was driven from their position and after a little confusion, surrendered en masse. General Hamblin, in his report of the battle, credited much of the success the brigade enjoyed that day to Olcott's skillful maneuver. "The success of the 6th instant is largely due to the prompt and splendid manner in which he maneuvered his regiment, charging under heavy fire and driving the enemy from our right flank."[52]

On the other side of the field, Sheridan's Cavalry met with similar success. By the end of the day roughly one third of Genearl Lee's army had been captured. An elated Captain Kidder recalled the moment.

> We started from camp about Monday noon, marched 14 miles and started again about 4 in the morning marching as far as we could in each day. Came up to the Rebs in the afternoon of the 6th at Sayler's Creek. Here we had a hard fight but we succeeded in driving them. . . . We captured Genl. Custis Lee and two stands of colors and over 1000 prisoners. This the 121st did. The men fought well, never done better.[53]

It was more like five hundred prisoners, but one can well appreciate how excited John S. Kidder must have been at this incredible victory. Custis Lee was indeed captured, and so were the colors. Private Harrison Hawthorne grabbed the son of the Confederate Commander-in-Chief and immediately demanded his sword. "I have not so much as a jackknife," replied Curtis Lee. Nonetheless, Hawthorne personally escorted Lee to General Wheaton's Headquarters.[54]

In the savage fight to capture flags, prizes equal to that of capturing generals, two men were killed outright before Private Warren Dockum was able to take the silk banner belonging to the 8th Savannah Guards. The flag was inscribed, To the Defenders of Our Altars and Our Hearts, Presented by the Ladies of Savannah Ga. to the Eighth Savannah Guards. Private Benjamin Gifford's prize was not as elegant and to this day it is not known whose flag it was that he captured. It was a wonderful feat, coming from a man who deserted from the 121st after General Burnside's Mud March, and returned to the regiment under the protection of Presidential Amnesty.[55]

Hawthorne, Dockum, and Gifford were all awarded the Medal of Honor for their services that day.

The Battle of Sayler's Creek, or Little Sayler's Creek, as the old-time veterans called it, was the last battle fought by the 121st and the VI Corps in the Civil War. Senior Captain Kidder was justifiably proud of the moment. The fact that the 121st assisted in vanquishing Ewell's Corps elated him. Ever since they crossed the Rapidan in May 1864, it was Ewell's men that the 121st New York faced. They locked horns with them in the Wilderness, punched through the Mule Shoe in the daring charge of May 10, and struck them at the Bloody Angle at Spotsylvania. It was always Confederate General Ewell's men. But the ultimate satisfaction for the 121st came in the total defeat of that portion of Ewell's Corps commanded by General Joseph B. Kershaw. It was Kershaw who soundly thrashed the 121st in their first battle at Salem Church two years earlier.

This rush to glory did not come without a price. The twenty-two men reported as killed and wounded represented one-fifth of the complement of the regiment that was present at Sayler's Creek.[56] Among the dead were two officers. John T. "Tracy" Morton was wearing his second lieutenant shoulder straps for less than a month when he was mortally wounded.[57] Capt. Ten Eyck Howland, who was previously wounded at Cedar Creek, had a musket ball crash into his chest, killing him before he staggered into the arms of his men. "No brave or gallant officer ever carried a sword," said Lt. Col. Olcott of the man who rose from private to captain.[58]

Sadly, one last casualty was unnecessary. That evening, as the men sat around the campfires in their underwear attempting to dry their wet trousers from fording Sayler's Creek, the order to fall in was given. Major Cronkite, acting on behalf of Olcott, who was absent, quickly mounted his horse and rode past the scattered campfires to rally the men. Suddenly, a shot rang out and Cronkite screamed with pain as he fell from his horse. While fumbling through stacked weapons, a recruit of the 95th Pennsylvania accidentally discharged his weapon. A horrified John S. Kidder

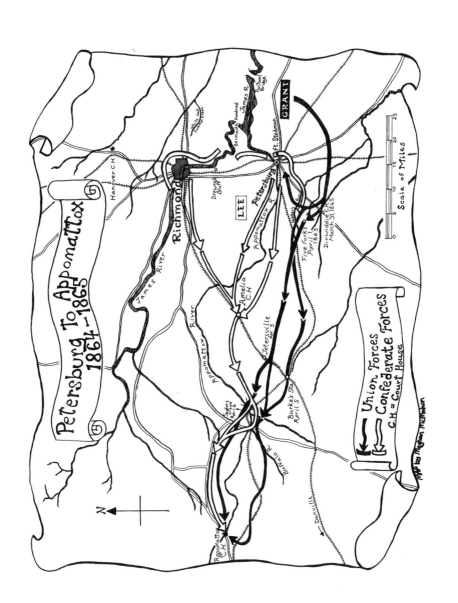

Petersburg To Appomattox
1864-1865

Union Forces
Confederate Forces
C.H. = Court House

rushed to the side of his old friend. The wound was serious but not fatal. The ball shattered the bone above Cronkite's left knee, leaving the surgeons little choice but to amputate. James W. Cronkite became the last casualty of the 121st New York in the Civil War.[59]

With the victory at Sayler's Creek came an avalanche of brevet, or temporary, promotions. Cronkite, Kidder, Jackson, VanScoy, Hassett and Lowe were all officially recognized for their bravery in several reports for the Petersburg breakthrough at Sayler's Creek. All of them advanced in rank.[60]

The coveted rank of major, which Kidder so earnestly sought and yearned for, was now due him through deeds of valor and not because of seniority. The only oversight was that of Olcott. Constantly recognized for his bravery and leadership abilities by General Wheaton and General Hamblin, from the fall of Petersburg to Sayler's Creek, Lt. Col. Olcott was denied a brevet promotion. He was never court-martialed for his Christmas drinking escapade, but he never received a brevet promotion in rank either.

For the next two days, the VI Corps marched hard in an effort to catch Lee's shattered army. By April 9, they were within four miles of Appomattox Court House when they were ordered to halt as rumors of General Lee's surrender began to circulate. About 4:00 P.M., Kidder received word from General Hamblin that Lee had surrendered.[61]

The news sent shock waves throughout the area. "We were perfectly wild with joy, such cheering you never heard," said Kidder of the moment. "The men threw up their hats, drums beat and cannons roared for about one hour. I never saw such a sight before." It wasn't until the next day that he was able to write his feelings down in a short letter to Harriet. "Victory is ours. Gen. Lee surrendered unconditionally with his whole Army of Northern Virginia yesterday. Thank God I have come through safe and sound."[62]

Harriet learned of the surrender long before she received her husband's letter. The church bells rang and all business in Laurens was suspended as a wild celebration got underway. William C. Strong recalled that, "All political animosities at once were forgotten; the celebration commenced by throwing a prominent man over the hotel bar, and after he had stood, another man was put over. This continued until about every one was gloriously drunk, Republicans, Democrats, Saints and Sinners." A makeshift parade was assembled, marched around the town and became so loud that Strong and the local schoolteacher, Mary Dietz, could not make their speeches. The rowdiness continued well into the evening and was highlighted by the antics of blacksmith, Morris Mead, whose son,

Damon, was in the 2nd New York Heavy Artillery. Morris Mead rode his horse into Eastons Hotel, where the frightened animal proceeded to kick out the panels of most of the doors in the hotel![63]

Meanwhile, back in Virginia, the VI Corps was unable to attend the formal surrender of the Army of Northern Virginia. Many of them claimed that their stunning victory at Sayler's Creek helped draw the war to a conclusion, and witnessing the surrender was an honor that was due them. In actual fact, the war was over, but only in Virginia. Further to the south there was still an army in the field that hadn't surrendered. The VI Corps was, once more, under marching orders to proceed south and intercept the army commanded by Gen. Joseph Johnston in North Carolina.

From Appomattox, the men retraced their steps, marching forty miles to Burkesville. When they arrived, the men of the 121st New York found their promised replacements waiting for them. They were a mixed lot that sharply contrasted with the seasoned veterans of Herkimer and Otsego Counties. Nineteen of them arrived under arrest for a variety of offenses, mostly desertion. One, it was discovered, had deserted the 44th New York and joined the 121st so he could collect another bounty. He was promptly returned to the 44th New York under arrest. Still others didn't quite make it to Burkesville, deserting as quickly as opportunities presented themselves, especially after hearing of the surrender of General Lee. Between April 9 and the end of May, more than fifty recruits simply walked away.[64]

There was another memory that was associated with Burkesville. It was here that the men heard the news of President Lincoln's assassination. The news stunned a volunteer soldier who answered the sixteenth president's call to help preserve the Union. Private John J. Ingraham called it, "The hardest blow that we've experienced yet. It is a horrible affair. The whole Army mourns his loss and asks for revenge."[65]

As the confusing details of the assassination became known, Kidder, unlike Ingraham, desired justice and not revenge. "We are glad to hear that Seward is recovering," he said of the botched attempt on the life of the Secretary of State that same evening. "I hope the villain who killed Lincoln will be caught."[66] A week later he got his wish. John Wilkes Booth was surrounded and killed in a tobacco barn in Maryland.

On April 19, the day of Lincoln's funeral, Lt. Col. Olcott approached Chaplain Adams and asked if some sort of service might be held in honor of the late President. "I tried to meet the occasion," said Adams. "The Brigade band discourses its dirges and plaintive airs. There has been a deep feeling in the army respecting the assassination."[67]

Of the somber affair, John S. Kidder added his own thoughts. "It appears more like Sunday at home than any day I have ever witnessed in the Army. All business is suspended throughout the army on account of the funeral of our beloved President."[68]

Remaining in camp at Burkesville for several days, the 121st New York saw the last of its recruits officially mustered into service. Olcott was sworn in as colonel and all that prevented Kidder from moving from major to lieutenant colonel was paperwork. Cronkite wrote a letter of resignation declining the offer so Kidder could move into the rank.

Meanwhile, there was other paperwork that Kidder gave a higher priority to. In a short while, he would return home to face the parents and loved ones of boys who had signed on with him in Company I. The most difficult of these meetings would, no doubt, be with those family members who had lost a son under his command. He could sympathize with those who had sons killed in battle, having lost his own brother.

What he found difficult to accept were those who had signed on in 1862, and then deserted. Some of these men were listed as being "absent without leave," and others simply as deserters. Kidder had to be absolutely sure that these men had, in fact, deserted. Once more he relied on his wife to make discreet inquiries around and about Laurens regarding the whereabouts of missing men from Company I. The wanderings of Charlie Dean worried Kidder, as did the vanishing act performed by wagoneer, Edward Pattengill.

Dean had been absent from the regiment since 1862. He was, in effect, a huge disappointment to Kidder. He wanted to groom Dean for more important duties within Company I, and then move him up the advancement ladder in much the same way Cronkite had. "What has Charlie Dean gone to Canada for?" asked Kidder while at Elmira. "Has he any relatives there?"[69]

It was a question that Harriet could not answer. Now, with the war all but over, he implored her to make the proper inquiries. "Tell Delos Dean that Charles is reported here as a deserter. I hope he will report to some Provost Marshall and return under the President's Proclamation. This is my advice to Charles and tell Delos to write him on the subject. I should think that every deserter would return with such a chance."[70]

Kidder didn't have the slightest clue as to where Pattengill was. He vanished on the eve of Burnside's Mud March, and hadn't been seen since.

Even without these two, there were more and more replacements coming into the 121st. While at Burkesville, Kidder received word that some were waiting for the unit at City Point. So while the 121st New York made preparations to march to Danville, with "12 days rations, 4 in haversacks and 8 in the wagons," John S. Kidder received permission to make the trip to City Point and collect these other men.[71]

There were several advantages to making this journey. First, there was the opportunity to visit James W. Cronkite in the hospital and have the necessary papers signed and sent to the Governor of New York for the promotion. Second, he could travel through Petersburg, an opportunity he did not have when the VI Corps scored their breakthrough a few weeks earlier. He had a few addresses and found friends waiting for him who were former prisoners from Elmira . "Two of them were merchants, one a lawyer, and a member of the Legislature of Virginia. . . . They were of the first class men of Petersburg and appeared to be as glad to see me as though I were one of their officers. I met a brother of one who was a Lieutenant of Lee's Army. They all treated me with kindness and urged me to call and make them a longer visit."[72]

Arriving at City Point, Kidder found Cronkite in good spirits. He "is gaining finely," he observed, noting that his old friend might be able to go home in four to six weeks.[73] It was a difficult visit for both of them. The two had been through several battles and were wounded together at Spotsylvania. Through a careless accident, Cronkite was now unable to perform the duties of a lieutenant colonel, and graciously stepped aside for Kidder. It was a gesture that John S. Kidder never forgot.

Before collecting his recruits, Kidder made one last stop in Petersburg. He promised Verona that he would check in on her husband, Charley Matteson. As expected, the one-armed Matteson was doing a brisk business. He was now constructing wooden boxes for the soldiers in City Point. These were in great demand as soldiers, including Kidder, began sending a variety of items back home now that the war had ended. Kidder purchased one right away and packed his overcoat and a recently purchased bedspread in it. He hoped that the bedspread would be a pleasant surprise for his wife, being very careful to mention that it was not stolen! "The present is a splendid white counterpiece or bedspread, much nicer than your best one. . . . One of my men bought [it] off a Negro, his master ran away and the Negro sold the things out of the house then ran away also."[74]

Kidder left City Point and together with his two hundred recruits, headed toward the railway at Burkesville only to be delayed. As the tracks were different widths, they had to wait until another train could be brought up for them. While they waited, they heard that General Joseph Johnston's forces had surrendered and the war was officially over. This, of course, was a great relief to all. Due to abundant rumors, though, Kidder harbored the theory that guerilla bands would still be about, harassing Union troops. This wasn't a pleasant prospect, considering his green recruits had so little training; they could hardly be counted upon to fend for themselves. Some of the reports about the guerilla activity he dismissed, but he couldn't afford to take unnecessary chances.

> *I have plenty of company and we are all armed so that if we should have to march [and not take the train] we shall be safe from all guerilla bands. In fact, I have not heard of any disturbance from any armed men since Lee surrendered. I think there are no guerilla bands in this section of Virginia. The paroled prisoners behave well. All appear to be glad that the war is over.*[75]

After bringing the recruits to Burkesville, Kidder had to turn them around and march toward Petersburg. Here, they were to guard the railroad lines while the rest of the army converged on Washington for the Grand Review. This passing of the armies in one immense parade would be the last official act of the volunteer army before its disbandment. The Army of the Potomac would be present, as well as Sherman's rugged-looking legions that had marched to the sea. All would be there except the VI Corps. Some felt slighted by this oversight, while others tried their best to be a little more optimistic. "The VI Corps was among the first in the field and the last to go out," said Private John J. Ingraham, "and if there is any hard fighting to be done they are always in front, and in case of a retreat we always cover the rear."[76]

John S. Kidder didn't care one way or the other. He was just proud of the fact that he was a part of the VI Corps. "I want you to wear a plain red cross on your hat," he reminded Harriet. "Something like this . . . ,"[77] and in the margin of one of his last letters home, outlined the corps patch of the VI Corps.

With the end of hostilities, and no apparent guerilla activity, Captain Kidder, and many of the other officers and men, took every opportunity to travel and explore the Virginia countryside. After all, any guard duty to be performed could be done by the new recruits. In the company of Capt. Lansing B. Paine and Sedate Foote, he took a leisurely ride out to the Sayler's Creek battlefield for the purpose of locating the graves of their fallen comrades. "I am glad that I went," wrote Kidder, "as some of the graves had only paper with names written. I put boards to all of them."[78]

The three were about to leave when several mounted men approached them. "I thought it was someone from Philadelphia looking for his brother . . . ," remarked Kidder.[79]

Whatever made him think that someone from Philadelphia would be looking over the Sayler's Creek battlefield for his brother is a complete mystery, but the thought probably escaped him when he noticed that the men on horseback were dressed in *grey* and not *blue*. The three were at first startled, but not alarmed, at the sight of these Confederates. They, too, were veterans of Sayler's Creek and were looking for cemetery markers. "We rode over the field and through the wood together and talked over the fight as friendly as *brothers*. I was not afraid of them. In fact, I could not induce them to take some guns that were on the field as they said some evil-minded person might report them with arms in their hands," said Kidder.[80]

Meeting these men was a pleasant diversion, and helped instill in John S. Kidder the fact that the war was over. It was only after he started to leave the field that he chanced upon a ravine and all the horrors of the war came back. "I found a ditch which was so full of dead Rebels that they had thrown dirt over them to bury them but the rain had washed some of them out and it was a shocking sight to behold—heads, arms and legs bleaching in the sun."[81] It was a ghastly scene that sickened him. When he returned to camp, he alerted his superiors as to what he had witnessed. It wasn't until June 15, eleven weeks after the battle, that Brevet Colonel S. R. Clark was able to bring a burial detail to the field. Here they found, just as Kidder described, seventeen bodies. The bodies were reburied.[82]

By mid-May, the 121st moved steadily from Burkesville, through Wellsville, then Petersburg, and eventually arrived in Manchester on May 20. With the regiment at rest, John S. Kidder, this time with Chaplain Adams, took in the sights. The two visited the remains of Fort Darling on the James River. The fort, located on a bluff above the river, was an obstacle to the Union advance during the Peninsular Campaign of 1862, and proved to be a thorn in General Butler's side during the 1864 campaign around Richmond. "It was a most formidable work," declared Chaplain Adams. "All the navies in the world could not take it from the water side."[83]

John S. Kidder was not as easily impressed. It was a strong fort, he admitted, but it lacked firepower. "There was not a rifled gun in it," he said after counting all fifteen guns, all of which were smoothbores.[84]

When he and Adams returned to the regiment, they discovered that Capt. Daniel Jackson had resigned his commission and started for home instead of waiting to be mustered out with the entire regiment. Kidder could hardly blame him, for there was nothing to hold him to the regiment [he wasn't waiting for a promotion], and besides, it was getting boring. For Kidder, his wait was over the next day. At noon, on May 22, 1865, John S. Kidder was mustered in as lieutenant colonel of the 121st New York Volunteers.[85] Other appointments and promotions were made that day, and an overall festive mood prevailed throughout the regiment. Kidder celebrated in grand style by purchasing a new horse, complete with saddle, at the cost of $125, and attending the theater in Richmond in the company of Col. James Hubbard of the 2nd Connecticut.[86]

Several days later, the VI Corps was reviewed by General Henry Halleck. It was Lieutenant Colonel Kidder's first official duty; he wanted to make a good impression on former President Lincoln's Chief of Staff. Kidder was nervous but he needn't have been. "We had drilled the new men only ten days but I was happily disappointed as they did much better than I thought they could as they marched like old troops. Colonel Olcott is entitled to the credit for it was by his energy and perseverance that [he] accomplished the results and every man had a knapsack and was fully equipped."[87]

Again on the march, the VI Corps made their way north, past battlefields whose names were recalled in blood, past Fredericksburg, where they received their first baptism in battle, to the carnage associated with the Wilderness and Spotsylvania.

At Hall's Hill, Virginia, near Georgetown, the 121st was mustered out of the United States service. Only those last minute replacements, the single-year recruits, stayed in the service. These men were transferred to the 65th New York. Of the over nine hundred officers and men who left Camp Schuyler in August 1862, only three hundred twenty returned. There were others, many of whom were still in hospitals, who would be discharged at a later date. As he had done after every battle, Lt. Col. Kidder went down the line and made a headcount, this one, his last. He and Delavan Bates brought ninety-three men in as Company I. Less than twenty were mustered out at Hall's Hill.

True to his word, Kidder remained behind with his men. He didn't resign his commission and go home the way some of the other officers did when they found Upton's methods of discipline not to their liking. He also didn't opt for the road to quick advancement in the United States Colored Troops the way some others had. In the end, of the original ten company Captains, he was the only one that remained. All the others either quit, resigned due to illness, or were killed.

In one of her last letters from home, Harriet wrote to her husband to tell him that the box with the bedspread arrived safely, but she was a little curious as to the walking stick that was tucked inside the folds of his overcoat. "You wonder what I want of that cane," he replied. "It will be good for me when I am old and infirm. I hope to live to talk to my great-grandchildren of the wars of this rebellion."[88]

On June 8, the VI Corps assembled in Washington for their Grand Review. They passed in review before a grandstand of dignitaries that included President Andrew Johnson, Secretary of War Edwin Stanton, and a cadre of high-ranking generals.

The parade was anticlimatic. The crowds were there to cheer and wave, but the veterans were barely excited. The war had been over for two months. President Lincoln had been assassinated, buried, and the conspirators presently on trial. Parading under the sweltering summer sun, the soldiers just wanted to go home. "I never heard an enlisted man enthuse over the memory of that review," recalled Lt. Isaac O. Best.[89]

Three weeks later, the 121st New York Volunteers boarded a train and headed north. Arriving in New York City on July 1, the regiment made a triumphant march down Broadway. The next day they arrived at the state capitol where they expected to receive their final pay and their mustering out of state service. They were in for a surprise.

Ever since General Robert E. Lee's surrender, rumors persisted in both Herkimer and Otsego Counties that the 121st New York would have to fulfill its three-year term of enlistment. This meant that the men could not officially be mustered out until August 1865. Soldiers wasted no time in writing letters to local newspapers, Albany politicians, and congressmen, in hopes of dispelling these rumors. The only troops that had an obligation to stay, they said, were the one-year men, and they were already transferred out of the regiment.

As Independence Day neared and with the issue still not resolved, a committee assembled in Little Falls for the purpose of welcoming back the boys in blue in grand style. H. P. Alexander and H. M. Burch went to Albany to ask if the regiment might be brought back to Little Falls on July 4. "They were handsomely refused," reported the committee treasurer. The two were not discouraged. "They made a flank movement in the War Office at Washington and were successful."[90]

With permission granted, the only thing that stood in their way was the necessary funds to bring the regiment home. The entire celebration would cost $792.24; the vast majority of the money being used to purchase round trip tickets for the soldiers. The money was quickly procured with the largest single donation of $269.29 coming from Little Falls native, Henry Galpin, who recently set himself up in the Bucklin Block selling "Stoves and Tinware."[91]

While the Little Falls Reception Committee prepared to roll out the red carpet for their own Grand Review, the 121st sat in Albany doing nothing, only because there was absolutely nothing to do. All routines duties were suspended. There were no more drills, assemblies or inspections. In fact, Col. Olcott put himself up in the comfort of a hotel rather than tenting with the regiment.

This idyllic boredom was shattered when an officer in command of the Albany district arrived at the camp of the 121st on Troy Road. The officer, noting the relaxed atmosphere, ordered the commanding officer of the 121st New York to resume the standard military routines of drills and parades. On the receiving end of this order was Lt. Col. John S. Kidder. He may have been a little amused at this order. The war was over, they had done their duty and the regiment was slated to be discharged at any moment. Kidder accepted the "order" and, not wishing to go over the head of his own commanding officer, sent word of the incident to Olcott.

He, too, saw that this was a ludicrous order and told John S. Kidder to ignore it. Again, the officer arrived and saw that nothing had changed. With no men in parade formation, he ordered that *all* the men be reported as absent without leave. It wasn't funny anymore. "There are no officers or men in this regiment absent without leave," growled Kidder. With this, the officer left and soon another arrived. A little more brazen than the first, this one ordered that the captured Rebel flags be turned over to the adjutant general of the state of New York. Now it had gone too far! Not only did Lt. Col. Kidder refuse to obey this order, but he refused to recognize the authority of the adjutant general. The battle flags were trophies earned by the men of the 121st New York and the property of the United States. Furthermore, said Kidder, they were loaned to the regiment by the Secretary of War and no one was taking them except the Secretary of War, the President, or General Ulysses S. Grant. When Kidder finished, the officer left. Kidder knew he hadn't seen the last of him and decided to make a few preparations of his own. With a portion of the regiment called out and armed with fixed bayonets in a skirmish line, Kidder stood by, sword in hand, ready to meet the officer once again. The officer arrived at the head of a company of men. "There are the Rebel flags," roared Lt. Col. Kidder, "and here are the soldiers who captured them. If you must have them you can give your men the command to take them away from their captors, and if they cannot defend them I will call out the entire regiment." The officer and his company of men beat a hasty retreat and were no longer any trouble to the 121st while they were in Albany.[92]

Meanwhile, back in Little Falls, the Reception Committee was seeing to last minute details. When Independence Day arrived, people were drawn to the city as early as 8:00 A.M. Within two hours, the population swelled to fifteen thousand; wagons and carriages arrived from all parts of the county, lining the parade route and filling the park to capacity.

At 10:45 A.M., the train arrived and slowly lurched to a halt. The crowd cheered and a brass band struck up a patriotic air as remnants of Upton's Regulars emerged from the rail cars. Officially welcomed by the Reception Committee with a short speech, Colonel Olcott brought the regiment into parade formation. The men closed ranks, snapped to attention and with the order, "Forward, March!" began their last official duty as volunteer soldiers in the service of their country. "Upton's Regulars" were home at last.

There were no second measures taken with this two division parade honoring the men of the 121st New York. There were three brass bands, two volunteer fire departments, a contingent of the Little Falls National Guard, complete with horse drawn cannon and caissons, plus fifteen aged veterans of the War of 1812. They marched triumphantly through the streets of Little Falls, passing under a series of flowered arches. One was inscribed, Welcome Home to Our Brave Boys, and another said, Welcome Brave 121st That's Never Known Defeat.[93] The captured Rebel flags, which caused so much controversy in Albany, drew cheers and applause from the crowd. The Savannah Guards banner, carried by Private Warren Dockum, was a particular favorite. Others gazed at the regimental flag of the 121st New York Volunteers. Riddled by shot and shell, it stood in mute testimony, a grim reminder of what the men had seen and done in three years of war.

The parade route ended at the park, and after a few more speeches, Col. Egbert Olcott was brought forward. Never one for making speeches of any kind, Olcott slowly made his way forward.

> I, for the officers and men of the 121st, earnestly thank you for this kind of reception and honest praise. Nothing is more pleasant than appreciation, nothing more delightful to a returned soldier than to meet warm hearts and open hands. Once again, I, for all, tender you our gratitude and grateful acknowledgement.[94]

After a thunderous applause, the politicians shook hands and the soldiers mingled with the crowd seeking out friends and loved ones. There was enough food for everyone that day, all donated by the grateful citizens of Little Falls. For men that had existed on a diet of beans, salt pork, hard tack, and coffee, it was truly a banquet fit for kings. *The Little Falls Journal and Courier* proudly reported that there were

> at least two large wash tubs full of pickles, more than two bushels of cold boiled eggs, quarters of mutton, boiled hams, fifty cold chickens, cold tongue, fifty lbs. of sugar, one hundred and fifty loaves of cake, a cart load of cookies, more than two hundred pies, many pounds of butter, sixty gallons of fresh milk, more than two hogsheads full of biscuits and bread and large quantities of scores of other articles, of which we had no time to take particular note.[95]

The entire community and surrounding countryside had come forward to say thank you to the boys in blue for what they had done for their country.

NINE

Laurens, the Port Warden and Retirement

1865-1905

When Lt. Col. Kidder finally returned to Laurens in the late summer of 1865, he noticed no new businesses and several that were experiencing financial difficulties. Although the Civil War served as a boon to the northern economy, small rural villages like Laurens saw little in the form of businesslike expansion. One of the businesses that certainly needed help was the Kidder and Fisher Carriage Shop.

From a financial standpoint, the Kidder money had always been divided into two accounts, one for the house and one for the shop. The household account, controlled by Harriet, appeared to be in good order. Her three year money balancing act paid the mortgage. She still rented out the spare room, and was able to pay a variety of store accounts on a monthly basis.[1]

The carriage shop was another matter. Now that John S. Kidder and Elisha Fisher were back in Laurens, the accounts that had been "put on hold" were suddenly active again. Not only were they faced with their creditors, but there were also very few orders for new wagons. The two had to either breathe new life into the shop or make other arrangements. For the next ten years, they worked hard to keep the shop in operation and their efforts did not go unnoticed. In the summer of 1878, the *Oneonta Herald* complimented them on their success. "We are glad to see them prosper."[2]

A year later, the business still appeared to be moving ahead. In the winter of 1878-79, Kidder and Fisher built and sold eight cutters, and small

189

one or two person sleighs; the *Herald* boasted were the finest in the area.[3] Unfortunately, this proved to be the last hurrah for the carriage shop.

Toward the end of January, in 1879, Leroy Tucker went bankrupt and a week later, on the last day of the month, the *Herald* sadly announced the end of the carriage shop.

> *Another failure to be added to our once prosperous village, Messrs. Kidder and Fisher have been compelled to make an assignment. William Widger assigned, liabilities about $5,000, assets nearly enough to pay. Messrs. Kidder and Fisher strove hard to weather the storm but the other failures destroyed the trust of the people and consequently they were driven to the wall.*[4]

Kidder and Fisher wanted to avoid the indignity of a public auction. Both decided to call it quits before the bank got involved. While they made arrangements with William Widger to transfer assets and material, the bank auctioned off the contents of Leroy Tucker's shop on the front steps of his former establishment.

In the face of this personal crisis, John S. Kidder managed quite well. Widger assumed the debts and liabilities of the business and in return, Kidder had the use of the tools, supplies, and whatever inventory was available. Widger was free to use his own name on the shop (which he did) and in return, rented the buildings from Kidder for $30 per month. This was beneficial to Widger as he had just purchased a home in Laurens, and by renting from Kidder he avoided an additional mortgage.

As the paperwork was being drawn up for the dissolution of the carriage business, Kidder began to set his sights on a new career. At forty-nine, he was far from retirement and well aware of the fact that he had a growing family to support. Unlike Fisher, who opened a shop of his own in Laurens in December 1879, John S. Kidder chose not to look back.

In May 1879, he made the first of several trips to New York City in search of employment. He made a series of inquiries regarding an upcoming position as Port Warden.[5] Why he aspired to this position is yet another family mystery. Family members speculated well into the next century as to his intentions. One granddaughter said that he liked things "military" after the war, that is, everything in good order. Others saw him in the same light as his father before him, a victim of the Industrial Revolution, forced to abandon an outmoded way of making a living to accept something more modern. Whatever his motive may have been, there was certainly more money to be made as a Port Warden than as a carriagemaker.

Throughout the spring and summer of 1879, Kidder set about collecting a portfolio of endorsements that he needed to convince the powers in Albany that he was the right man for the job. As one of the founders of the Republican Party in Otsego County, he had plenty of political connections. Congressman David Wilbur of Milford, an old acquaintance, was just one of twenty-two members of Congress who sent letters, along with twenty-one members of the New York State Senate and scores of Otsego County officials. From far away Fortress Monroe, Virginia, came a letter that John S. Kidder prized above all others.[6]

> Fort Monroe, Va
> Dec. 3rd, 1878
> To the Hon. A. B. Cornell
> Dear Sir:
>   The friends of Col[onel] John S. Kidder are presenting his claims for the appointment as one of the Harbor Masters in the Port of New York. During the war I knew him as a faithful efficient and most gallant officer. At Salem Heights, Chancellorsville, Rappahannock Station, the Wilderness, and Spotsylvania C. H. his conduct was specially commendable. I will say no more except to add that no fitter tribute could be paid to the surviving officers and men of the 121st New York than be rewarding their commander at Appomattox with the gift of a public office.
>   I have the honor to be Very Truly Yours
>   E. Upton
>   P.S. I might add that Col. Kidder has the evidence of his service in preserving the Union. At Spotsylvania C.H. on the 12th of May while in command of his Regiment he received a severe wound in the head.[7]

On April 22, 1880, after months of waiting, John S. Kidder was appointed Port Warden for a term of three years. The appointment didn't arrive without controversy. There was some discussion in executive session in Albany whether the candidates had the qualifications needed for the position. One Senator questioned whether these appointees, "know anything about the duties of a Harbor Master or a Port Warden."[8] The majority of the Senators felt that these candidates were just as good as any of the others who had been nominated to the position in the past. Only one Senator outwardly voiced his disapproval, trying valiantly to save the position for a friend. He failed, and as the *New York Times* said, "was obliged to accept the Democratic doctrine that 'to the victors belong the spoils.'"[9]

The news of the appointment created a great deal of excitement in the village of Laurens as well as within the Kidder household. The *Oneonta Herald* lauded the appointment while at the same time poked fun at the change in lifestyle that Kidder would, no doubt, experience. "We are glad of his good fortune and he left behind him many friends who wish him the best possible success in his new undertaking. It will be quite a change from the society of home to that of dock hands and wharf rats."[10]

The situation was not that humorous in the Kidder home. When he received the appointment, John S. Kidder expected to pack up bag and baggage and relocate to New York City. He saw nothing tying him to Laurens. Harriet's father, Joshua, whom they had cared for since they were married, died three years earlier. The children were also growing up. Clara, his "Little Diamond," was no longer little but a young lady of nineteen, and second daughter, Mary, was now fifteen. Rounding out the family was a nine-year-old son, George, named after his late uncle.[11]

Despite the fact that the position of Port Warden would be a windfall for the family financially, Harriet steadfastly refused to move to the big city. Laurens was her home. It was where her friends were and where her family was. She was determined to stay and stay she did. Husband and wife worked out a compromise. Both became commuters. They traveled to see each other on weekends, alternating between New York City and Laurens. It was an arrangement they kept up for twenty years until his retirement in 1901.

Leaving Laurens in the summer of 1880, John S. Kidder set himself up in a New York brownstone apartment and went to work. From all reports, he had no problem adjusting to city life or his new position. As one of nine Port Wardens, his primary function was to grant seaworthiness to departing vessels and to inspect the cargoes of those vessels that had recently docked in New York. In this regard, he had to maintain a good working relationship with the sea captains, cargo owners, and insurance companies. The most challenging aspect of his work was the final say he had over the fate of damaged goods. As Port Warden, Kidder had to judge the fitness of the cargo and determine if the goods were too damaged to be of any use and whether they should be sold outright on the docks to the highest bidder, "for the benefit of whom it may concern."[12]

His pay was determined by the inspection fees charged to each vessel. As all fees were to be divided equally among the nine Port Wardens, it was in their own best interest to inspect as many cargoes as possible and keep excellent records of all transactions. This was their only record of pay, as none of them received a salary from the state of New York or the city of New York.[13]

John S. Kidder's service as a Port Warden, from 1880 to 1901, was interrupted only once. In April 1893, Democratic Governor, Rosewell Flower, replaced Kidder with Dubois Collier. From that time until his reappointment by Republican Governor, Levi P. Morton in 1886, Kidder remained in New York offering his services to the other Port Wardens as an "expert." This did not go unnoticed. *The New York Times* reported that, "his long term of service and familiarity with the duties of the position render[ed] him nearly indispensable to the board, and it was the fact that he was retained as an expert that saved the Board of Port Wardens at one time from being entirely ignored by the Board of Marine Supervisors of the Port of New York."[14]

His removal prompted many protests, mainly from shipowners, merchants, and agents of steamship lines. All wrote letters on Kidder's behalf urging the politicians to reinstate him as Port Warden.

Records kept by the Port Wardens of their activities and fees during this period have long since vanished, but it is probably safe to assume that they all enjoyed a very flexible work schedule.[15] A quick glance at the arrival and departure lists, published in all the newspapers, could easily determine the work load for the nine wardens. The fewer the ships, the fewer the wardens that were needed. It is easy to see how Kidder could absent himself from New York on a number of occasions.

On June 11, 1885, he made a special trip to Laurens to escort his "Little Diamond" down the aisle in her marriage to George Ainslee. Two years later, on August 4, Mary Salina married Fayette Allen. The youngest, George, married Bertha Brainard on September 25, 1890. George and Bertha relocated to Brooklyn near his father where he entered the butter and egg business.

There was also plenty of time for a Port Warden to take extended vacations. In 1899, when John S. Kidder was sixty-nine years old and Harriet a spry sixty-three, the two embarked on a cross-country tour. This would be his last opportunity to visit his younger brothers, Edward and Major. Edward and his family had resided in Little Sioux, Iowa since 1883, while Major and his family lived in Mondamin, Iowa.

The high point of the trip, however, was a journey to Shasta, California. It was the first time in forty-three years that John S. Kidder saw his brother William, now an ordained Baptist minister. As truly happy as he was to see his brother, nonetheless, Kidder was unimpressed with Shasta.

Family legend has it that Kidder, in his typical right to the point style asked, "William, what crime did you commit that you had to come to this God forsaken place?"[16]

When he wasn't traveling with Harriet or working in New York, John S. Kidder spent almost all of his spare time absorbed in reunion activities. During the nation's Centennial in 1876, the 121st Regimental Association was formed. The group met each year in different communities in Herkimer and Otsego Counties. As one of the highest ranking surviving officers, John, always in the company of Harriet, was an honored guest. When the Grand Army of the Republic Posts began to spring up throughout central New York, he joined Hall Post No.139 in Laurens and also associated himself with the George Kidder Post No. 224 in nearby Morris.

The largest task facing the 121st Regimental Association was a project they undertook in 1885. Gettysburg, now recognized as the turning point in the War of the Rebellion, had the distinction of being named a military park. Regiments who participated in the three day battle were now invited to place monuments at their respective positions on the field. A special committee was formed for the purpose of raising the necessary funds to construct a suitable memorial. James W. Cronkite, now a custom house agent in New York City, was elected chairman of this committee, and John S. Kidder, its treasurer. The state of New York set aside $1,500 to help defray the cost of the project and the committee estimated that they had the formidable task of raising an additional $1,000.[17]

The surviving members of the 121st New York regiment, that had been severely thinned in battle, were denied funds by both the Herkimer and Otsego County Boards of Supervisors. They would have to raise the $1,000 by themselves.

Kidder and Cronkite canvassed the state and nation seeking out the former members of Upton's Regulars. Donations arrived from as far west as Los Angeles and as far north as Ontario, Canada.[18]

It wasn't only veterans who made contributions to the memorial fund. All of John S. Kidder's children, as well as James W. Cronkite's made donations as well. Money was received from mothers, like Mrs. B. Z. Fox whose son, Robinson, was killed at Salem Church. Brothers and cousins of the late Capt. John D. Fish also made donations. There were many contributions made by individuals who had no connection to the regiment. Dr. Addison A. P. Strong of Laurens, who followed the activities of the regiment in the local newspapers and through Kidder's letters, donated money to the cause. Over five hundred people contributed to the fund during the next five years with amounts that ranged anywhere between $.50 to $500. The total cost of the project eventually reached $2,900.[19]

The year 1889 proved to be a very busy and exciting time for John and Harriet. On July 8, they became grandparents with the birth of Mary's first child. The very next day, Clara gave birth to her first child. In the years that followed, there were ten more grandchildren.

In October 1889, John and Harriet, in the company of their son George, journeyed to Gettysburg to attend the dedication and unveiling of the regimental monument on the slope of Little Round Top. It was a day filled with handshakes, long speeches, and plenty of photographs. For many of the old veterans, it was the first time they had been to Gettysburg since those pivotal days in July 1863.

In 1901, John S. Kidder retired as Port Warden and returned to Laurens. With only one exception, he served in that position longer than any other person.[20] He looked forward to a quiet retirement. There would be no more long trips to New York City or far away southern battlefields. The farthest he and Harriet traveled was to Schuyler Lake to visit Clara's family.

When they returned from one of these Schuyler Lake visits, the couple was fêted with a surprise party in honor of their fiftieth wedding anniversary. There was music, plenty of food, and well-wishers. "Their cheerfulness," noted one who attended the event, "must have been an inspiration to all present."[21]

In the years that followed, John's health gradually failed. On May 19, 1905, he died in Laurens. According to the attending physician, his brief illness became more complicated, "due to general debility as a result of a gunshot wound of the left ear and resulting disease of the throat and as a result of the lowered vitality developed a carbuncle on the back of the neck and this, together with the previous debility as stated, was the cause of death."[22] His funeral was attended by many of his former comrades in arms. He was buried in the Laurens Cemetery.

John S. Kidder left no will, however, he left Harriet in a comfortable financial situation. Various promissory notes and a few scattered land holdings in Otsego County valued his estate at $15,935.72.[23]

Harriet continued to live in Laurens in the house she always loved. She remained active in community affairs and never failed to miss a reunion of the 121st New York Volunteers, of which she was a dues paying member. One of her last big projects in Laurens was typical of her. Appalled at the condition of the Laurens Cemetery, she organized the women of the village to form a Cemetery Association. Harriet and her group of women saw to the beautification of the cemetery, including the placing of flags on veterans graves. The women of Laurens continued to dominate the Cemetery Association until the 1940s.

As Harriet's health failed, it became impossible for her to care for her large house. George and his family moved in. Occupying a room on the first floor, granddaughter, Frances Warren, recalled how her grandmother Harriet would sit for hours staring at the bureau chest. Displayed on it in perfect order were the epaulets, sword, medals, reunion ribbons, and pictures of her husband in uniform, mementos of a long ago era that changed their lives forever.[24]

Harriet died at the age of eighty-six, on August 2, 1922. She is buried next to her husband in the Laurens Cemetery.

Appendix A

Ainslie, Clara Ameila Kidder—"The Little Queen Diamond," mentioned so often in her father's letters, married George Ainslie on June 11, 1885. Like her mother, Clara refused to leave Laurens and with her husband George, opened a lumber, lath, and shingle business in Laurens. Clara died on August 30, 1908, and is buried next to her mother and father in the Laurens Cemetery. Of the seven Ainslie children, five grew to maturity.

Allen, Mary Salina Kidder—After her marriage to Fayette Allen on August 4, 1887, the second child of John and Harriet Kidder relocated to the village of Morris. Here, they operated a local hardware store. Eventually, the couple took up residence in Schuyler Lake where they bought out the local grocery store, added a hardware store, and found time to devote themselves to a variety of community concerns. Fayette Allen was instrumental in linking the villages of Richfield Springs and Schuyler Lake with telephone service and worked tirelessly to secure railroad and trolley lines between the neighboring villages. Mary Salina died on December 9, 1949, in the Clark Nursing Home in Richfield Springs, NY; she is buried in the Laurens Cemetery. Her two children, not surprisingly, were named John and Harriet.

Bates, Delavan—With his departure from the 121st New York Volunteers, the career and fortune of Worcester native, Delavan Bates, was literally on the rise. Taking command of the 30th United States Colored Troops on March 1, 1864, Bates drilled and trained his men until they were battle ready. While leading his troops at Cemetery Hill near Petersburg on July 30, 1864, Bates was struck no less than five times in the head, chest, and arms. The most serious wound was a .58 caliber bullet that struck him in the right cheek and exited under his left eye. Rendered unconscious, his men carried him from the field. Bates miraculously survived and was awarded the Medal of Honor and a promotion to Brevet Brigadier General in July 1864.[1]

After the war, Delavan Bates took advantage of the Homestead Act and secured for himself a 160 acre tract of land in Nebraska. For the remainder of his life, he became actively involved in the development of the community of Aurora. At one point, he was the Superintendent of Schools, a member of the City Council, and Mayor. He became one of the first members of the Board of Trustees when the town was incorporated and was chief advocate of the building of the City Court House. He later served as the Vice President of the First National Bank.[2]

Bates kept up a lively correspondence with John S. Kidder while the latter was a Port Warden. He maintained a membership with the 121st Regimental Association and sent Kidder a check for $100 to be used for the Gettysburg Monument. With the check he enclosed a letter declaring, "That battlefield is to be a Mecca for coming generations. We were there and our position should be marked."[3]

General Bates died in Aurora, Nebraska on December 18, 1918.

Cronkite, James W.—When he took over the duties of company clerk from the errant Charlie Dean, John S. Kidder said that Orderly Sergeant James W. Cronkite was, "the best one in the regiment." While Kidder was ill, from the end of October until November 28, 1862, Cronkite was in command of Company I (Bates was also ill at this time). From that moment on, Cronkite climbed the ladder of promotions within the regiment, as battles and sickness decimated the officer ranks. He, like Captain Kidder, was promoted to lieutenant colonel. Cronkite recovered from his leg amputation after Sayler's Creek and later went on to become Deputy Collector of the Custom House in New York City. While in New York, he was a frequent visitor at the house of John and Harriet. As chairman of the 121st Monument Committee, he worked with John S. Kidder to secure the necessary funds needed to mark their spot in history at Gettysburg.

Cronkite died in Plainfield, New Jersey on June 16, 1903, and is buried in Washington, D.C. His first wife, the former Mariette Gleason, died on December 2, 1878, in Brooklyn. He then married Alice Reed on October 20, 1881, in Syracuse, New York. It was Harriet Kidder who assisted Alice Cronkite in completing her widow's pension.[4]

Dean, Charles—With the 121st New York Volunteers in the field barely two months, John S. Kidder felt that his neighbor, Charlie Dean, was the best clerk in the entire regiment. "Could not have got one in the whole regiment that would do the work of his office as well as he can," wrote Kidder on October 4, 1862. In time, his admiration would turn to bewilderment and then finally to disgust with the twenty-seven-year-old Dean. The former merchant from Laurens managed to take his clerking skills from Company I up to the regimental level. On September 16, 1863, Dean fell ill and from that time onward never returned to the 121st New York. In and out of hospitals from Baltimore to Washington, Dean did manage to serve for a short while as a clerk in the Judge Advocate's Office in Washington (February to July 1864), only to be readmitted to Judiciary Square Hospital. When he was declared fit for "light duty," he deserted the hospital on August 19, 1864, presumably on a furlough. He returned to the hospital and was once more readmitted only to desert one last time. Despite the plea of John S. Kidder, Dean never came back to the regiment and is listed in every official report as a deserter. He never came back to Laurens either, and later settled in Albany, New York. On December 21, 1891, he applied for a government pension. On the application, he did not deny that he was a deserter but did claim "over 90 days in the War of the Rebellion." Dean was granted a partial pension and his claim was discontinued a year later.[5]

Charlie Dean died on October 27, 1909.

Fields, William Craig—Born on February 13, 1804, in New York City, William C. Fields was one of the leading citizens, as well as one of the wealthiest, in the village of Laurens, New York. He was associated with woolen and cotton manufacturing in Laurens. Very active in local politics, Fields was one of the founders of the Republican Party in Otsego County. He was the Justice of the Peace for sixteen years, Otsego County Clerk from 1852–55 and Supervisor of Otsego County from 1865–66. Fields also served in the Fortieth Congress from 1867–69.

He died on October 27, 1882, and is buried in the Laurens Cemetery.[6]

Fish, John D.—John S. Kidder would have been truly saddened if he learned, and it is doubtful that he ever did, the fate of family friend, John D. Fish, of Frankfort, New York. The youngest of the Fish girls, Annie, died, at the age of three, on August 30, 1865. Her mother, Sophie Nichols Fish, died penniless on October 11, 1872, after a lengthy illness. National Archives Records indicate that at least a half dozen Frankfort residents petitioned the government in an effort to seek reimbursement for their services to Sophie Fish. Bills ranged from $67.50 for "Board and Nursing," to $4.50 for the grave digger. Sophie and her daughter Annie lie in unmarked graves in the Frankfort Cemetery.

The only surviving daughter of John and Sophie Fish, Estella, affectionately called "Etta" by her father, was sent west where she was married off at the age of fifteen. She divorced, reappeared in Frankfort and married Charles R. Crosby on November 11, 1882. This union also ended in divorce. She then married a third time to Judge Baillette of Lilydale, New York. She tried, unsuccessfully, to sue several Frankfort residents on September 3, 1903, in an attempt to recover money from the sale of her late mother's home. In Lilydale, Estella became a certified medium and continued to search for the grave of her late father via the spirit world.[7]

Fisher, Elisha—A blacksmith by trade, thirty-year-old Elisha Fisher worked as hard as he could, while John S. Kidder was in the army, to keep the carriage shop in working order. There were times when Kidder had nothing but praise for him, and others when he was totally frustrated with him. The most memorable being the time when Fisher wanted John S. Kidder to advance him the necessary funds to pay the commutation fee. When Fisher did eventually join the army, he never got farther than guarding Confederate prisoners of war at Hart Island in New York City. Like

John, he returned to Laurens with hopes of resurrecting the carriage shop. When the business dissolved in January 1879, Fisher struck out on his own and opened his own carriage and repair shop that December. This business venture lasted approximately two years. Then he moved to Unadilla, New York, and worked for the Hanford Wagon Works for the next twenty-five years.

His first wife, the former Ruth C. Chapin, died in Laurens on January 21, 1870. He then married the former Mary A. Steere on September 27, 1870.[8]

Elisha Fisher died on December 10, 1880, and is buried in the Laurens Cemetery.[9]

Foote, Sedate—Twenty-five-year-old Sedate Foote participated in every battle and skirmish with Company I until he was wounded in the arm at Cold Harbor on June 2, 1864. After making the usual hospital tour (Lincoln Hospital, then to City Point and finally to Alexandria), Foote was transferred to the Veteran Reserve Corps and eventually returned to the 121st New York where he was present at the surrender of General Robert E. Lee's Army of Northern Virginia. He was mustered out with the entire regiment at Hall's Hill, Virginia on June 25, 1865. After the war, he continued to farm and was very active in the George Kidder G.A.R. Post No. 224 in Morris.

He died March 6, 1916, and is buried in Morris, New York.[10]

Galpin, Henry—John S. Kidder thought very highly of Henry Galpin; he was upset when his friend was passed over for promotions due to, what Kidder felt, were political influences. After Kidder said goodbye to Henry Galpin at the Little Falls July 4 celebration, he never saw him again. Galpin remained in Little Falls, operating a stove and tin business and, by 1867, relocated to Jackson, Illinois. Here, he applied for an Invalid Pension. Still suffering from multiple wounds, especially those received at Cedar Creek, Henry Galpin contracted pneumonia and died in Jackson on March 9, 1871. He is buried in Albany, New York.[11]

Hall, Leroy—Former drummer boy Leroy Hall, who survived a brief imprisonment at the hands of the Confederates after the Battle of Salem Church, was mustered out with the entire regiment at Hall's Hill, Virginia, on June 25, 1865. The Hall family would know nothing but tragedy in the years following the Civil War. Leroy was killed in a railroad accident in Oneonta, New York on July 27, 1882. His wife, the former Mary Ritter, died on October 10, 1896. Their two children, William and Goldie, were placed in the care of their aunt, Emma R. Ritter, who secured a government pension on their behalf. The papers described William as "incapable from earning his support by reason of physical and mental incapacity. He is small in stature and has no palate and is a mere child in intellect and judgment and requires the same care of a child 7 or 8 years of age."

Leroy and his brother James are both buried in the Laurens Cemetery. G.A.R. Post No. 139 in Laurens is named in their honor.[12]

Kidder, Ann Elizabeth Starr—In dire financial straits following the death of her husband, George, Ann Kidder submitted the necessary paperwork to Washington to receive a government pension. Her parents, Ruggle and Ann Starr, who served as witnesses to her marriage to George Kidder on February 6, 1855, signed their names as witnesses to her widow's pension. The $8 a month she received seemed hardly enough to provide for herself and her two children, Hobart and Mary Ann. When Ann discovered that this amount was due a sergeant, she had the application amended. As George had been a newly commissioned second lieutenant at the time of his death, it raised the pension to $17 per month. Ann and the children wandered after this. They resided in St. Joseph, Missouri in 1864, and eventually moved to Elmira, New York to live near her sister. She died on March 22, 1895, and is buried in the Woodlawn Cemetery in Elmira.[13]

Kidder, Clara—See, **Ainslie, Clara Amelia Kidder.**

Kidder, Edward—Discharged for disability on January 26, 1864, from Finley Hospital, Washington, D.C., Edward Kidder returned to the family farm. He and his wife, the former Louise Josephine Thompson, and their son, Rushton Edward, later relocated to Little Sioux, Iowa. Still suffering from the effects of being wounded in the left arm at Salem Church, Edward managed to earn a living as a plasterer and mason. He applied for a pension on March 22, 1922, when he was eighty-two years old. He died on June 15, 1922, and is buried in the Little Sioux Cemetery.[14]

Kidder, George—After his marriage to Bertha Brainard, the only son of John and Harriet Kidder moved to Brooklyn, New York and entered into the butter and egg business. He moved back to Laurens when his father retired as Port Warden and remained there until 1918 when he moved to nearby Canadarago Lake. He died of complications from a farming accident on April 16, 1931. He is buried in the Laurens Cemetery.[15]

Kidder, Major Henry Payne—The youngest of the Kidder clan and the only one born in America, Major Henry Payne Kidder volunteered his services to the Union Army in the late summer of 1864. Signing on for one year, he enlisted on August 20, 1864, in Norwich, New York. Due to a mix-up in paperwork, he found himself attached to the predominantly Irish 69th New York Volunteers. A unit that saw some hard fighting early in the war, older brother, John S. Kidder, never expressed much concern for Major's safety after he enlisted. It is quite possible that the nineteen year old saw little action and could have been on the disabled list or in the hospital. Medical records do not exist for his Company E, but pension records indicate that his time in the service added to his "debilitating condition." In 1865, he and his wife, the former Emma Jenette Mickle, bought a farm in Mondamin, Iowa. By 1913, the couple moved to Boulder, Colorado, to be near their children. Major died on June 30, 1925, and is buried in the Green Mountain Cemetery, Boulder, Colorado.[16]

Kidder, Mary Salina—See, **Allen, Mary Salina Kidder**

Kidder, William Samuel—The most traveled of all the Kidders, William arrived in San Francisco in 1858 and immediately set out for the Shasta Gold Fields to make his fortune. In addition to mining, he taught school in Whiskeytown and was affiliated with the Whiskeytown Baptist Church, which eventually changed its name to the Mount Shasta Baptist Church. William Kidder became an ordained Baptist minister on September 9, 1860. He enlisted as a private in the 7th Regiment California Volunteers on November 10, 1864; he was discharged on March 31, 1866, in Presidia, California. His service career was spent going from post to post guarding against Indian attacks. He almost died from heat stroke when he collapsed while crossing the Mojave Desert in June 1865. He married the former Mary Elizabeth McFarlin and the couple had eight children. William died on March 16, 1911, and is buried in the Ono Cemetery, Ono, California.[17]

Lewis, Henry Delos—Brother-in-law, Delos Lewis, who had been an occasional thorn in Kidder's side, never recovered from the wound he received on May 10, 1864. Discharged on August 3, 1865, he returned to Morris, New York. He died at the home of Edward Kidder with his wife Frances at his side, on October 19, 1873. His pension of $4 per month was received on October 11, 1879, made retroactive from August 5, 1865. He is buried in Hillington Cemetery, Morris, New York.[18]

Mather, Andrew—When twenty-five-year-old Mather signed on with the 121st New York, he became the first lieutenant of Capt. Sacket Olin's Company K. Kidder lacked the real political clout that young Mather possessed. His father, Andrew A. Mather, was the Sheriff of Otsego County. As a result, no other junior officer advanced in rank faster than Mather did the first year the 121st was in the field. Promoted to captain on January 14, 1863, Andrew Mather advanced to the rank of major after the Battle of Salem Church. Kidder's opinion of Mather changed from time to time depending on the circumstances. He admired his bravery at Salem Church when he stood by the colors, but later declared, "He is such a fop," after he was promoted to major over the heads of officers with more seniority. When Mather resigned to accept the rank of lieutenant colonel in the 20th United States Colored Troops, John S. Kidder expressed no remorse or regret. This only paved the way for Henry Galpin to be the new major, a move that Kidder felt was justified all along. After the war Mather went into business in Albany, New York. He died on October 2, 1913, and is buried in the Butternut Valley Cemetery, Town of Lisbon, which is north of Garrettsville in Otsego County.[19]

Matteson, Charles—While in Elmira as a ring seller and boatman, and later in Petersburg in the lumber business, one-armed Charley Matteson constantly amazed John S. Kidder with his resourcefulness. After the Civil War, Charley moved to Georgia and then back to upstate New York; he became a frequent lecturer on the Battle of Gettysburg. He was able to earn a living as a stone mason but was seriously injured on August 4, 1894; he fell three stories from a swinging scaffold while cleaning the brickwork at the Normal School in Oneonta (now Oneonta State University). He never recovered from his injuries. Surrounded by his wife and six children, it was a scene, the local paper said, "that would melt the hardest heart." Matteson died from his injuries and is buried in the Laurens Cemetery. The other brickworkers at the Normal School helped raise $114 for the family and later sponsored a grand invitational ball at the Metropolitan Theater in Oneonta to raise additional funds for the family. "As long as men are men no family of a veteran, who bore the blue to the honor of himself and the saving of the nation, will be allowed to remain long in need," said the *Oneonta Herald* of the event.[20]

Olcott, Egbert—When Egbert Olcott bid his farewell to the citizens of Little Falls, New York after the July 4 celebration, he assured them that he would begin work immediately on a regimental history of the 121st New York. It wasn't to be. Aggravated by the effects of the gunshot wound to the head he received at the Wilderness, his mental state slowly deteriorated. On October 25, 1872, Olcott was admitted to Kings County Lunatic Asylum in Utica, New York. To hasten the pension application of his wife, Susan, John S. Kidder submitted an affidavit on her behalf on April 7, 1875. Olcott died in Willard's Asylum, Willard, New York in February 1882. Susan Olcott died on April 30, 1884, leaving three orphaned children.[21]

Upton, Emory—The last time John S. Kidder saw Emory Upton was right before the May 12 assault on the Bloody Angle. By the time Kidder returned to the 121st in January of 1865, Upton had already recovered from the wound he received in the Shenandoah Valley Campaign, and was in command of a cavalry division in Alabama. Continuing in the regular army after the war, General Upton wrote several works on military history and policy. If Kidder was able to meet his former commander at the time his letter of recommendation was written in 1878, he would have been shocked at the sight. The once upbeat, ramrod straight disciplinarian, who transformed the 121st New York Volunteers into a cohesive fighting unit, had turned into a paunched, overweight recluse. He suffered deep bouts of depression, due in part to the loss of his young wife and the constant worry about public acceptance of his books. On March 15, 1881, while in command of the 4th U.S. Artillery at the Presidio in California, Upton put a gun to his head. He was forty-two years old. General Upton is buried in Fort Hill Cemetery, Auburn, New York.[22]

Appendix B

John Kidder and Delavan Bates signed on the following men in what became Company I of the 121st New York Volunteers. This appears in the *Annual Report of the Adjutant General of the State of New York* for the year 1903.

ALGER, CHESTER:

Age twenty-two, teacher, enlisted August 9, 1862 in Hartwick, New York. Died of chronic diarrhea in Belle Plain, Virginia on December 16, 1862.

BABCOCK, SAMUEL A.:

Age eighteen, farmer, enlisted August 6, 1862 in Laurens, New York. Killed in action on September 21, 1864 in Charleston, Virginia.

BECKER, ROBERT

Age twenty-three, farmer, enlisted July 31, 1862 in Milford, New York. Deserted on July 16, 1863 in Middletown, Maryland.

BEMIS, LEVI:

Age eighteen, farmer, enlisted August 13, 1862 in Pittsfield, New York. Transferred to the Veterans Reserve Corps, November 13, 1863.

BENNETT, RICHARD:

Age twenty-two, farmer, enlisted on August 11, 1862 in Laurens, New York. Killed in action on June 1, 1864 in Cold Harbor, Virginia.

BERNER, HUMPHREY:

Age twenty-two, shoemaker, enlisted on August 8, 1862 in Worcester, New York. Discharged on November 16, 1863 from the hospital, Fort Schuyler, New York Harbor.

BOLT, STEPHEN:

Age twenty-one, farmer, enlisted on August 6, 1862 in Morris, New York. Mustered out on June 14, 1865 from Whitehall Hospital, Philadelphia, Pennsylvania.

BOWEN, ZEBULON:

Age thirty-two, farmer, enlisted on August 5, 1862 in Laurens, New York. Wounded in action on May 10, 1864 in Spotsylvania. Mustered out with the regiment on June 25, 1865 in Hall's Hill, Virginia.

BRUCE, WILLIAM:

Age twenty-seven, carpenter, enlisted on August 7, 1862 in Worcester, New York. Mustered out with the Regiment on June 25, 1865 in Hall's Hill, Virginia.

BULL, GEORGE:

Age thirty-four, laborer, enlisted on August 13, 1862 in Worcester, New York. Deserted on January 21, 1863 and returned on July 14, 1863. Absent, under sentence of court-martial, at the mustering out of the regiment.

BUSHNELL, DAVID:

Age twenty-one, harness maker, enlisted on August 7, 1862 in Worcester, New York. Died of fever on October 8, 1862 in Burkesville, Maryland.

BUTLER, EDWIN:

Age eighteen, enlisted on August 6, 1862 in Morris, New York. Wounded in action on May 10, 1864 in Spotsylvania, Virginia. Transferred to the Veteran Reserve Corps on January 9, 1864.

CAMP, CHARLES G.:

Age twenty-one, enlisted July 29, 1862 in Morris, New York, to serve three years. Mustered in as a private in Co. I, August 23, 1862. Died of typhoid fever, no date, in Windmill Point, Virginia.

CAMP, HIRAM:

Age twenty-eight, enlisted, August 4, 1862 in Morris, New York. Served three years. Mustered in as a private in Co. I, August 23, 1862. Discharged for disability, March 27, 1862, from Convalescent Camp, Virginia.

CAMP, NELSON L.:

Age twenty-five, enlisted, July 29, 1862 in Morris, New York. Mustered in as a private in Co. I, August 23, 1862. Died of typhoid fever, March 23, 1863, in White Oak Church, Virginia.

CARD, REUBEN:

Age twenty-one, farmer, enlisted on August 11, 1862 in Pittsfield, New York. Killed in action on May 3, 1863 in Salem Church.

CARYL, MOSE:

Age twenty-seven, farmer, enlisted on July 30, 1862 in Worcester, New York. Mustered out with entire regiment on June 25, 1865 in Hall's Hill, Virginia.

COLE, WILLIAM:

Age nineteen, farmer, enlisted on August 12, 1862 in Worcester, New York. Transferred to First New York Independent Battery on December 5, 1863.

COLTON, CHAUNCEY:

Age thirty-two, carpenter, enlisted on August 6, 1862 in Laurens, New York. Killed in action, May 6, 1864 at the Wilderness.

CURRY, NELSON:

Age forty-four, farmer, enlisted on August 4, 1862 in Laurens, New York. Discharged on December 6, 1862 as "worthless" from hospital in Washington.

CRONKITE, JAMES W.:

Age twenty-one, carriage maker, enlisted on August 5, 1862 in Milford, New York. Wounded in action at Spotsylvania on May 10, 1864, and at Sayler's Creek on April 6, 1865.

DARLING, JOSEPH:

Age twenty-one, farmer, enlisted on July 31, 1862 in Worcester, New York. Died of liver disease on February 10, 1863 in White Oak Church, Virginia.

DEAN, CHARLES:

Age twenty-seven, mechanic, enlisted on August 5, 1862 in Laurens, New York. Deserted on expiration of furlough while on detached service in Washington, D.C.

DINGMAN, ELIJAH:

Age twenty-one, farmer, enlisted on August 6, 1862 in Milford, New York. Killed in action on October 19, 1864 in Cedar Creek, Virginia.

DIXON, GEORGE:

Age eighteen, farmer, enlisted on August 4, 1862 in Morris, New York. Transferred to the Veteran Reserve Corps on September 30, 1862.

DOWNING, CHARLES:

Age twenty-six, farmer, enlisted on August 2, 1862 in Morris, New York. Wounded in action on May 10, 1864 in Spotsylvania, Virginia. Mustered out of the service on June 10, 1865 from Emory Hospital, Washington, D.C.

EDSON, JOSEPH:

Age thirty-five, farmer, enlisted on August 16, 1862 in Milford, New York. Wounded in action on June 1, 1864 in Cold Harbor, Virginia. Transferred to the Veteran Reserve Corps. Discharged on July 12, 1865 at Broome Street Barracks, New York City.

EDWARDS, WILLIAM:

Age twenty-two, farmer, enlisted on August 4, 1862 in Morris, New York. Transferred to the Veteran Reserve Corps.

FANNING, BENJAMIN:
Age eighteen, farmer, enlisted on August 12, 1862 in Worcester, New York. Killed in action on May 3, 1863 in Salem Church, Virginia.

FENTON, SAMUEL:
Age twenty-seven, enlisted on July 20, 1862 in Laurens, New York. Served three years as a private. Killed in action on May 3, 1863 in Salem Church, Virginia.

FOOTE, SEDATE:
Age twenty-five, farmer, enlisted on August 4, 1862 in Morris, New York. Wounded in action on June 1, 1864 in Cold Harbor, Virginia.

FOOT, ZEPHARIAH:
Age thirty-five, farmer, enlisted on August 5, 1862 in Morris, New York. Died of measles on February 9, 1863 in White Oak Church, Virginia.

FOX, ROBINSON:
Age twenty-two, merchant, enlisted on August 5, 1862 in Laurens, New York. Killed in action on May 3, 1863 in Salem Church, Virginia.

FULLER, ALBERT:
Age eighteen, farmer, enlisted on August 11, 1862 in Oneonta, New York. Wounded in action on May 3, 1863 in Salem Church, Virginia. Transferred to the Veteran Reserve Corps on February 15, 1864.

GARDNER, JAMES:
Age nineteen, farmer, enlisted on July 30, 1862 in Laurens, New York. Killed in action on May 10, 1864 in Spotsylvania, Virginia.

GENUNG, BURDETT:
Age twenty-three, farmer, enlisted on August 4, 1862 in Morris, New York. Wounded in action on May 15, 1864 in Spotsylvania, Virginia. Discharged on June 9, 1865 from the hospital in Washington, D.C.

GOODRICH, HENRY:
Age twenty, farmer, enlisted on August 29, 1862 in Worcester, New York. Discharged, no date.

GREEN, ORLIN:
Age eighteen, enlisted on July 31, 1862 in Milford, New York. Served three years as a private. Promoted to corporal on March 1, 1865. Discharged on June 25 at Hall's Hill, Virginia.

GRIGGS, WILLIAM:
Age twenty-four, farmer, enlisted on August 11, 1862 in Worcester, New York. Killed in action on February 6, 1865 in Hatcher's Run, Virginia.

HALL, JAMES:
Age twenty-two, farmer, enlisted on August 5, 1862 in Laurens, New York. Died of typhoid fever on December 23, 1862 in White Oak Church, Virginia.

HALL, LEROY:

Age twenty-four, mechanic, enlisted on August 13, 1862 in Laurens, New York. Mustered out with the entire regiment on June 25, 1865 in Hall's Hill, Virginia.

HENIKER, HENRY:

Age twenty-eight, farmer, enlisted on August 5, 1862 in Laurens, New York. Wounded in action on October 19, 1864 in Cedar Creek, Virginia. Mustered out with the entire regiment on June 25, 1865 in Hall's Hill, Virginia.

HOGABOOM, LARRY:

Age twenty-one, farmer, enlisted on August 21, 1862 in Oneonta, New York. Killed in action on May 3, 1863 in Salem Church, Virginia.

HOLLISTER, LEROY:

Age thirty-seven, carpenter, enlisted on August 6, 1862 in Milford, New York. Wounded in action on May 10, 1864 in Spotsylvania, Virginia. Discharged for wounds on May 23, 1865.

HOUSE, SAMUEL:

Age nineteen, manufacturer, enlisted on August 6, 1862 in Pittsfield, New York. Died of chronic diarrhea on December 31, 1862 in Hagerstown, Maryland.

JAYCOX, ADELBERT:

Age twenty-one, farmer, enlisted on August 12, 1862 in Worcester, New York. Mustered out with the entire regiment on June 25, 1865 in Hall's Hill, Virginia.

JENKS, MASON:

Age thirty-three, farmer, enlisted on August 8, 1862 in Laurens, New York. Wounded in action on October 19, 1864 in Cedar Creek, Virginia. Mustered out of the service on June 29, 1865 from McClellan General Hospital, Philadelphia, Pennsylvania.

JEWELL, MYRON:

Age twenty-five, farmer, enlisted on August 6, 1862 in Milford, New York. Deserted on February 3, 1863 from hospital in Antietam, Maryland.

LAMONT, ASBELL:

Age twenty-one, farmer, enlisted on July 29, 1862 in Worcester, New York. Killed in action on November 7, 1863 in Rappahannock Station, Virginia.

LATIMER, HARRISON:

Age twenty-eight, farmer, enlisted on August 8, 1862 in Milford, New York. Wounded in action on May 3, 1863 in Salem Church, Virginia. Died of wounds on May 11, 1863.

LEWIS, EDWIN: Age twenty, farmer, enlisted on July 28, 1862 in Morris, New York. Killed in action on April 6, 1865 in Sayler's Creek, Virginia.

LEWIS, HENRY DELOS: Age twenty-one, farmer, enlisted on August 4, 1862 in Morris, New York. Wounded in action on May 10, 1864 in Spotsylvania, Virginia. Transferred to the Veteran Reserve Corps on January 25, 1865.

LYON, ALONZO: Age thirty-four, farmer, enlisted on July 29, 1862 in Hartwick, New York. "Did absent himself without leave from his regiment and the service of the United States Jan. 17th and remained absent till Feb. 9, 1863, when he returned to his Reg. near White Oak Church, Va . . . 'Court-Martialed, found *Guilty* of absence without leave'" and sentenced "'to forfeit to the U[nited] States one months pay' the proceedings of the court are disapproved and the prisoner will be released from arrest" (Day Books of the 121st New York Volunteers, 188). Deserted on July 8, 1863 in Middletown, Maryland.

MARIHEW, DAVID: Age nineteen, farmer, enlisted on August 8, 1862 in Hartwick, New York. Wounded in action on May 3, 1863 in Salem Church, Virginia and in Petersburg, Virginia on March 25, 1865. Discharged from Finley Hospital, Washington, D.C. on August 2, 1865.

MCINTYRE, JAMES: Age thirty-three, shoemaker, enlisted on July 26, 1862 in Laurens, New York. Discharged for disability on April 11, 1863 from hospital in Maryland.

MCINTYRE, PARLEY: Age twenty-two, farmer, enlisted on August 4, 1862 in Morris, New York. Wounded in action in Cedar Creek, Virginia on October 19, 1864. Discharged for disability on February 10, 1865.

NICHOLS, CHARLES: Age twenty, farmer, enlisted on July 30, 1862 in Laurens, New York. Wounded in action. Discharged for wounds on August 27, 1863.

OLDS, GILBERT: Age twenty-two, farmer, enlisted on August 6, 1862 in Morris, New York. Wounded in action on May 3, 1863 in Salem Church, Virginia. Transferred to the Veteran Reserve Corps.

OSTRANDER, EDWARD:

Age twenty-one, farmer, enlisted on August 6, 1862 in Morris, New York. Mustered out with the entire regiment on June 25, 1865 in Hall's Hill, Virginia.

PATRICK, JAMES:

Age twenty-one, enlisted on July 31, 1862 in Worcester, New York. Promoted to corporal on March 1, 1865. Discharged at Hall's Hill, Virginia on June 25, 1865.

PATTENGILL, CHARLES:

Age twenty-four, farmer, enlisted on August 9, 1862 in Morris, New York. Wounded in action on May 10, 1864 in Spotsylvania, Virginia. Died of his wounds on May 11, 1864.

PATTENGILL, EDWARD:

Age twenty-two, farmer, enlisted on August 21, 1862 in New Lisbon, New York. Deserted on January 20, 1863 in White Oak Church, Virginia.

PECK, ISAAC:

Age nineteen, blacksmith, enlisted on August 5, 1862 in Milford, New York. Mustered out with the entire regiment on June 25, 1865 in Hall's Hill, Virginia.

PEET, SHERMAN:

Age eighteen, farmer, enlisted on August 5, 1862 in Laurens, New York. Discharged for disability on March 16, 1863 from Chester Hospital, Philadelphia, Pennsylvania.

PERINE, PETER:

Age forty, mechanic, enlisted on August 2, 1862 in Morris, New York. Captured at the Wilderness on May 6, 1864. Paroled on December 6, 1864. Mustered out with the entire regiment on June 25, 1865 in Hall's Hill, Virginia.

PIERSON, GEORGE:

Age eighteen, farmer, enlisted on August 9, 1862 in Worcester, New York. Wounded in action. Discharged for wounds on October 13, 1863 from Armory Square Hospital, Washington, D.C.

POTTER, HENRY:

Age thirty-four, teacher, enlisted on August 11, 1862 in Laurens, New York. Mustered out of the company on May 16, 1865.

POTTER, PHILLIP:

Age twenty-one, farmer, enlisted on August 6, 1862 in Morris, New York. Wounded in action. Discharged for wounds on August 1, 1863.

POWERS, LEVI:

Age twenty-one, farmer, enlisted on August 23, 1862 in Worcester, New York. Wounded in action on May 3, 1863 in Salem Church, Virginia and died of those wounds on May 6, 1863.

POWERS, SAMUEL:
Age eighteen, farmer, enlisted on August 8, 1862 in Worcester, New York. Mustered out with the entire company on June 25, 1865 in Hall's Hill, Virginia.

REMMEL, CALEB:
Age eighteen, enlisted on September 19, 1862 in Albany, New York. Wounded in action in Petersburg, Virginia.

REMMEL, WILLIAM:
Age nineteen, farmer, enlisted on August 20, 1862 in Fairfield, New York. Missing in action in Cedar Creek, Virginia on October 19, 1864.

RICHARDSON, GEORGE:
Age thirty-seven, farmer, enlisted on August 5, 1862 in Laurens, New York. Wounded at Salem Church, Virginia. Mustered out with the entire regiment on June 25, 1865 in Hall's Hill, Virginia.

ROBERTS, JOSEPH:
Age twenty-seven, farmer, enlisted on August 7, 1862 in Morris, New York. Discharged for disability on June 6, 1865 from Emory Hospital, Washington, D.C.

ROCKEFELLER, MATTHEW:
Age twenty, farmer, enlisted on August 11, 1862 in Worcester, New York. Killed in action on May 3, 1863 in Salem Church, Virginia.

ROSE, FREEMAN:
Age eighteen, farmer, enlisted on August 11, 1862 in Milford, New York. Died of fever on November 21, 1862 in hospital in Washington, D.C.

ROUSE, CLARK:
Age twenty, farmer, enlisted on July 30, 1862 in Laurens, New York. Mustered out with the entire regiment on June 25, 1865 in Hall's Hill, Virginia.

SHOVE, THOMAS:
Age twenty-four, farmer, enlisted on August 2, 1862 in Morris, New York. Discharged for disability on January 12, 1863 from VI Corps Hospital.

SNEDEKER, HENRY:
Age eighteen, cotton manufacturer, enlisted on July 26, 1862 in Laurens, New York. Discharged for disability on June 21, 1863.

SNEDEKER, SAMUEL:
Age twenty-five, farmer, enlisted on August 8, 1862 in Laurens, New York. Killed in action on May 10, 1864 in Spotsylvania, Virginia.

STONE, NORMAN S.:	Age twenty-seven, enlisted on August 6, 1862 in Milford, New York. Mustered out with the entire regiment on June 25, 1865 at Hall's Hill, Virginia.
TEEL, AUSTIN:	Age eighteen, farmer, enlisted on July 29, 1862 in Worcester, New York. Transferred to fill battery on December 5, 1863.
TEEL, GEORGE:	Age thirty-five, farmer, enlisted on July 29, 1862 in Laurens, New York. Wounded in action on October 19, 1864 in Cedar Creek, Virginia.
TERRIL, PETER:	Age twenty-eight, farmer, enlisted on August 12, 1862 in Worcester, New York. Mustered out with the entire regiment on June 25, 1865 in Hall's Hill, Virginia.
TERRY, LEROY:	Age twenty-one, farmer, enlisted on August 9, 1862 in Morris, New York. Transferred to the Veteran Reserve Corps, no date.
THURSTON, CHARLES:	Age eighteen, farmer, enlisted on July 30, 1862 in New Lisbon, New York. Discharged for disability in December 1862.
TRACY, JULIUS:	Age twenty-five, enlisted on August 5, 1862 in Morris, New York. Killed in action on May 3, 1863 in Salem Church, Virginia.
WATERMAN, SILAS:	Age twenty-seven, farmer, enlisted on August 9, 1862 in Worcester, New York. Killed in action on May 9, 1864 in Spotsylvania, Virginia.
WEBB, FLETCHER:	Age nineteen, farmer, enlisted on August 7, 1862 in Butternuts, New York. Killed in action on May 3, 1863 in Salem Church, Virginia.
WESTCOTT, CYRUS:	Age twenty, farmer, enlisted on July 31, 1862 in Worcester, New York. Mustered out with the entire regiment on June 25, 1865 in Hall's Hill, Virginia.
WESTCOTT, HAMILTON:	Age thirty-four, farmer, enlisted on August 7 1862 in Worcester, New York. Discharged for disability on January 6, 1863 from Camden Street Hospital, Baltimore, Maryland.
WILSEY, CHARLES:	Age eighteen, farmer, enlisted on July 30, 1862 in Worcester, New York. Transferred to the Veteran Reserve Corps on September 30, 1863.

WILSEY, JOHN:

Age twenty-six, farmer, enlisted on August 23, 1862 in Worcester, New York. Wounded in action on May 3, 1863 in Salem Church, Virginia. Mustered out with the entire regiment on June 25, 1865 in Hall's Hill, Virginia.

WILSON, HOMER:

Age eighteen, farmer, enlisted on August 4, 1862 in German Flats, New York. Deserted on September 27, 1862 from Camp Schuyler, Herkimer, New York.

WINTON, AMASA:

Age twenty-one, farmer, enlisted on July 28, 1862 in Milford, New York. Discharged for disability on February 2, 1863 from Calvert Street Hospital, Baltimore, Maryland.

WRIGHT, MOSES:

Age eighteen, farmer, enlisted on July 28, 1862 in Laurens, New York. Dishonorably discharged on October 17, 1864 for "misbehavior before the enemy." Pardoned in August 1865.

YAGER, SYLVESTER:

Age twenty-one, farmer, enlisted on July 31, 1862 in Milford, New York. Deserted on October 18, 1862 in Burkittsville, Maryland.

YOUNG, TREAT:

Age twenty-eight, carpenter, enlisted on August 12, 1862 in Worcester, New York. Wounded and captured in action on May 6, 1864 at the Wilderness. Escaped in September 1864. Wounded in Petersburg on March 25, 1865. Mustered out with the entire regiment on June 25, 1865 in Hall's Hill, Virginia.

Notes

ONE: *The New Americans* (1830-1862)

1. John S. Kidder to Harriet M. Kidder, Letter, 4 October 1862. (Hereafter referred to as JSK to HMK).

2. Howard B. Furer, ed., *The British in America 1578-1970* (Dobbs Ferry, New York: Oceana Publications, Inc., 1972), 36.

3. Carl Wittke, *We Who Built America: The Saga of the Immigrant* (Ohio: Case Western Reserve University, 1967), 112-13.

4. *Conveyance Book 71* (Cooperstown, New York: Otsego County Clerks Office), 172.

5. Ibid., 75, 204.

6. John S. Kidder, Account Books, Kidder Family Papers, Harrie Washburn, Sharon Springs, N.Y.

7. Bureau of Census, Census Records (Cooperstown, New York: Otsego County Clerks Office, 1855).

8. *Biographical Review. Biographical Sketches of the Leading Citizens of Otsego County, New York* (Boston: Biographical Review Publishing Company, 1893), 467.

9. Bureau of the Census, Census Records (Otsego County Clerks Office, 1855).

10. Bernice Wardell, *History of Laurens Township* (Laurens, New York: Bernice Wardell, 1975), 89.

11. Ibid., 90.

12. JSK to HMK, Letter, 20 November 1861.

13. Wardell, *History of Laurens Township*, 94.

14. Allan Nevins, *The War for the Union: War Becomes Revolution 1862–1863* (New York: Charles Scribner's Sons, 1960), 144.

15. *Little Falls Journal and Courier*, 17 July 1862, 2. (Hereafter cited as LFJC).

16. *LFJC*, 31 July 1862, 3.

17. Frederick Phisterer, *New York State in the War of the Rebellion*, vol. 4 (Albany, New York: J. R. Lyon, 1912), 3423.

18. *Biographical Dictionary of the American Congress, 1774–1989* (Washington, D.C.: Government Printing Office, 1989), 967.

19. *LFJC*, 31 July 1862, 3.

20. JSK to HMK, Letter, August 26, 1863.

21. Ibid.

22. Ibid.

23. Delavan Bates, "War and Reminicences," *Otsego Republican*, 8 July 1895.

24. Delavan Bates, "Worcester's Quota in the 121st N.Y. Volunteers," *Otsego Republican*, 10 February 1896.

25. *LFJC*, 28 August 1862, 2.

26. *LFJC*, 31 July 1862, 3.

27. Bureau of Census, Census Records for Laurens (Cooperstown, New York: Otsego County Clerks Office, 1860), 60. As late as 1865, the average farm laborer in the same election district as John S. Kidder could only expect to earn $300 per year, or $32.50 for work during "the summer months."

28. Silas Burt, *My Memoirs of the Military History of the State of New York During the War of the Rebellion 1861–1865* (Albany, New York: J. B. Lyon Company, 1902), 148.

29. *Oneonta Herald*, 30 July 1862, 3.

30. Cassius Delavan Diary, 28 August 1862. Walt Dingman Collection, Middleville, N.Y.

31. Burt, *My Memoirs*, 105.

32. *Regimental Day Books of the 121st New York Infantry* (Washington, D.C.: National Archives, Company I), 295.

33. *LFJC*, 14 August 1862, 2.

34. Cassius Delavan in a letter to his sister, 11 August 1862, Walt Dingman Collection, Middleville, N.Y.

35. *LFJC*, 14 August 1862, 2.

36. Ibid., 11 September 1862, 2.

37. Delavan Bates in a letter to his father, 5 September 1862. John G. Saint Collection, Springfield, Ill.

38. Cassius Delavan Diary, 3 September 1862, Walt Dingman Collection, Middleville, N.Y.

39. *Memorial and Letters of Rev. John R. Adams* (Cambridge, Mass.: University Press, 1890), 66.

40. Isaac O. Best, *History of the 121st New York State Infantry* (Chicago: Lt. James H. Smith, 1921), 10–11.

41. JSK to HMK, Letter, 15 September 1862. Cooley's Hill is a steep hill in Laurens near Kidder's Carriage Shop.

42. Best, *History of the 121st*, 26.

43. Cassius Delavan Diary, 24 September 1862, Walt Dingman Collection, Middleville, N.Y.

44. JSK to HMK, Letter, 4 October 1862.

45. Ibid.

46. *Oneonta Herald* newspaper article, no date, Kidder Papers, Jerry Reed Collection, Whitesboro, N.Y.

47. JSK to HMK, Letter, 4 October 1862.

48. Ibid.

49. Ibid.

50. Ibid.

51. *A Surgeon's Civil War: The Letters and Diary of Daniel M. Holt, M.D.,* James M. Greiner et al., eds. (Ohio: Kent State University Press, 1994), 4.

52. JSK to HMK, Letter, 17 October 1862.

53. Richard Franchot File, National Archives, Washington, D.C.

54. JSK to HMK, Letter, 4 October 1862.

55. Ibid.

56. Ibid.

57. JSK to HMK, Letter, 17 October 1862.

58. Ezra J. Warner, *Generals in Blue: Lives of the Union Commanders* (Baton Rouge: Louisiana State University Press, 1964), 519.

59. Burt, *My Memoirs*, 105. Silas Burt claims, in his memoirs, that Franchot purposely resigned so that Colonel Upton could take the position. Burt says that Franchot, "had accepted the command '*locum tenens*' for Lieutenant Emory Upton of the Fourth Regiment Artillery, United States Army." At the time of the appointment, Upton was a captain, not a lieutenant and he was attached to the Fifth, not Fourth Artillery.

60. Delavan Bates to his mother, 27 November 1862, John G. Saint Collection, Springfield, Ill.

61. JSK to HMK, Letter, 4 October 1862. Kidder may have had his newspapers confused. Charlie Dean, in a letter to the *Oneonta Herald*, 24 October 1862, stated that the, "*New York Tribune* is not brought into camp."

62. *Oneonta Herald*, 20 October 1862.

63. Best, *History of the 121st*, 34.

64. JSK to HMK, Letter, 27 November 1862.

65. Delavan Bates in a letter to his mother, 27 November 1862, John G. Saint Collection, Springfield, Ill.

66. JSK to HMK, Letter, 27 November 1862.

67. Ibid.

68. *Annual Report of the Adjutant General of the State of New York for the Year 1903*, series no. 36 (Albany, New York: Oliver Quayle, 1904), 186. (hereafter referred to as the *Adjutant General's Report*)

69. John Quinby to his parents, 1 December 1862, Herkimer County Historical Society (hereafter cited as HCHS), Herkimer, N.Y.

70. Best, *History of the 121st*, 34.

71. JSK to HMK, Letter, 9 December 1862. *Adjutant General's Report*, 186.

72. Delavan Bates, "War and Reminiscence," *The Otsego Republican*, 22 August, 1895, 25 March, 1895. "Coal Heavers" was rather mild compared to the tongue lashing given to the 96th Pennsylvania by Assistant Surgeon Daniel M. Holt of the 121st New York. To him they were "Saerkrout Lunkheads" and "Cowards." See: Holt, *A Surgeon's Civil War*, 13–14.

73. JSK to HMK, Letter, 4 October 1862.

74. Delavan Bates in a letter to his mother, 27 November, 1862, John G. Saint Collection, Springfield, Ill.

75. JSK to HMK, Letter, 30 November 1862.

76. John J. Ingraham, *Civil War Letters*, Edward C. Ingraham ed. (Frankfort, New York: Phoenix Printing Corporation, 1986). Letter written at White Oak Church, no date.

77. JSK to HMK, Letter, 30 November 1862.

78. Best, *History of the 121st*, 55.

79. JSK to HMK, Letter, 30 November 1862.

Two: *"You must not fret about me"*
(November 1862–April 1863)

1. JSK to HMK, Letter, 4 October 1862.

2. JSK to HMK, Letter, 27 November 1862.

3. JSK to HMK, Letter, 6 January, 1863.

4. JSK to HMK, Letter, 9 December 1862.

5. Ibid.

6. John J. Ingraham, Letter, 9 December 1862.

7. JSK to HMK, Letter, 9 December 1862.

8. John J. Ingraham, Letter, 9 December 1862.

9. JSK to HMK, Letter, 9 December 1862.

10. Ibid.

11. Ibid.

12. JSK to HMK, Letter, 11 December 1862.

13. Ibid.

14. Ibid.

15. Cassius Delavan Diary, 11 December, 1862, Walt Dingman Collection, Middleville, N.Y.

16. JSK to HMK, Letter, 11–12 December 1862.

17. JSK to HMK, Letter, 12 December 1862.

18. Ibid.

19. Ibid.

20. Ibid.

21. Best, *History of the 121st*, 44.

22. JSK to HMK, Letter, 14 December 1862.

23. Ibid.

24. Ibid.

25. JSK to HMK, Letter, 18 December 1862.

26. *The War of the Rebellion: A Compilation of the Official Records of the Union and Confederate Armies*, Ser. 1, vol. 21 (Washington, D.C.: Government Printing Office, 1880-1901), 523-24. (hereafter referred to as OR with Series and vol.)

27. JSK to HMK, Letter, 14 December 1862.

28. JSK to HMK, Letter, 18 December 1862.

29. Ibid.

30. JSK to HMK, Letter, 6 January, 1863.

31. Ibid.

32. Ibid.

33. Phisterer, *New York State in the War of the Rebellion*, 929.

34. JSK to HMK, Letter, 6 January, 1863.

35. Ibid.

36. JSK to HMK, Letter, 17 October 1862.

37. JSK to HMK, Letter, 30 November 1862.

38. JSK to HMK, Letter, 6 January, 1863.

39. Ibid.

40. Ibid., drill—coarse linen or cotton bails—"hoop handles."

41. JSK to HMK, Letter, 4 October 1862.

42. JSK to HMK, Letter, 26 August 1863.

43. JSK to HMK, Letter, 16 January, 1863.

44. JSK to HMK, Letter, 6 January, 1863.

45. Ibid.

46. Ibid.

47. Ibid.

48. Ibid.

49. Ibid.

50. JSK to HMK, Letter, 16 January 1863.

51. Ibid.

52. Phisterer, *New York State in War of the Rebellion*, 3423–39. Best, *History of the 121st*, 53–54.

53. Nevins, *The War for the Union: War Becomes Revolution (1862–1863)*, 434.

54. *Oneonta Herald*, 4 March 1863, 3. The same letter and list appeared in the *Herkimer County Journal*, 19 February, 1863.

55. Ibid.

56. JSK to HMK, Letter, 30 November 1862.

57. JSK to HMK, Letter, 25 February 1863.

58. JSK to HMK, Letter, 19 March 1863. The "Rip-raps" was a prison near Norfolk, Virginia. See: Bell Irvin Wiley, *The Life of Billy Yank* (Baton Rouge: Louisiana State University Press, 1952), 215.

59. JSK to HMK, Letter, 25 February 1863. Dr. Bently could have been a contract surgeon, hired by the government. There is no record of a Dr. Bently in New York state.

60. *New York Adjutant General's Report*, series no. 36; 127.

61. JSK to HMK, Letter, 25 February, 1863.

62. John S. Kidder Papers, Jerry Reed Collection, Whitesboro, N.Y. On March 10, 1863, Lincoln issued a special proclamation regarding those soldiers who had deserted. He offered them complete amnesty if they returned to their regiments before April 1. OR, Series 1, Vol. 40: 137.

63. JSK to HMK, Letter, 25 February 1863.

64. Ibid.

65. Ibid.

66. Ibid. Kidder makes several references here. A shin plaster is paper money that was made almost worthless due to inflation. Ohio politician and outspoken critic of the Lincoln administration, Clement Vallandingham (1820–1871),

publicly urged soldiers to desert and return home. See: Allan Nevins, *The War for the Union: The Organized War 1863–1864* (New York: Charles Scribner's Sons, 1971), 176.

67. Ibid.

68. JSK to HMK, Letter, 21 May 1865.

69. JSK to HMK, Letter, 25 February 1863.

70. Ibid.

71. *Regimental Day Books of the 121st New York Volunteers*, 26 August 1862.

72. Mark M. Boatner III, *Civil War Dictionary* (Revised, New York: David McKay Company, 1988), 266.

73. JSK to HMK, Letter, 17 October 1862. See: Holt, *A Surgeon's Civil War*, 36–37.

74. JSK to HMK, Letter, 19 March 1863.

75. Ibid.

76. Phisterer, *New York State in War of the Rebellion*, 3438.

77. JSK to HMK, Letter, 19 March, 1863.

78. *Regimental Day Books of the 121st New York Volunteers*, 5 April 1863.

THREE: *"A most terrible battle"* (MAY 1863–JULY 1863)

1. OR, series 1, part 1, vol. 25:857.

2. Ralph Happel, *Salem Church Embattled* (Washington, DC: National Park Service, 1980), 22.

3. OR, series 1, part 1, vol. 25:581.

4. OR, series 1, part 1, vol.25:858.

5. C. E. Rice, *The Letters and Writings of the Late Lieutenant Adam Clarke Rice* (Little Falls, New York: *Journal and Courier*, 1864), 73. It is interesting to note that Kidder never mentioned this act to his wife.

6. OR, series 1, part 1, vol. 25:589.

7. Ibid., 590.

8. See: OR, series 1, part 1, vol. 25:561. The 43rd New York did participate in the storming column attack on the heights. The New Jersey troops Captain Kidder speaks of were probably those of Brig. Gen. Thomas Nellis' 3rd Brigade and the Vermonters, those of Brig. Gen. Albion Howes' 2nd Brigade.

9. Hamilton D. Hurd, *History of Otsego County, New York* (Philadelphia: Everts and Fariss, 1878), 174. Willis Hillsinger, a neighbor from Laurens, was a member of the 43rd New York Volunteers; he was killed at Fredericksburg, as Kidder stated, on May 3.

10. OR, series 1, part I, vol. 25: 578–79. The 23rd New Jersey did manage to get to the woods but came under heavy fire in much the same way as the 121st New York had.

11. *New York Adjutant General's Report*, series no. 36; 18. Although Captain Kidder was disappointed with the thirty-two-year-old Laurens farmer, Zebulon Bowen did serve with distinction throughout the rest of the war and was wounded at Spotsylvania.

12. Col. William Lessig of the 96th Pennsylvania made no note of this rally around the colors in his official report of the battle.

13. It is not clear who Captain Kidder is referring to, for there was only one lieutenant assigned to Company I at this time and that was Delavan Bates.

14. OR, series 1, part 1, vol. 25:858. Confederate losses at Salem Church have often been overlooked. Confederate Gen. Cadmus Marcellus Wilcox in his official report of the battle, states that his victory was "dearly earned." He reported 495 men killed, wounded, and missing.

15. Holt, *A Surgeon's Civil War*, 92. Leroy Hall and Sedate Foote were no doubt with Dr. Irving Hotaling, a newly appointed assistant surgeon of the 121st New York. Tragically, the regiment had only the services of Hotaling and Holt at this battle. Hotaling had the lion's share of the work that day as Dr. Daniel Holt and the entire Drum Corps were captured and held by the Confederates for ten days until they were released.

16. *Report of the 35th Annual Reunion of the 121st New York Volunteers* (1911), 19–20. The colors changed hands four times during the battle.

17. John S. Kidder was wrong. The Union cavalry performed a raid as a diversion during the Chancellorsville Campaign. This raid is still the subject of debate among historians.

18. See Phisterer, *New York State in the War of the Rebellion*, 3432. Lieutenant Gorton was promoted to captain immediately after the battle.

19. The forty-year-old Peter S. Perine never did get promoted after this battle or any other. He was mustered out of the regiment as a sergeant.

20. Stephen W. Sears, *Chancellorsville* (Boston and New York: Houghton Mifflin Company, 1996), 394. Mayre's Heights, which Captain Kidder refers to, was retaken by Confederate Gen. Jubal A. Early's troops on May 4.

21. Eventually, the VI Corps did retreat in this manner.

22. JSK to HMK, Letter, 8 May 1863. Delavan Bates Letters, John G. Saint Collection, Springfield, Ill.

23. JSK to HMK, Letter, 16 May 1863.

24. John S. Kidder Papers, Equipment List, Battle of Salem Church, July 27, 1863, Kidder Family Papers, Jerry Reed Collection, Whitesboro, N.Y.

25. JSK to HMK, Letter, 16 May 1863.

26. Ibid.

27. Edward Kidder file, National Archives Pension records.

28. JSK to HMK, Letter, 16 May 1863. Other officers agreed with Captain Kidder in the placement of troops at Salem Church. "I must say that some one of our Generals, either Brooks or Sedgwick, committed a great error, in thus crowding our forces into that Hell-hole on Sunday afternoon, without first ascertaining the strength and position of the enemy," wrote Lt. Adam Clarke Rice. *Letters and Writings of Adam Clarke Rice*, 14 May 1863.

Kidder was, naturally, proud of the efforts of his own regiment, but was perhaps unduly harsh in his assessment of the fighting abilities of the Jersey Brigade. As they retreated from the fighting, so did the 121st New York.

For the first, and certainly not the last, time, Captain Kidder expresses his particular disdain for the predominantly German XI Corps. This Corps received the brunt of Stonewall Jackson's celebrated flanking movement of May 2, 1863.

29. JSK to HMK, Letter, 1 June 1863.

30. Newton Martin Curtis, *From Bull Run to Chancellorsville: The Story of the Sixteenth New York Infantry* (New York: G. P. Putnam's Sons, The Knickerbocker Press, 1906), 302.

31. JSK to HMK, Letter, 1 June 1863.

32. Stephen Ambrose, *Upton and the Army* (Baton Rouge: Louisiana State University Press, 1964), 22–23.

33. JSK to HMK, Letter, 1 June 1863.

34. Ibid. Captain Gorton was still recovering from his wound when he accepted this promotion but eventually resigned on October 5, 1863. Phisterer, *New York State in the War of the Rebellion*, 3432.

35. JSK to HMK, Letter, undated, but probably written in late May or early June 1863.

36. Ibid.

37. Ibid.

38. Phisterer, *New York State in the War of the Rebellion*, 3439. Robert D. Wilson had been a staff officer on Brigade Commander Gen. Joseph Bartlett's staff. It should be also noted that Lt. Lewis C. Bartlett was a brother to the brigade commander. Official records indicate that James P. Wilson accepted the commission of major but never served in the position.

39. John J. Ingraham Letters, 1 June 1863.

40. JSK to HMK, Letter, undated.

41. Ibid.

42. JSK to HMK, Letter, 1 June 1863.

43. Ibid.

44. JSK to HMK, Letter, 12 June 1863.

45. JSK to HMK, Letter, 17 June 1863. A sulkey is a light two-wheeled carriage or chaise.

46. Ibid.; Elisha Hunt Rhodes, *All for the Union*, ed. Robert Hunt Rhodes (New York: Orion Books, 1985), 113. Elisha Hunt Rhodes of the 2nd Rhode Island Infantry recorded the same scene in his diary.

47. JSK to HMK, Letter, 17 June 1863.

48. JSK to HMK, Letter, 12 June 1863.

49. JSK to HMK, Letter, 17 June 1863.

50. Ibid.

51. Ibid.

52. Ibid.

53. JSK to HMK, Letter, 1 July 1863.

54. Ibid.

55. Ibid.

56. Ibid.

57. OR, series 1, part 3, vol. 27:465, 567.

58. Ibid.

59. JSK to HMK, Letter, 17 June 1863.

60. JSK to HMK, Letter, 9 July 1863. According to the Regimental History of the 121st, Captain Kidder was well within his authority to act in this manner. "Orders were given the officers to shoot stragglers, and every man

was impressed with the seriousness of the situation." See Best, *History of the 121st*, 88.

61. OR, series 1, part 1, vol. 27:251. Maj. Gen. Abner Doubleday, who had assumed command of the I Corps after the death of Maj. Gen. John F. Reynolds, reported staggering casualties for the corps on the first day of fighting at Gettysburg. "The First Corps only consisted of about 8,200 men when it entered the battle. It was reduced at the close of the engagement to about 2,450." The XI Corps had been pushed through the center of town and eventually held their ground at Cemetery Hill.

62. OR, series, 1, part 1, vol. 26:180. Captain Kidder is making reference to Brig. Gen. Romeyn B. Ayre's division of the V Corps, which contained two brigades of U.S. Regulars. As to the role of the Pennsylvania Reserves, Kidder was commenting on the activities of Col. William McCandles. His men charged down the north side of Little Round Top into the Wheat Field.

63. The cannonade Captain Kidder is referring to is the massive bombardment that preceded Pickett's Charge. The combination of about 150 Confederate and an almost equal number of federal field pieces could be heard as far away as Harrisburg.

64. Phisterer, *New York State in War of the Rebellion*, 2797–2813. The 76th New York was, indeed, "badly cut up" as Kidder stated. At the Battle of Gettysburg, the unit, which drew men from Cortland and Otsego County, suffered 234 casualties including Maj. Andrew Jackson Grover. Four other officers died of their wounds and an additional thirteen were wounded. Although his arm was amputated, Charlie Matteson did not fall into the hands of the enemy.

65. One of the most serious I Corps losses on the first day of the battle was that of Corps Commander Gen. John F. Reynolds. While placing his troops into position along McPherson's Ridge, he was killed. John S. Kidder was, perhaps, overly critical of the popular I Corps commander. Reynolds was reacting to a desperate situation. Kidder would be just as severe with his reaction to the loss of his own commander in less than a year's time.

66. Boatner, *Civil War Dictionary*, 275. The cavalry action Captain Kidder witnessed was the Union attack on the right wing of Longstreet's Corps near the Big Round Top. It was led by Brig. Gen. Elon Farnsworth who had been wearing his stars for just five days. Farnsworth advised his superiors that the attack was unwise given the rough terrain. This observation proved all too true. The attack was foolhardy, accomplished nothing, and deprived the cavalry of a good officer. The twenty-six-year-old Farnsworth was mortally wounded having been hit five times.

67. The Confederate prisoner he spoke to may have exaggerated this number to impress Kidder. When Lee marched north on June 30, he had about 79,880 men.

68. Boatner, *Civil War Dictionary*, 339. Now it was Kidder's turn to exaggerate. In addition to the erroneous rumor that Longstreet had been captured, the prisoner count is too great for that day. Confederates listed as missing or captured for the three day battle number between 5,150 and 5,425.

69. These would be the guns of Battery C, 3rd Massachusetts Artillery.

70. The "high hill" Captain Kidder refers to is Little Round Top.

71. The rocks Kidder speaks of are a collection of boulders known as Devil's Den. This was a perfect location for rebel sharpshooters. The general that was killed was Brig. Gen. Stephen Weed (1834-1863). An 1854 graduate of West Point, Weed was mortally wounded when a Rebel sharpshooter's bullet passed through both shoulders and severed his spine. As he lay dying, he summoned his friend, Lt. Charles Edward Hazlett. A witness, Lt. Col. David T. Jenkins of the 146th New York, reported that Weed said, "My sister." In an instant, another bullet crashed through Hazlett's brain, killing him. Weed died later that day in excruciating pain. See: Glenn Tucker, *High Tide at Gettysburg* (Ohio: Morningside Bookshop, 1973), 264. The news of Hazlett's death probably stunned Col. Emory Upton. Both of them graduated from West Point in May 1861. See *Cullum Memorial Edition Register of Graduates and Former Cadets United States Military Academy* (West Point, New York: West Point Alumni Foundation, 1960).

72. Warner, *Generals in Blue*, 426-28. Prussian born Carl Schurz came to the United States in 1852. A staunch abolitionist, he campaigned for Abraham Lincoln in 1860 and was commissioned a Brigadier General of Volunteers two years later. This move pleased the great number of German-Americans who were already serving in the Union Army.

73. OR, part 1, vol. 27:173-85.

74. Edwin B. Coddington, *The Gettysburg Campaign* (New York: Charles Scribner's Sons, 1968), 151. Captain Kidder is being overly critical. New York's Governor Horatio Seymour did send 13,500 militia to assist in the crisis in Pennsylvania. "New York, however, was the only state in the northeast to send any large number of troops to the threatened area."

75. Boatner, *Civil War Dictionary*, 339. But the numbers were not equal. Although both sides had been mauled after three days of fighting, General Robert E. Lee had an effective strength of about forty-seven thousand men and General George G. Meade could count on about sixty-five thousand men.

76. Ibid., 273-74. While at the same time building pontoon bridges to recross the Potomac River, Lee had, indeed, fortified his position at Williamsport.

77. Philip Randall was in Company I of the 144th New York Infantry.

78. JSK to HMK, Letter, 9 July 1863.

79. Ibid.

80. Ibid.

81. Ibid.

82. Ibid.

83. Ibid.

84. Ibid.

FOUR: "*I do not wish to boast, but . . .*"
(AUGUST 1863–APRIL 1864)

1. JSK to HMK, Letters, 12 August 1863 and 12 October 1863.

2. JSK to HMK, Letter, 12 August 1863.

3. Jeffry D. Wert, *Mosby's Rangers* (New York: Simon and Schuster, 1990), 32.

4. JSK to HMK, Letter, 12 August 1863.

5. Ibid.

6. Ibid.

7. Ibid.

8. Ibid.

9. Ibid.

10. Ibid.

11. Ibid.

12. *Historical and Statistical Gazetter of New York State* (Syracuse, New York: J. H. French, 1860), 150. Otsego County had a very small black population of 172, five years before the Civil War. According to the 1860 census, there was only one black living in Laurens, nine year old Henry Johnson.

13. Holt, *A Surgeon's Civil War*, 60–61, 77.

14. JSK to HMK, Letter, 12 August 1863.

15. Ibid.

16. JSK to HMK, Letter, 26 August 1863.

17. Nevins, *The War for the Union: War Becomes Revolution 1862–1863*, 463–64.

18. JSK to HMK, Letters, 25 February, and 1 March 1863.

19. Nevins, *The War for the Union: War Becomes Revolution 1862–1863*, 463–64.

20. JSK to HMK, Letter, 27 September 1863.

21. Nevins, *The War for the Union: War Becomes Revolution 1862–1863*, 465.

22. JSK to HMK, Letter, 26 August 1863.

23. John S. Kidder Paper, undated, Kidder Obituary. Kidder Family Papers, Jerry Reed Collection, Whitesboro, N.Y.

24. JSK to HMK, Letter, 4 October 1862.

25. JSK to HMK, Letter, 27 September 1863.

26. JSK to HMK, Letter, 14 October 1863.

27. *Biographical Dictionary of the Governors of the United States*, eds. Robert Sobel and John Raimo, vol. III (Connecticut: Meckler Books, 1978), 1210.

28. Ibid.

29. JSK to HMK, Letter, 14 October 1863; see Andrew Gregg Curtin (1815–1894), "Soldier's Friend," *Dictionary of American Biography*, vol. II (New York: Charles Scribner's Sons, 1928), 606.

30. *Dictionary of American Biography*, vol 9, 8. Horatio Seymour (1810–1886) states that he, "was tireless at filling up the state quotas for the Union Armies." His letter to Lincoln was published on page one of the 10 August 1863 issue of *The New York Times*.

31. JSK to HMK, Letter, 12 August 1863.

32. JSK to HMK, Letter, 18 October 1863. According to the 1860 Census of Laurens, William Comstock had real estate valued at $22,000 and employed three full-time farm hands, 34.

33. JSK to HMK, Letter, 18 October 1863.

34. JSK to HMK, Letter, 12 August 1863.

35. Bureau of the Census, *1865 Laurens Township Census*, 60.

36. JSK to HMK, Letter, 18 October 1863.

37. *New York Adjutant General's Report*, series no. 36; 23.

38. Ibid., 78.

39. JSK to HMK, Letter, 12 August 1863.

40. *New York Adjutant General's Report*, series no. 36; 23, 78.

41. JSK to HMK, Letter, 16 August 1863.

42. Robert I. Alotta, *Civil War Justice: Union Army Executions Under Lincoln* (Shippensburg, Pa.: White Mane, 1989), 75–76.

43. Ibid., 204.

44. JSK to HMK, Letter, 12 October 1863.

45. Ingraham Letters, 9 October 1863.

46. JSK to HMK, Letter, 27 August 1863.

47. JSK to HMK, Letter, 16 October 1863.

48. Here, John S. Kidder freely uses the quote made famous during the Battle of Lake Erie during the War of 1812, by U.S. Naval officer hero, Oliver Hazzard Perry.

49. It was a bothersome wound for Captain Casler; he resigned on October 14, 1864. *New York Adjutant General's Report*, series no. 36; 31.

50. OR, series 1, part 1, vol. 29:593.

51. Douglas Southall Freeman, *Lee's Lieutenants: A Study in Command*, vol. 3 (New York: Charles Scribner's Sons, 1942–1944), 267. According to Freeman, the affair at Rappahannock Station sent, "shock waves throughout Lee's Army."

52. Francis B. Morse, *Personal Experiences in the War of the Great Rebellion: the Memoirs of Adjutant Francis W. Morse* (Albany, New York: Munsell, Printer, 1866), 55.

53. *Hamilton County Register*, 27 December 1918.

54. Henry B. Walker Letters, 8 November 1863, Bird Library, Syracuse University, Syracuse, New York. Walker also mentioned that the day of the battle just happened to be his birthday.

55. Best, *History of the 121st New York*, 106.

56. Warner, *Generals in Blue*, 161–62.

57. JSK to HMK, Letter, 5 December 1863.

58. Ibid.

59. OR, series 1, part 1, vol. 29:777.

60. JSK to HMK, Letter, 5 December 1863.

61. OR, series 1, part 1, vol. 29:788. In reality, both units fought well that day and both sustained casualties. The 87th Pennsylvania had a, "very brisk

fight," and lost one man killed and had eleven others wounded. The 106th New York was compelled to retreat about sixty to seventy yards before being able to establish a line of battle. This, they held until dusk at the cost of four killed and fifteen wounded.

62. JSK to HMK, Letter, 5 December 1863.

63. OR, series 1, part 1, vol. 29:796. Sedgwick said that he was on the march by midnight and was in position by daylight.

64. John Quinby, Letter to his sister, father and mother, 11 November 1863. HCHS, Herkimer, N.Y.

65. JSK to HMK, Letter, 27 October 1863.

66. Ingraham Letters, 5 December 1863.

67. Ibid.

68. JSK to HMK, Lettr, 5 December 1863.

69. OR, series 1, part 1, vol. 29:796.

70. Ibid., 796–97.

71. JSK to HMK, Letter, 5 December 1863.

72. Boatner, *Civil War Dictionary*, 869.

73. JSK to HMK, Letter, 5 December 1863.

74. Ibid.

75. Ibid.

76. Freeman, *Lee's Lieutenants*, vol. 3, 275; see OR, series 1, part 1, vol. 29:16.

77. JSK to HMK, Letter, 5 December 1863.

78. Freeman, *Lee's Lieutenants*, vol. 3:276; see Freeman Cleaves, *Meade of Gettysburg* (Ohio: Morningside Bookshop, 1980), 212.

79. JSK to HMK, Letter, 5 December 1863.

80. OR, series 1, part 1, vol. 25:184. The 10th Vermont was in Washington from January 31 to May 31, 1863.

81. Ibid., 780.

82. Ibid., 682.

83. Ibid.

84. JSK to HMK, Letter, 5 December 1863.

85. OR, series 1, part 1, vol. 25:747; see Cleaves, *Meade of Gettysburg*, 209.

86. JSK to HMK, Letter, 18 December 1863.

87. Cleaves, *Meade of Gettysburg*, 212.

88. JSK to HMK, Letter, 18 December 1863.

89. JSK to HMK, Letter, 5 December 1863.

90. Best, *History of the 121st New York*, 112–13.

91. *35th Annual Report of the 121st New York Regimental Association*, 29; Wiley, *The Life of Billy Yank*, 57.

92. The description of the winter camp for 1863 was vividly recalled in the *35th Annual Report of the 121st New York Regimental Association*, 29; see JSK to HMK, Letter, 27 December 1863.

93. JSK to HMK, Letter, 18 October 1863.

94. JSK to HMK, Letter, 18 December 1863.

95. John J. Ingraham Letters, January 1864.

96. JSK to HMK, Letter, 27 December 1863.

97. Ibid.

98. *New York Adjutant General's Report*, series no. 36; 124.

99. Henry J. Walker Letters, 5 January 1864, Bird Library, Syracuse University, Syracuse, New York.

100. JSK to HMK, Letter, 2 October 1863.

101. Ibid.

102. Ibid.

103. John J. Ingraham Letters, 29 February 1864.

104. George W. Collins, Letter to his cousin, 17 December 1863. Mr. and Mrs. Earle Schwaiger, Clinton, New York.

105. JSK to HMK, Letter, 7 January 1864; see Phisterer, *New York in War of the Rebellion*.

106. Wiley, *The Life of Billy Yank*, 252.

107. Holt, *A Surgeon's Civil War*, 32.

108. Henry B. Walker Letters, 18 September 1863, and 30 September 1863, Bird Library, Syracuse University, Syracuse, New York.

109. Cassius Delavan Diary, 27 November 1862, Walt Dingman Collection, Middleville, N.Y.

110. JSK to HMK, Letter, 27 December 1863. Floating islands are custards with floating masses of whipped cream.

111. Egbert Olcott File, National Archives, Washington, D.C.

112. JSK to HMK, Letter, 27 December 1863. The regimental history did not mention the incident and neither did the Regimental Association notes.

113. JSK to HMK, Letter, 7 January 1864.

114. Best, *History of the 121st New York*, 113.

115. JSK to HMK, Letter, 18 December 1863.

116. Ibid.

117. Ibid. Too bad for Captain Kidder that David Winter didn't share his enthusiasm. He never did join the 121st New York.

118. Kidder File, Military, National Archives, Washington, D.C.

119. JSK to HMK, Letter, 7 January 1864.

120. John J. Ingraham, Letter to his sister, 22 February 1864.

121. JSK to HMK, Letter, 23 January 1864.

122. JSK to HMK, Letter, 7 January 1864.

123. JSK to HMK, Letter, 20 February 1864. National Archives.

124. Elisha Fisher File, National Archives, Washington, D.C.

125. JSK to HMK, Letter, 23 January 1864.

126. Bates to JSK, Letter, 17 March 1864, John G. Saint Collection, Springfield, Ill.

127. Bates to JSK, Letter, 4 March 1864, John G. Saint Collection, Springfield, Ill.

128. Fish to JSK, Letter, 30 March 1864, John G. Saint Collection, Springfield, Ill.

129. Ibid.

130. JSK to HMK, Letter, 24 April 1864.

131. Ibid.

132. *New York Adjutant General's Report*, series no. 36; 157, 72.

FIVE: *"I rec'd a severe wound in the face."* (MAY 1864)

1. Mary Wallitt DeYoung, *Drummer Boy* (Spencer, Iowa: DeYoung Press, 1990), 258.

2. Bruce Catton, *A Stillness at Appomattox* (Garden City, New York: Doubleday, 1953), 47–48.

3. JSK to HMK, Letter, 19 May 1864.

4. John J. Ingraham to Mary Green, Letter, 31 March 1864.

5. OR, part 1, vol. 36:493. Douglas Southall Freeman cites several sources, stating that Lee had between sixty-one thousand and sixty-five thousand men. See: Freeman, *Lee's Lieutenants,* 270.

6. JSK to HMK, Letter, 22 April 1864.

7. JSK to HMK, Letter, 16 April 1864.

8. JSK to HMK, Letter, 25 May 1864; see Holt, *A Surgeon's Civil War,* 180.

9. JSK to HMK, Letter, 25 May 1864.

10. OR, part 1, vol. 36:665.

11. Ibid.

12. Ibid., 605.

13. Ibid., 665.

14. Best, *History of the 121st New York,* 120–21. John S. Kidder had perfect attendance with one mysterious exception. Pvt. Richard Clifford, a trumpeter from the 16th New York, was listed as a deserter on May 4, 1864 at the Germanna Ford Crossing in the *1903 Annual Report.* However, the *121st Descriptive Books* in the National Archives, list him as a transfer to the 1st Massachusetts Artillery, and the June 2, 1864, *LFJC* lists him as killed in action at the Wilderness on May 6, 1864, 2.

15. John S. Kidder Papers, Jerry Reed Collection, Whitesboro, N.Y.

16. *New York Adjutant General's Report,* series no. 36; 39, 147, 213. Sergeant Colton had been paroled from a Confederate prison camp in December. Treat D. Young eluded his captors in September and returned to the regiment.

17. Boatner, *Civil War Dictionary,* 592–93.

18. JSK to HMK, Letter, 19 May 1864.

19. OR, series 1, vol. 36:608.

20. JSK to HMK, Letter, 19 May 1864.

21. OR, series 1, vol. 36:601.

22. Henry Roback, *History of the 152nd New York Volunteers* (Little Falls, New York: Henry Roback, 1888), 70-71.

23. William D. Matter, *If It Takes All Summer* (University of North Carolina Press, 1988), 107. Matter claims that the march to Chancellorsville was unusually long, perhaps due to the two days of hard fighting and forced marches. Issac O. Best makes no mention of it and neither does Colonel Upton in his official report.

24. Ibid.

25. JSK to HMK, Letter, 14 May 1864.

26. Colonel Upton to Adam Badeau, Letter, 26 December 1873, Library of Congress, Washington, D.C.

27. Matter, *If It Takes All Summer*, 156-58.

28. Ambrose, *Upton and the Army*, 31.

29. Upton to Adam Badeau, Letter, 26 December 1873, Library of Congress, Washington, D.C.

30. This order was reflected in a report filed by Captain Kidder after the May 10 charge. Kidder reported the loss of only "17 rifles, bayonets and cartridge boxes." John S. Kidder Papers, Jerry Reed Collection, Whitesboro, N.Y.

31. Boatner: *Civil War Dictionary*, 641. In the Civil War, a "capped" weapon was one that had a small metal cap with powder placed over the nipple of the rifle. When the hammer struck the cap, a spark was produced that discharged the weapon.

32. OR, series 1, part 1, vol. 36:602-603.

33. Upton to Adam Badeau, Letter, 26 December 1873, Library of Congress, Washington, D.C.

34. Best, *History of the 121st New York*, 129.

35. JSK to HMK, Letter, 30 May 1864.

36. JSK to HMK, Letter, 14 May 1864.

37. William Fox, *Regimental Losses in the Civil War* (Albany, New York, 1889), 78. The use of the bayonet in attacks was very rare in the Civil War and their effectiveness has often been debated. Colonel Upton later said, "Bayonet and sabre cuts are very rare. But at Spotsylvania there were plenty of bayonet wounds."

38. Colonel Upton to Adam Badeau, Letter, 26 December 1873, Library of Congress, Washington, D.C.

39. JSK to HMK, Letter, 30 May 1864.

40. Ibid.

41. Best, *History of the 121st New York,* 132.

42. Fox, *Regimental Losses in the Civil War,* 229, 446.

43. JSK to HMK, Letter, 14 May 1864.

44. Phisterer, *New York State in the War of the Rebellion,* 3436.

45. *New York Adjutant General's Report for 1903,* series no. 36; 116. Delos Lewis File, National Archives, Washington, D.C.

46. JSK to HMK, Letter, 30 May 1864.

47. *Utica Daily Herald,* 24 May 1864, pg. 2.

48. Best, *History of the 121st New York,* 133.

49. OR, series 1, part 1, vol. 36:1029.

50. Ulysses Grant, *Memoirs and Selected Letters* (New York: The Library of America, 1990), 549.

51. Catton, *A Stillness at Appomattox,* 116.

52. Best, *History of the 121st New York,* 144.

53. There is a little confusion as to the exact time Colonel Upton assembled his men. In his official report, he claimed to have assembled at 7:00 A.M. and fighting at 9:30 A.M. Still, other sources say he attacked at 6:00 A.M.

54. *Battles and Leaders of the Civil War,* eds. Robert Underwood Johnson and Clarence Clough Buel, vol. 4 (New York, 1887), 172; Best, *History of the121st New York,* 145.

55. Reverend George W. Bicknell, *History of the Fifth Maine Volunteers* (Portland: Hall L. Davis, 1971), 320. The night before the battle, John D. Fish penned his last letter to his wife. In it he predicted his own death.

56. *Regimental Day Books,* NA. An exact time frame does not exist of the day's actions on May 12 for the 121st New York.

57. JSK to HMK, Letter, 14 May 1864.

58. Matter, *If It Takes All Summer,* 256.

59. OR, series 1, part 1, vol. 36:200.

60. Ibid., 213.

61. Ibid., 230.

62. JSK to HMK, Letter, 27 September 1864.

63. *Letters and Writings of Adam Clarke Rice*, 11–12.

64. JSK to HMK, Letter, 14 May 1864.

65. Ibid.

66. Ibid.

67. OR, series 1, part 1, vol. 36:270.

68. Ibid.

69. George T. Stevens, *Three Years in the VI Corps* (Albany, New York: S. R. Gray, Publishers, 1866), 340.

70. Catton, *A Stillness at Appomattox*, 102–107. OR, series 1, part 1, vol. 36:227.

71. JSK to HMK, Letter, 14 May 1864. Silas Pierce is buried just outside Fredericksburg in the National Cemetery, grave # 1985.

72. Holt, *A Surgeon's Civil War*, 187.

73. *LFJC*, 19 May 1864, pg. 2.

74. JSK to HMK, Letter, 24 April 1864.

75. Ibid.

76. JSK to HMK, Letter, 14 May 1864.

77. OR, series 1, part 1, vol. 36:211.

Six: *U.S. General Hospital, Annapolis, Maryland* (MAY 1864–JUNE 1864)

1. *The Crutch*, 21 May 1864.

2. U.S. Naval Institute Proceedings, vol. 63, no. 11, November 1937, 1612, "Civil War Annapolis."

3. JSK to HMK, Letter, 25 May 1864.

4. John McElroy, *This Was Andersonville* (New York: McDowell, Oblensky, Inc., 1957), 286. Assuming that everyone was treated in the same manner, I relied on the experience of John McElroy.

5. JSK to HMK, Letter, 30 May 1864. Captain Kidder called him, "an old Surgeon of the 155th New York." When he met Dr. William Comstock, the doctor was a fifty-five-year-old graduate of the University of Indiana, Class of 1833. Kidder noted that Comstock was, "quite lame." He was discharged for dis-

ability *twice*, once on October 17, 1864, only to be reinstated one month to the day later. He was discharged a second time on November 26, 1864. *New York Adjutant General's Report*, and Phisterer, *New York State in the War of the Rebellion*, 3810.

6. JSK to HMK, Letter, 25 May 1864.

7. Ibid.

8. JSK to HMK, Letter, 22 May 1864.

9. JSK to HMK, Letter, 19 May 1864.

10. JSK to HMK, Letter, 30 May 1864.

11. JSK to HMK, Letter, 22 May 1864.

12. JSK to HMK, Letter, 30 May 1864.

13. Ibid.

14. JSK to HMK, Letter, 8 June 1864.

15. Phisterer, *New York State in the War of the Rebellion*, 3434.

16. *The Crutch*, 21 May 1864.

17. Ibid., 11 June 1864.

18. Ibid., 18 June 1864.

19. JSK to HMK, Letter, 30 May 1864.

20. Ibid.

21. JSK to HMK, Letter, 22 May 1864.

22. JSK to HMK, Letter, 30 May 1864.

23. JSK to HMK, Letter, 6 June 1864.

24. JSK to HMK, Letter, 30 May 1864.

25. JSK to HMK, Letter, 22 May 1864.

26. Phisterer, *New York State in the War of the Rebellion*, 3778.

27. JSK to HMK, Letter, 22 May 1864.

28. Ibid.

29. JSK to HMK, Letter, 8 June 1864. Phisterer, *New York State in the War of the Rebellion*, 3774.

30. Thomas R. Petrie to John Quinby, Letter, 1 July 1864, HCHS, Herkimer, N.Y. JSK to HMK, Letter, 22 May 1864.

31. Phisterer, *New York State in the War of the Rebellion*, 3778.

32. Ibid., 4104–10.

33. Delavan Hewitt to John Quinby, Letter, 21 February 1865, HCHS, Herkimer, N.Y.

34. James Cronkite to JSK, Letter, 7 June 1864, Kidder Papers, Harrie Washburn Collection, Sharon Springs, N.Y.

35. OR, series 1, part 1, vol. 36:671.

36. *New York 121st Regimental Day Books*, National Archives, Washington, D.C. *New York Adjutant General's Report*, series no. 36; 58, 68.

37. Cronkite to JSK, Letter, 7 June 1864, Kidder Papers, Harrie Washburn Collection, Sharon Springs, N.Y.

38. JSK to HMK, Letter, 30 May 1864.

39. Ibid.

40. Ibid.

41. Ibid.

42. Phisterer, *New York State in the War of the Rebellion*, 2437, 2441, 3186, 3200, 4263–64, 4309; George Worthington Adams, *Doctors in Blue* (New York: Henry Schuman, 1952), 84.

43. JSK to HMK, Letter, 30 May 1864.

44. Ibid.

45. JSK to HMK, Letter, 6 June 1864.

46. Ibid.

47. JSK to HMK, Letter, 30 June 1864.

48. JSK to HMK, Letter, 24 June 1864.

49. Ibid.

50. John S. Kidder File, National Archives, Washington, D.C.

SEVEN: *Elmira Prison* (JULY 1864–DECEMBER 1864)

1. *Oneonta Herald*, April or May 1912, Dick Rose Scrapbook, Kidder Papers, Jerry Reed Collection, Whitesboro, N.Y.

2. Bureau of the Census, Census Records, Laurens, 1860, 1865. Cooperstown, New York: Otsego County Clerk's Office.

3. JSK to HMK, Letter, 8 June 1864.

4. Edward Kidder File, National Archives Pension Records, Washington, D.C. Otsego Census. Otsego County Clerk's Office, Cooperstown, New York.

5. *Boulder Daily Camera*, 1 July 1925. Major Henry Payne Kidder Obituary.

6. *Boulder Daily Camera*, 1 July 1925. Major Henry Payne Kidder File, National Archives Pension Records, Washington, D.C.

7. This letter, printed in its entirety, is in the Pension File of George Kidder in the National Archives, Washington, D.C.

8. Anne Kidder to HMK, Letter, 17 July 1864.

9. A besom is a broom.

10. Anne Kidder to HMK, Letter, 20 July 1864. The diary that Anne Kidder mentions has never been found.

11. JSK to HMK, Letter, 21 July 1864.

12. John S. Kidder File, National Archives, Special Orders 249, July 26, 1864, Washington, D.C.

13. OR, series 1, part 1, vol. 7:146.

14. Phisterer, *New York State in the War of the Rebellion*, 4110.

15. OR, series 1, part 1, vol. 7:604–605.

16. JSK to HMK, Letter, 28 July 1864.

17. JSK to HMK, Letter, 10 September 1864.

18. JSK to HMK, Letter, 28 July 1864.

19. OR, series 2, vol. 7:151.

20. Ibid.

21. OR, series 2, vol. 7:1093.

22. OR, series 2, vol. 7:683; see Clay Holmes, *The Elmira Prison Camp* (New York and London: G. P. Putnam's Sons, 1912), 104.

23. JSK to HMK, Letter, 10 September 1864; *New York Adjutant General's Report for 1901*, Charles Matteson File, National Archives Pension Records, Washington, D.C.

24. JSK to HMK, Letter, 25 September 1864.

25. JSK to HMK, Letter, 13 November 1864.

26. Holmes, *The Elmira Prison Camp*, 44; see Phisterer for a brief description of each regiment.

27. City of Elmira historian, Carl Morrell, "Elmira Prison," no date.

28. *Miller's Photographic History of the Civil War: Prisons and Hospitals*, vol. 7 (New York: The Review of Reviews Co., 1911), 147.

29. JSK to HMK, Letter, 13 November 1864. The *Official Records* have no mention of prisoners from Elmira being shot while escaping.

30. Holmes, *The Elmira Prison Camp*, 161.

31. JSK to HMK, Letter, 25 September 1864.

32. Glenn H. Worthington, *Fighting for Time* (Baltimore, Md.: Baltimore Day Printing Company, 1932), 194.

33. JSK to HMK, Letter, 25 September 1864.

34. Warner, *Generals in Blue*, 416–17.

35. Warner, *Generals in Blue*, 519–20. Placed on sick leave, Colonel Upton never returned to the Army of the Potomac. He later commanded a division of cavalry in Georgia. When the Civil War ended, he was one of the few officers to have successfully commanded units of infantry, cavalry, and artillery.

36. Jeffry Wert, *From Winchester to Cedar Creek* (Pennsylvania: South Mountain Press, Inc., 1987), 237.

37. JSK to HMK, Letter, 21 October 1864.

38. Best, *History of the 121st New York*, 199.

39. JSK to HMK, Letter, 10 November 1864.

40. Henry Galpin File, National Archives, Washington, D.C.

41. *34th Reunion of the 121st New York*, 10 August 1910, 14. Letter from Ida Remmel Benson, sister of William Remmel, n.p.

42. JSK to HMK, Letter, 4 November 1864.

43. Moses Wright File, National Archives, Washington, D.C.

44. JSK to HMK, Letter, 10 November 1864.

45. JSK to HMK, Letter, 4 November 1864.

46. *History of Otsego County*, 174.

47. JSK to HMK, Letter, 4 November 1864. *History of Otsego County*, 174.

48. JSK to HMK, letter, 4 November 1864.

49. *Utica Herald*, April or May 1912. John S. Kidder Papers, Jerry Reed Collection, Whitesboro, N.Y.

50. JSK to HMK, Letter, 25 September 1864.

51. JSK to HMK, Letter, 10 November 1864.

52. JSK to HMK, Letter, 13 November 1864.

53. JSK to HMK, Letter, 28 July 1864.

54. JSK to HMK, Letter, 13 December 1864.

55. JSK to HMK, Letter, 1 October 1864.

56. JSK to HMK, Letter, 30 December 1864; See OR, series 2, vol. 2:127.

57. JSK to HMK, Letter, 30 December 1864.

58. James Cronkite to S. Thomas, Letter, 24 December 1864, *Regimental Day Books of the 121st New York*, National Archives, Washington, D.C.

59. Holmes, *The Elmira Prison Camp*, 330.

60. *9th Virginia Cavalry*, compiled by Robert Krick (Lynchburg, Virginia: H. E. Howard, 1982), 1:71.

61. John A. Evans died on June 21, 1921 in Stafford County, Virginia. Krick, *9th Virginia Cavalry*, 71.

EIGHT: *"Victory is ours"* (JANUARY 1865–APRIL 1865)

1. Best, *History of the 121st New York*, 203.

2. JSK to HMK, Letter, 30 January 1865.

3. Best, *History of the 121st New York*, 204.

4. *History of Otsego County*, 173-74.

5. Best, *History of the 121st New York*, 204; JSK to HMK, Letter, 30 January 1865.

6. Best, *History of the 121st New York*, 204.

7. Phisterer, *New York State in the War of the Rebellion*, 2043-44.

8. *Regimental Day Books of the 121st New York*, Cronkite to Bartlett, Letter, 31 December 1864, 40. National Archives, Washington, D.C.

9. *Regimental Day Books of the 121st New York*, Cronkite to Fenton, Letter, 2 January 1865, 41. National Archives, Washington, D.C.

10. JSK to HMK, Letter, 30 January 1865.

11. John S. Kidder Papers, voucher no. 5, February 3, 1865, "Camp in the field at Petersburg." Jerry Reed Collection, Whitesboro, N.Y.

12. Adams, *Memorial and Letters of Rev. John R. Adams*, 199.

13. JSK to HMK, Letter, 30 January 1865.

14. Noah Adam Trudeau, *The Last Citadel, Petersburg, Virginia, June 1864–1865* (Boston: Little Brown and Company, 1991), 312.

15. Warner, *Generals in Blue*, 553. Wheaton had *real* Civil War connections. His father-in-law was ranking Confederate General Samuel Cooper and his mother-in-law was sister to James Mason of the famous Mason and Slidell affair, a major diplomatic flap that almost involved the Lincoln administration in a war with England.

16. Adams, *Memorial and Letters of Rev. John R. Adams*, 199–200.

17. OR, series 1, vol. 46:298.

18. Ibid.

19. Adams, *Memorial and Letters of Rev. John R. Adams*, 200.

20. Trudeau, *The Last Citadel*, 322.

21. OR, series 1, vol. 46:300; Phisterer, *New York State in the War of the Rebellion*, 3424.

22. Adams, *Memorial and Letters of Rev. John R. Adams*, 201.

23. JSK to HMK, Letter, 12 March 1865.

24. Ibid.

25. Adams, *Memorial and Letters of Rev. John R. Adams*, 212.

26. Ibid.

27. Ibid., 205–206.

28. John J. Ingraham to his sister, Letter, 23 February 1865.

29. Adams, *Memorial and Letters of Rev. John R. Adams*, 203.

30. JSK to HMK, Letter, 12 March 1865.

31. John J. Ingraham to his sister, Letter, 23 February 1865.

32. Adams, *Memorial and Letters of Rev. John R. Adams*, 205.

33. OR, series 1, vol. 46:100.

34. Adams, *Memorial and Letters of Rev. John R. Adams*, 203.

35. OR, series 1, vol. 46:300.

36. Best, *History of the 121st New York*, 207.

37. Adams, *Memorial and Letters of Rev. John R. Adams*, 213. *Otsego Biographical Review*, 311.

38. *Otsego Biographical Review*, 311.

39. Boatner, *Civil War Dictionary*, 647.

40. OR, part 3, vol. 46:498.

41. JSK to HMK, Letter, 10 April 1865.

42. Ibid.

43. OR, series 1, vol. 46:936; Best, *History of the 121st New York*, 209.

44. Best, *History of the 121st New York*, 211.

45. OR, series 1, vol. 46:904.

46. OR, series 1, vol. 46:938.

47. *New York Adjutant General's Report*, series no. 36; 47; Interview with granddaughter, Mary Jo Dasey, Little Falls, New York.

48. Best, *History of the 121st New York*, 202; *New York Adjutant General's Report*, series, no., 88.

49. OR, series 1, vol. 46:932.

50. Best, *History of the 121st New York*, 212.

51. OR, series 1, vol. 46:921.

52. Ibid., 933.

53. JSK to HMK, Letter, 10 April 1865.

54. OR, series 1, vol. 46:938. Years later, Harrison Hawthorne's claim would be disputed by members of the 37th Massachusetts despite several eyewitness accounts to the contrary, including a statement made by Chaplain Adams.

55. Pvt. Benjamin Gifford deserted on New Year's Day, 1863, and did not return to the 121st until April 1, 1863. He was arrested on his father's farm and returned to the unit with no charges being filed against him. Benjamin Gifford File, National Archives, Washington, D.C.

56. Best, *History of the 121st New York*, 216; Phisterer, *New York State in the War of the Rebellion*, 3424.

57. *New York Adjutant General's Report*, series no. 36; 133.

58. OR, series 1, vol. 46:937.

59. James W. Cronkite File, National Archives Pension Records, Military Service Records, Washington, D.C.

60. Phisterer, *New York State in the War of the Rebellion*, 3428.

61. JSK to HMK, Letter, 10 April 1865.

62. Ibid.

63. John S. Kidder Papers, undated newspaper article, Jerry Reed Collection, Whitesboro, N.Y.

64. *New York Adjutant General's Report*, series no. 36.

65. John J. Ingraham Letter, 19 April 1865.

66. JSK to HMK, Letter, 19 April 1865.

67. Adams, *Memorial and Letters of Rev. John R. Adams*, 219.

68. JSK to HMK, Letter, 19 April 1865.

69. JSK to HMK, Letter, 1 October 1864.

70. JSK to HMK, Letter, 19 April 1865.

71. JSK to HMK, Letter, 25 April 1865.

72. Ibid.

73. JSK to HMK, Letter, 29 April 1865.

74. JSK to HMK, Letter, 25 April 1865.

75. JSK to HMK, Letter, 29 April 1865.

76. John J. Ingraham Letter, 19 May 1865.

77. JSK to HMK, Letter, 21 May 1865.

78. Ibid.

79. Ibid.

80. Ibid.

81. Ibid.

82. Noah Adam Trudeau, *Out of the Storm* (Baton Rouge: Louisiana State University Press, 1955), 356-57.

83. Adams, *Memorial and Letters of Rev. John R. Adams*, 223.

84. JSK to HMK, Letter, 21 May 1965.

85. John S. Kidder File, National Archives, Washington, D.C.

86. JSK to HMK, Letter, 28 May 1865.

87. Ibid.

88. JSK to HMK, Letter, 21 May 1865.

89. Best, *History of the 121st New York*, 225.

90. *LFJC*, 30 August 1865, pg. 2.

91. Ibid.

92. New York Monuments Commission for the Battlefields of Gettysburg and Chattanooga, *Final Report on the Battlefield of Gettysburg* (Albany, New York: J. B. Lyon Company, Printers, 1900), 842–43; Lt. Col. J. W. Cronkite, *Report of the Gettysburg Monument Committee, of the 121st New York Volunteers* (Otsego Republican Press, N.D.), 80–81.

93. *LFJC*, 6 July 1865, pg. 1.

94. Ibid.

95. Ibid.

NINE: *Laurens, the Port Warden and Retirement* (1865–1905)

1. The 1865 Laurens Census indicates that one of the boarders was also employed as a domestic servant. This was Mary Secor.

2. *Oneonta Herald*, 12 July 1878, pg. 3.

3. Ibid., 10 January 1879, pg. 3.

4. Ibid., 31 January 1879, pg. 3.

5. Ibid., 12 December 1879, pg. 3.

6. John S. Kidder Papers, April 11, 1896 news article from the *New York Herald*.

7. Kidder Papers, handwritten copy, Jerry Reed Collection, Whitesboro, N.Y.

8. *New York Times*, 23 April 1880, pg. 8.

9. Ibid.

10. *Oneonta Herald*, 30 April 1880, pg. 3.

11. Bureau of the Census, *Census Records, Laurens Township*, 1880.

12. Edgar A. Werner, *Civil List and Constitutional History of the County and State of New York* (Albany, New York: Weed, Parsons and Co. Publishers, 1886), 219.

13. Ibid., 200.

14. *The New York Times*, 11 April 1896, pg. 9.

15. The New York State Archives has only one set of Port Warden Records, 1903-1928.

16. Kidder Genealogy, Jerry Reed Collection, Whitesboro, N.Y.

17. *Report of the Gettysburg Monument Committee*, compiled by Lt. Col. J. W. Cronkite, *Otsego Republican Press*, no date, 9.

18. Ibid., 56-59.

19. Ibid., 18.

20. Undated newspaper clipping, most likely the *Utica Globe*, Jerry Reed Collection, Whitesboro, N.Y.

21. Ibid.

22. John S. Kidder File, National Archives Pension Records, Dr. Francis Winsor was the attending physician.

23. Otsego County Clerk, *Letters of Administration*, Book 13:320.

24. Author's interview with Frances Warren, 15 January 1995, Mohawk Homestead, Mohawk, New York.

Appendix A

1. *Hamilton County Register*, 20 December 1918.

2. Ibid.

3. Delavan Bates to JSK, Letter, 27 January 1889, Kidder Papers, Jerry Reed Collection, Whitesboro, N.Y.

4. James W. Cronkite File, National Archives, Washington, D.C.

5. Charles Dean File, National Archives Pension and Service Records, Washington, D.C.

6. *Who's Who in American History* (Chicago: A. N. Marquis Company, 1967), 249.

7. John D. Fish File, *National Archives Pension Records*, Washington, D.C., Herkimer County Courthouse *Probate Records*, Herkimer, New York.

8. Elisha Fisher File, National Archives Pension Records, Washington, D.C.

9. *Oneonta Herald*, 12 December 1908.

10. Sedate Foote File, National Archives Pension Records. Washington, D.C.

11. Henry Galpin File, National Archives, Washington, D.C.

12. Leroy Hall File, National Archives, Washington, D.C.

13. George Kidder File, National Archives, Washington, D.C.

14. Edward Kidder File, National Archives, Washington, D.C.

15. Kidder Family Genealogy, Jerry Reed Collection, Whitesboro, N.Y.

16. Major Henry Payne Kidder File, National Archives Pension Records, Washington, D.C. See: the *Boulder Daily Camera*, 1 July 1925.

17. William Kidder File, National Archives Pension Records, Washington, D.C.

18. Edward Kidder File, National Archives, Washington, D.C.

19. Andrew Mather File, National Archives, Washington, D.C.

20. *Oneonta Herald*, 4 and 6 August 1894.

21. Egbert Olcott File, National Archives Pension Records, Washington, D.C.

22. Warner, *Generals in Blue*, 519–20.

Bibliography

Manuscript Collections

Cassius Delavan Papers. Walt Dingman, Middleville, New York.

Delavan Bates Papers. John G. Saint, M.D., Springfield, Illinois.

Emory Upton Letters. Library of Congress, Washington, D.C.

George W. Collins Letters. Mr. and Mrs. Earle Schwaiger, Clinton, New York.

Henry B. Walker Letters. Byrd Memorial Library, Syracuse University, Syracuse, New York.

John Quimby Letters. Herkimer County Historical Society, Herkimer, N.Y.

Kidder Family Papers. Harrie Washburn, Sharon Springs, New York.

Kidder Family Papers. Jerry Reed, Whitesboro, New York

United States Department of the Interior. Pension Records, Military Service Records Archives, Washington, D.C.

Primary Sources

Conveyance Books 71, 76. Otsego County: County Clerk's Office.

Johnson, Robert Underwood, and Clarence Clough Buel, eds. *Battles and Leaders of the Civil War.* 4 vols. New York, 1887.

Letters of Administration, Book XIII. Otsego County: County Clerk's Office.

Otsego County Census for 1855. Otsego County: County Clerk's Office.

Otsego County Census for 1860. Otsego County: County Clerk's Office.

Regimental Day Books of the 121st New York Infantry. National Archives, Washington, D.C.

The *War of the Rebellion: A Compilation of the Official Records of the Union and Confederate Armies.* 128 vols. Washington, D.C.: Government Printing Office, 1880–1901.

SECONDARY SOURCES

Adams, John Ripley. *Memorial and Letters of Rev. John R. Adams.* Cambridge, MA: University Press, 1890.

Adams, John Worthington. *Doctors in Blue.* New York: Henry Schuman, 1952.

Alotta, Robert I. *Civil War Justice: Union Army Executions Under Lincoln.* Shippensburg, PA: White Mane, 1989.

Ambrose, Stephen. *Upton and the Army.* Baton Rouge, LA: Louisiana State University Press, 1964.

Annual Report of the Adjutant General of the State of New York for the Year 1903. Ser. no. 36 Albany, NY: Oliver Quayle, 1904.

Beers, F. W., A. D. Ellis, and G. G. Soule, eds. *Atlas of Otsego County.* New York: n.p., 1868.

Best, Isaac O. *History of the 121st New York State Infantry.* Chicago, IL: Lt. James H. Smith, 1921.

Bicknell, Rev. George W. *History of the Fifth Maine Volunteers.* Portland, ME: Hall L. Davis, 1871.

Bigelow, John Jr. *The Campaign of Chancellorsville.* New Haven, CT: Yale University Press, 1910.

Biographical Dictionary of the American Congress, 1774–1989. Washington, D.C.: Government Printing Office, 1989.

Biographical Dictionary of the Governors of the United States. Vol. III. Edited by Robert Sobel and John Raimo. Westport, CT: Meckler Books, 1978.

Biographical Sketches of the Leading Citizens of Otsego County, New York. Boston, MA: Biographical Review Publishing Company, 1893.

Boatner, Mark M. III. *Civil War Dictionary.* Revised, New York: David McKay Company, 1988.

Bolander, Louis H. "Civil War Annapolis." In *U.S. Naval Institute Proceedings.* Vol. 63, No.11 (November 1937).

Burt, Silas. *My Memoirs of the Military History of the State on New York During the War of the Rebellion 1861–1865.* Albany, NY: J. B. Lyon, 1902.

Catton, Bruce. *A Stillness at Appomattox*. Garden City, NY: Doubleday, 1953.

Cleaves, Freeman. *Meade of Gettysburg*. Ohio: Morningside Bookshop, 1980.

Coddington, Edwin B. *The Gettysburg Campaign: A Study in Command*. New York: Charles Scribner's Sons, 1968.

Cronkite, J. W. *Report of the Gettysburg Monument Committee*. Cooperstown, NY: The Otsego Republican, n.d.

Cullum Memorial Edition Register of Graduates and Former Cadets United States Military Academy. West Point, NY: West Point Alumni Foundation, 1960.

Curtis, Newton Martin. *From Bull Run to Chancellorsville: The Story of the Sixteenth New York Infantry*. New York: G. P. Putnam's Sons, The Knickerbocker Press, 1906.

DeYoung, Mary Wallitt. *Drummer Boy*. Iowa: DeYoung Press, 1990.

Dictionary of American Biography, Vols. 2, 9. New York: Charles Scribner's Sons, 1928.

Foote, Shelby. *The Civil War, A Narrative, Red River to Appomattox*. New York: Random House, 1974.

Fox, William. *Regimental Losses in the American Civil War*. Albany, NY: 1889.

Freeman, Douglas Southall. *Lee's Lieutenants: A Study in Command*. 3 Vols. New York: Charles Scribner's Sons, 1942-1944.

Furer, Howard B., ed. *The British in America 1578-1970*. Dobbs Ferry, NY: Oceana Publications, Inc., 1972.

Grant, Ulysses. *Memoirs and Selected Letters*. New York: The Library of America, 1990.

Happel, Ralph. *Salem Church Embattled*. Washington, DC: National Park Service, 1980.

Hesseltine, William Best. *Civil War Prisons: A Study in War Psychology*. New York: Frederick Unger Publishing Co., 1964.

Historical and Statistical Gazetter of New York State. Syracuse, NY: J. H. French, 1860.

Holmes, Clay. *The Elmira Prison Camp*. New York: G. P. Putnam's Sons, 1912.

Holt, Daniel M. *A Surgeon's Civil War: The Letters and Diary of Daniel M. Holt, M.D.* Edited by James M. Greiner, Janet L. Coryell, and James R. Smithers. Ohio: Kent State University Press, 1994.

Hurd, D. Hamilton. *History of Otsego County, New York*. Philadelphia: Everts and Fariss, 1878.

Hyde, Thomas W. *Following the Greek Cross*. New York: Houghton and Mifflin Company, 1894.

Ingraham, John James. *Civil War Letters*. Edited by Edward C. Ingraham. Frankfort, New York: Phoenix Printing Corporation, 1986.

Krick, Robert. *Ninth Virginia Cavalry*. Virginia: H. E. Howard, 1982.

McElroy, John. *This Was Andersonville*. New York: McDowell, Obolensky, Inc., 1957.

McPherson, James M. *Battle Cry of Freedom: The Civil War Era*. New York: Oxford University Press, 1988.

Matter, William D. *If It Takes All Summer: The Battle of Spotsylvania*. Chapel Hill: University of North Carolina Press, 1988.

Michie, Peter S. *The Life and Letters of Emory Upton*. New York: D. Appleton and Company, 1885.

Miller, Francis Trevelyan. *Photographic History of the Civil War*. 10 Vols. New York: The Review of Reviews Company, 1911.

Morrell, Carl. "Elmira Prison." n.p.

Morse, Francis B. *Personal Experiences in the War of the Great Rebellion, the Memoirs of Adjutant Francis W. Morse*. Albany, NY: Munsell Printer, 1866.

Nevins, Allan. *The War for the Union: War Becomes Revolution 1862–1863*. New York: Charles Scriber's Sons, 1960.

———. *The War for the Union: The Organized War 1863–1864*. New York: Charles Scribner's Sons, 1971.

———. *The War for the Union: The Organized War to Victory 1864–1865*. New York: Charles Scribner's Sons, 1971.

New York at Gettysburg. 3 Vols. Albany, NY: J. R. Lyon, 1902.

Phisterer, Frederick. *New York State in the War of the Rebellion*. Albany, NY: J. R. Lyon, 1912.

Rhodes, Elisha Hunt. *All for the Union*. Edited by Robert Hunt Rhodes. New York: Orion Books, 1985.

Roster of the 121st New York Volunteer Association. Ilion, NY: Citizen Publishing Co., Printers, 1904.

Report of the 29th Annual Reunion of the 121st New York Volunteers. Herkimer, NY: Citizen Publishing Company, 1905.

Report and Roster of the 30th Annual Reunion of the 121st New York Volunteers. Oneonta: NY: The Herald, 1906.

Report of the 31st Annual Reunion of the 121st New York Volunteers. Oneonta, New York: The Herald, 1907.

Report of the 32nd Annual Reunion of the 121st New York Volunteers, n. p. 1908.

Report of the 33rd Annual Reunion of the 121st New York Volunteers, n.p. 1909.

Report of the 34th Annual Reunion of the 121st New York Volunteers, n.p. 1910.

Report of the 35th Annual Reunion of the 121st New York Volunteers, n.p. 1911.

Report of the 36th Annual Reunion of the 121st New York Volunteers, n.p. 1912.

Rice, C. E. *The Letters and Writings of the Late Lieutenant Adam Clarke Rice.* Little Falls, NY: *Journal and Courier,* 1864.

Roback, Henry. *History of the 152nd New York Volunteers.* Little Falls, NY: Henry Roback, 1888.

Sears, Stephen W. *Landscape Turned Red: The Battle of Antietam.* New Haven, CT: Ticknor and Fields, 1983.

———. *Chancellorsville.* Boston, MA and New York: Houghton Mifflin Company, 1996.

Steere, Edward. *The Wilderness Campaign.* Pennsylvania: The Stackpole Company, 1960.

Stevens, George T. *Three Years in the Sixth Corps.* Albany, NY: S. R. Gray Publishers, 1866.

Thomas, Howard. *Boys in Blue from the Adirondack Foothills.* Prospect, NY: Prospect Books, 1960.

Trudeau, Noah Adam. *The Last Citadel.* Boston, MA: Little, Brown and Company, 1991.

Trudeau, Noah Adam. *Out of the Storm.* Baton Rouge, LA: Louisiana State University Press, 1955.

Tucker, Glenn. *High Tide at Gettysburg.* Ohio: Morningside Bookshop, 1973.

Wardell, Bernice. *History of Laurens Township.* Bernice Wardell, 1975.

Warner, Ezra J. *Generals in Blue: Lives of the Union Commanders.* Baton Rouge, LA: Louisiana State University Press, 1964.

Werner, Edgar A. *Civil List and Constitutional History of the County and State of New York.* Albany, NY: Weed, Parsons and Company, 1886.

Wert, Jeffry. *From Winchester to Cedar Creek.* Carlisle, PA: South Mountain Press, Inc., 1987.

———. *Mosby's Rangers.* New York: Simon and Schuster, 1990.

———. "Rappahannock Station." *Civil War Times Illustrated*, December 1976, 5.

———. "Spotsylvania: Charge on the Mule Shoe." *Civil War Times Illustrated*, (April 1983): 12.

Who's Who in American History. Chicago: A. N. Marguis Company, 1967.

Wiley, Bell Irvin. *The Life of Billy Yank.* Baton Rouge, LA: Louisiana State University Press, 1952.

Willard, Sylvester. *Regimental Surgeons of the State of New York in the War of the Rebellion, 1861–3.* Albany, NY: n.p., 1863.

Wittke, Carl. *We Who Built America, The Saga of the Immigrant.* Ohio: Case Western Reserve University, 1967.

Worthington, Glenn H. *Fighting for Time.* Baltimore: Day Printing Company, 1932.

Index